I0411813

INDIEN ETHNOLOGY:

Grounded, Gendered, Meaningful

Cultural Traditions

Jay Miller, Ph.D.

Indiens of North America

2

© 2016

Apt images by Owen Shaffer for these ethnological comparisons appear in
North American Indian Arts, Andrew Whiteford, Golden Press. 1970 +

2

TABLE OF CONTENTS

2

Foreword

Culture is always engaging, the same, similar, and different among all human communities, just like life itself. For the past to be carried into the present, though, it is sifted down to relevant and remembered details. In written traditions, however, basic documents remain behind to fill in nuanced complexities, but for oral traditions, especially when reported by outsiders, much is lost in sorting and translating from these complex information systems apportioning profound ideas, derived from the prosaic, among community rankings.

To convey such fragile richness and variety, this book attempts to do many things while concentrating on engendered variations in Native North America. Further, our present collective world is huge, with North America just part of this whole. Events and attitudes involving natives often developed in other places and contexts. Too often, texts about Native Americans lose sight of the larger anthropological context of all humanity. For that reason, this book includes some examples and illustrations from other places and times to better examine Native American contributions to our total world.

While most tribes use four as their sacred number, seven expresses completeness because it combines the four directions with the three of up, down, and center, the pivot of, from, for all. This book, therefore, has seven chapters, beginning with an imaginary dialog to set the tone.

The first, Sheltered by the Land looks at North America as an engendered whole, as theme and variations under a variety of topics such as families, geography, languages, and archaeology.

The second, as background to better understand the tribal presentations, summarizes any culture in terms of my struckon model recognizing an all-pervading Man/Woman echo reverberating through a range of matrices categorized by exclusive, inclusive, and inclosive attributes.

The third, Tribal Isolates, treats specifically each of the tribes whose languages have had a long period of independent existence and can not be easily related to the major American language stocks.

The fourth, Invasions and Evasions, considers, from the broadest possible view, particular early examples of Spanish and Native American conflict, trials, and tribulations over the past five hundred years. Since colonization began before the Roman Empire, Tacitus serves to set this tone, followed by glimpses of the Spanish invasion which tried to revive a Roman model. Since the history of English, French, Dutch, Swedish, and Russian conflict are treated in other sources, the less well known Moravian and Russian colonies will be discussed, along with trend setting intellectual interests of Thomas Jefferson with regard to Native America. Lastly, as a reminder that natives continue to contribute to the diversity of America, the 1994 National Heritage Fellowship Awards week will be described briefly.

The fifth, Timeline, brings a comparative perspective to the fore, pulling together historical bits and pieces that often get left out of comprehensive works.

As the preface makes clear, ordinary complexity requires many names. While Native American in the United States and First Nations in Canada are currently the politically correct terms, ochers, Indiens, and tribal designations will also be used interchangeably. Similarly, European, chalk, and settlers will be used for the newcomers, colonists, and misnamed pioneers.

After several decades devoted to understanding Native North America, no definitive conclusions have been reached, yet four useful decisions have had to be made to provide useful terms for basic Americanist concepts.

A word already accepted in a limited way has been extended because it already solves a difficulty most others still debate and struggle with. Adopting the French spelling of <u>Indien</u> clearly distinguishes the natives of the West Indies and Americas from those of the subcontinent of India.

Similarly, the all-pervading concept of power-force-potency-energy-vitality pervading the engendered cultures of the Americas will be called *powha*, blending terms from Algic languages of the east and Numic ones of the west to indicate its special significance. Capitalized names serve to indicate immortal species rather than biological mortals, so Raven is a mythic character but raven scavanges on the beach.

Two terms, needed to convey the organizational complexities of these native lifeways, are anagrams of <u>sig(er)</u> from "special interest group (leader)" and of <u>tysic</u> from "time space center" with vowels pointing down (y) and up (i). Yup'ik Eskimos of Alaska nicely capture this temporal and spacial union in their ubiquitous use of a decorative circle with a central dot, as their language does with words like *ciuliaq* = "ancestor, leader" from *ciu-* meaning the forepart of a body, front area, or time before; in contrast to *kingu-* meaning rear end, back area, or time after.[1]

Elders often complain about the young, for good reason. In seeking their own way in the world, youngsters often bend to selfish, self-serving, solipsistic desires. Anthropology and academia is in such a mode with its present critical cultural theorizings to deny the validity of structures, judgements, and true understandings. While it is abundantly clear that Europeans have seriously failed to grasp the basis for other cultures, that is not the fault of those adhering to their own tenets.

Any language must have a grammar composed of units of sound, meaning, expression, and interconnecting logic using universal, pan-human conceptual relationships that serve to imbed and nest less expansive notions within broader ones. Such a nested series will be called a matrix consisting of specific, generic, and categoric members. A culture, it will be argued, goes farther by informing similar building blocks and interlinking logic with an articulating overall tension. For the Americas, this structuring tension is most often an explicit engendering by Man/Woman bridged by Mind. Throughout the Americas, however, relations between these genders and matrices are rarely if ever the same, providing a full scale outlet for human creativity, variety, and diversity.

---

[1] Ann Fienup-Riordan, <u>Eskimo Essays</u> 1990: 202, 212.

DEFINITIONS

Special words with agreed upon meaning are important for clarity in the exchange of ideas. They must be mastered in order to grasp the principles and intent of a particular outlook. All fields have such argots, including sports. For example, consider the next two paragraphs.

In 71 words: This guy carrying a fat stick walked up to this rubber square and stood with his knees slightly bent into a crouch. This other guy standing on top of a pile of dirt in the center of the field threw a white ball at the first guy, who hit it. Then he ran around a diamond shape with rubber squares at the corners until he got back to where he started.

In 17 words: The batter stepped to the plate, slammed the pitch, and ran the bases for a home run.

That is why we need definitions, particularly in anthropology where we cross all kinds of boundaries between cultures and disciplines.

ACADEMIC − Someone who has qualified through a formal course of study, holds a recognized degree, and is employed in a research related career.

AFFIX − A grammatical particle that must be attached properly to other word forms in order to convey its meaning. Affixes are usually divided into prefixes (as in English re-volve, de-volve), infixes (as in English sit, sat), and suffixes (as in English look-ed, look-ing) .

AGE GRADE − A social group based on the close ages of its members, who are sometimes further divided into age sets that are even nearer in age.

AGNATIC − Relationships traced through the father or males.

AMBILATERAL − Tracing descent through both parents such that one must choose to activate membership in one of a fixed number of descent groups. Some Salish people have options in any of eight descent groups through their great grand parents, only a few of which are activated at any given time.

AMERIND − A contraction formed of American + Indian.

AMITATE − Special relationship between children and someone in the category of paternal aunt, father's sister (FZ).

AVUNCULOCAL − Residence with a maternal uncle, usually of the groom, in anticipation of matrilineal inheritance from a mother's brother to a sister's son.

BEHAVIORISM − Perspective which holds that the world is understandable in concrete, empirical terms as the result of cause and effect relationships.

BERDACHE − A man who adopts the clothing and activities of females, although the role may not involve either homosexual or heterosexual relations. The justification for assuming a berdache position is usually both supernatural and personal. Among urban gay natives, "two spirit" is the preferred term.

BILATERAL − tracing descent through both parents equally.

BIOME − The largest biological community as recognized by its climax character, including seral stages, such as tundra, desert, deciduous forest, etc.

CACIQUE − A Jamaican term borrowed by Spanish explorers to refer to the native, often religious, leader of a town, especially a Southwestern Pueblo.

CLAN − A unilineal descent group tracing descent from an ancestor or entity who is often not just human, such as a plant, animal, star, or mythic figure. Clan members share mystic ties and common leaders.

COUP, Counting Coup – The Plains practice of earning military honors by recklessly touching an enemy, stealing a horse, or otherwise risking one's life for the welfare of the group.

COMPLEX – A convenience term for an assemblage of archaeological features and artifacts from a particular area during a specific time period.

CONFIGURATIONISM – The study of the culture-whole in terms of the key features of its integration.

COUSIN TERMINOLOGIES – The six types of kinship terminologies for categorizing close relatives in the generation of Ego: HAWAIIAN (everyone is brother or sister), ESKIMO (siblings are distinguished from cousins), IROQUOIS (siblings and parallel cousins are combined (lumped together), cross cousins are distinct), SUDANESE (siblings, parallel, and cross cousins are distinct), OMAHA (Patrilineage members are separated out, MB=MBS=MBSS), and CROW (Matrilineage members separated out, FZ=FZD=FZDD).

COUVADE – A cultural practice in which the father of a new born simulates the process of giving birth, lying-in, or joins his wife in following various food, work, or clothing taboos.

CROSS COUSINS – The children of siblings of opposite sexes: FZch and MBch.

CULTURE – The human species-specific adaptation consisting of an integrated conceptual system defining a particular human society, such as the widening relationship between Echo, Matrix, and Emanations.

CULTURE AREA – A mega-cultural region showing similar patterns of ecological adaptation, social structure, and constituent philosophies, often further divided into provinces on the basis of closer similarities.

CULTURAL RELATIVITY – The tenet of anthropology that every society and culture is as good as any other in terms of satisfying the needs of its members.

DIALECTIC – The dynamic process of viewing an entity as simultaneously itself, its opposite, and a synthesis resolving these.

DIBBLE – a digging stick, used in traditional subsistence activities.

DOUBLE DESCENT – tracing descent from either of both parents such that one parent provides one affiliation and the other parent another membership. Among the Keres, clans are inherited maternally, while religious group (kiva, priesthood) are a paternal inheritance.

EGO – the point of reference for tracing kinship, Latin word for "I."

EMIC – the attempt to parallel or approximate the viewpoint of a native participant in a community, generally by embedded linguistic terms, conceptual categories, logical relationships, and rationalist arguments.

ENVIRONMENTAL DETERMINISM – The discredited theory that the environment of a people automatically establishes personality (hot, cold humors) and social patterns. Current ecological opinion recognizes only that the environment will permit or discourage any of a range of possibilities.

ENDOGAMY – Marriage within a specific social group.

ETHNOCENTRISM – The conceit that one culture or society is inherently better than others; usually that one society is your own.

ETHNOGRAPHY – Careful descriptions of human lifeways and expressions.

ETHNOLOGY – Comparative analysis of human lifeways and expressions.

ETIC – the attempt to present an objective, acultural, "scientific", outsider viewpoint on particular phenomena, generally in term of measurable, behavioral, universal, comparative arguments.

EXCLUSIVE/INCLUSIVE – The symbolic cultural opposition between a category defined as bounded, closed, limited, specific, and exclusive; while the opposite category is defined as unbounded, open, ambiguous, general, generic, and inclusive.

EXOGAMY – Marriage outside of one's own social group.

GRAMMAR – The structure of all human languages, generally viewed as composed of a sound system (phonology), a meaning system (morphology), and rules for ordering all these elements (syntax).

GUILD – Social grouping based on occupation and attendant rituals.

INDIEN – A native whose ancestry is rooted in the Americas, the Indies by extension, according to continenal European spelling.

INFLECTIVE – Languages characterized by changes in form that convey grammatical distinctions such as case, gender, number, tense, aspect, voice, etc.

HYPERGAMY – Marriage to someone of higher status.

INTELLECTUAL – A sustained thinker with intuitive ability and probing curiosity.

INTERGLACIAL – A time period of glacial retreat between major glacial advances.

INTERSTADIAL – A time period within a glacial advance represented by minor fluctuations or retreat.

JOKING RELATIONSHIP – Kinspeople, who are often already affines, obligated to ease tensions by making ribald or obscene insults because they are potential spouses.

KILL SITE – An archaeological site associated with the killing and butchering of large animals.

KINDRED – A kinship grouping (personal, nodal, stem, prestige) based on bilateral descent. In American society, everyone has a "personal kindred" composed of all known relatives. Some Americans also have a "prestige kindred" composed of those relatives who trace a relationship to someone wealthy, famous, or notable.

KINSHIP SYSTEMS – Patterned ways of recognizing descent or relationship with humans and other beings based on marriage and shared substances such as blood, flesh, bone, or spirit.

KIVA – A semi-subterranean square or round building used for religious and ritual activities by Pueblo peoples, also as a clubhouse by men.

LANGUAGE FAMILY – A collection of languages sharing a common ancestry and considerable internal similarity.

LANGUAGE STOCK – A collection of languages sharing a remote common ancestry and showing considerable internal diversity.

LEXICAL – A linguistic unit of sound and meaning as affix, root, stem, or word.

LEVIRATE – Marriage type in which a man married the widow of his 'brother'.

LINEAGE – A unilineal descent group, usually three generations in depth, GF = F = S or GM = M = D.

MANLY-HEARTED WOMAN – Northern Plains women who are noted for their aggressive, outspoken personalities and warrior attributes.

MARKED/UNMARKED – The linguistic opposition between words or concepts which are specific, demarcated, closed, exclusive (marked) and those which are general, ambiguous, open, inclusive (unmarked).

MATRILINEAL – Kinship system in which descent is traced through women, inheritance comes from the mother, and authority passes from someone in the category 'mother's brother' to someone in the category of 'sister's son.'

MATRILOCAL – Residence with the descent group of the bride = mother.

MOIETY – A social structure based on the division of the world into halves such as right/left (Kansa), sky/earth (Hochungara), summer/winter (Tewa), light/dark (Sauk), and so forth.

MYSTIC BUNDLE, Power Pack – A container generally of hide in which are kept metonymical aspects of various things, such as feet, claws, birds, stones, plants, etc., which in combination serve to concentrate various cosmic powha at this one place for a given purpose. One Native intellectual once likened a Power Pack to a radio: useless as individual pieces but a powerful means of communication when correctly combined, much as a computer on the "web."

NATIVE – an indigenous, deeply-rooted inhabitant of Native North America.

NEOLOCAL – Independent residence established by a married couple.

NODAL KINDRED – A bilateral kinship grouping composed of parents, siblings, and spouses clustering around a node of parents, then siblings.

OLACHEN – An anadromous smelt-like fish (Thaleichthys pacificus, Candlefish, Eulachon, ulakon, Oolachon) noted for its very high oil content, and once plentiful in the Nass River during spring runs.

PAIDEUMA (Greek for 'that which is instilled') – The all pervasive property (echo) of a culture whole, considered, throughout this text, to be dyadic categories in tension.

PARALLEL COUSIN – The children of siblings of the same sex: FBch and MZch.

PATRILINEAL – Kinship system in which descent is traced through males, inheritance comes from the father, and authority passes from the categories of 'father' to 'son.'

PATRILOCAL – Residence with the descent group of the groom = father.

PHRATRY – A cluster of linked clans.

PIKA – A high altitude lagomorph (Ochotona princeps in the Rockies and O. collaris in the Yukon) related to rabbits and hares, and noted for drying various grasses and twigs in the sun for storage as winter food.

POLYANDRY – Marriage type permitting wife to have more than one husband, generally serving as a means to retain scarce resources among males and children.

POLYGYNY – Marriage type permitting a husband to have more than one wife, generally correlated with high male status and requirements of hospitality and generosity upon his household.

POTLATCH – A formalized redistribution of crests, privileges, people, and resources before a body of witnesses, who are given food and gifts to validate changes in the fabric of Pacific Northwest societies.

POWER PACK – See Mystic Bundle.

PRECOPERNICAN – A world view which is anthropocentric: pervaded by the human metaphor based on the complementarity of Man and of Woman.

PRONGHORN – An ungulate which is not a true antelope but rather the last surviving member of its class (Antilocapra americana), noted for its swiftness and horns on both sexes.

PTARMIGAN – A gallinaceous bird (Lagopus spp.) with completely feathered feet, related to grouse, common in arctic conditions.

RATIONALISM – Perspective which holds that the world is understandable in logical terms, which means that nothing is ever only what it seems.

SCHOLAR – Someone who has left a record of his/her thought, experiences, and reflections.

SHAMAN – A part-time specialist able to clarify any ambiguity so that he (rarely she) is adept at mystical journeys, curing, divination, and cosmological mediation.

SIG, SIGER – Special interest group; someone in charge of same.

SITE – An archaeological unit associated with human activities, such as a Habitation Site indicating some type of domestic occupation or a Kill Site indicating the slaughter, butchering, and processing of larger animals.

SODALITY – A social group which recruits on a voluntary basis, members share only a willingness to have joined and served that organization.

SORORATE – Marriage type in which a woman marries the widower of the deceased 'sister.'

STRUCTURALISM – The study of discrete human productions, often mental ones, in terms of pervasive relationships, which are frequently found to be dyadic after analysis.

TASKER, Task Leader – A group leader who functions for the duration of a specific activity by virtue of his spiritual powha, experience, and abilities.

TRADITION – That which holds a community together, generally but not always some belief or practice that is regarded as ancient and venerable.

TRANSHUMANCE – Seasonal movement among a series of fixed camps at resource areas, usually associated with the husbanding of animal herds.

TRANSLATOR – An adept Native intellectual who provides insights and information about the community in which he / she resides as a member, often from birth.

TYSIC – anagram of time space center, a crucial pivot, node, or nexus orienting people to all dimensions.

UNILINEAL – tracing descent through only one parent.

UTERINE – Relatives traced through the mother or females.

WAPITI (Cervus canadiensis) – Large American mammals, compared to European elk, which are antlered, unspecialized plant feeders.

The English language allows for certain modifications to any word such as those used here, mostly as a suffix at the end of the word. In this way, -ist means someone interested in something, as a Puebloist is interested in reseach among the Pueblo Nations of New Mexico and Arizona; -ic refers to language, as Tsimshianic is the language of the Tsimshian; -an makes a noun into a more encompassing adjective, as Puebloan means a wide range of things having to do with the Pueblos.

Similarly, punctuation has been added to extend a meaning of the written text. For directness, the = indicates significant equivalences. Parentheses () after a word presents a more correct, clarifying, or precise way of saying the same thing, such as medicine bundle (power pack). Quotation marks " " mean that the word or phrase should not be taken at face value because irony, distortion, historical bias, or misunderstanding are involved. Words like " primitive" and "beast of burden" are used only because they reflect prejudice of another (European ethnocentric) time. Words for important concepts or spiritual forces appear with a capitol first letter (Spider the trickster, spider the bug) to distinguish them, as noted.

For ease of presentation, several icons are used to express varied interrelationships.

= the same as, equivalent, translated as
< derived from
- connected with, linked in a series
+ closely linked with, overlapping
/ opposed to, in contrast with, intensed division betwee
() another way of saying this, substitute word, component parts, means the same as this word in another language

PREFACE
Setting the Tone

A small car approaches a farm house set back off the road. An old woman rocks on the porch. The car stops and a young man, an anthropologist (#), gets out to visit with this elder (*) of an unnamed tribe. While thoroughly versed in the language and traditions of her people, she has been, during a long life, an advocate of learning and understanding for her people and interested outsiders, including her visitor. She speaks.

* Welcome back, dear. What's on your mind? Didn't you ask all of your questions last time?

No, ma'am, I didn't and I don't think I ever will. There is so much to learn that there are always going to be more questions. I just hope you let me ask you as many as I can.

* Well, that's OK with me. I'm old and not many people come by or seem interested in what I know. I was raised the real old way, you know – I guess you do or you wouldn't keep coming back. Now-a-days they call me an Elder, but I'm really more of a Younger since all that I am and know came to me because of the way I was raised as a child.

I know that and I really appreciate your willingness to talk to me. I enjoy it, even if it's a record for science and scholarship, you know.

* Well, I don't know about that college stuff. I had a native education, school of hard knocks and advanced disappointments. I went to school some and always did well, but life had more to teach me. All I know is that I can talk to you the way the elders talked to me in the old days – except I wasn't allowed to come right out and ask a lot of straight on questions. It's interesting to me and worthwhile for you, so I guess it's all right. Besides, it gives me company. There are very few people of my own tribe around here who have any interest in these old time things. We all visit and we talk, but we don't remember and ponder the way you and I do. That's what makes your visits so special. At first they were just a novelty, but now I understand more of what you're after and I'd like to encourage more of it. Now I think about Indien stuff a lot more. You've got us all thinking. The other old heads, old timers at elders lunches, are talking a lot more about our memories when we get together, and we like it.

That means a lot to me. I don't want to be just doing something that will be reduced to writing and then collect dust in some library. If I can get people thinking about these things and realizing how significant they are, then maybe some more traditions can be brought back.

* No, it's too late for that. Those times are gone and we need to adapt to new ones, like I keep telling my kids. But we must do so in a way that makes sense in terms of respecting the old ways. We have to conquer the white people, learn what we can that is useful and yet stay faithful to our own ways. That's the hard part.

No, it's not. You're talking about the fallout from colonialism, the European take over of the world, with the victim adopting the arguments of the oppressor. I don't want to get into this, but it is a fact of tribal life that native people never get appreciated on their own terms by most Americans.

* Yeah, I guess so, but we try hard to ignore outside demands. It makes things easier to deal with.

Sure, it's a solution, but it's not a safe one. Always remember that the aim of colonialism is to distortion and deny. Only by subverting, belittling, dehumanizing, and denying native people could an European vanguard, usually by military might of fire power, of one country take over another. Distortion works its insidious way into all aspects of this encounter.

As a strategy, it is also assumed by the colonialized as a way of holding their own.

* And it makes me mad. Our holy places have been insulted and destroyed. Look how they rename them. Sacred stones, peaks, and lakes are now called things like Spook Rock, Demon Mountain, and Devil's Lake. That is wrong. Spirits of this very land lived here long before anyone ever heard of a devil. Only by sticking together can we keep our strength and resolve to persist. The hardest part is that this land, our mother, was taken away from us. We lost our support.

True, land is the source of all things, but only at the end was land alienated. In the Americas, the colonial exchange went through several stages. Initially, the newcomers wanted food, goods, and services. Among these (ironically named) goods were gold and (to Europeans) other valuables, like furs, crops, and minerals – along with novel conveniences like tobacco, hammocks, and canoes. After European settlement, native middlemen developed to bring the goods from the hinterlands to the traders. Such was the origin for Iroquois and Osage and Chinook ascendancy by trading items into their hinterlands.

* Yeah, but they still took our land.

Getting land of their own was what brought over most English and other people I call "chalks" because their land hunger had been stifled in Europe by a so-called "landed gentry" of nobles. Therefore, the land "exchange" loomed large in the history of the Americas. While conquest by denial played its part in beating natives into submission, along with overwhelming diseases and discouragements, the actual exchange was legalized by treaties. Most "reserved" to the natives some of their former territory, usually later further cut up by subsequent demands. This is the origin of the reservations of the United States and the reserves in Canada. This was land kept by Indiens themselves, with the rest exchanged for goods, money, gifts, and services promised by representatives of the national government.

* You're talking about our treaty rights, honored when the treaties were made, but more and more maligned as the native population has become a tiny minority. We learned the hard way that numbers count unless you take the long and righteous view.

Unfortunately, that's the way many Chalks see it. With the loss of natural resources, most of the land, and much of their communal wellbeing, natives were left with their labor to exchange, just like any other citizen. In addition, of course, they also had whatever "valuables" were left on their reserves. While these places often appeared barren and desolate in the Far West, hidden reserves of oil, gas, minerals, and gems were sometimes unintentionally included. Thus, occasional tribal wealth (Quapaw zinc, Osage oil, Navaho coal, Laguna uranium) receive disproportionate attention than their population numbers would merit, either to highlight a missed opportunity on the part of American business ("If we had only known, those Indiens would have never been allowed to keep that land.") or the divine land-right of Indiens ("The Great Spirit put that oil there to help us poor Indien people."). Even so, the capitalist system has a way of exploiting every and all resources.

* Things have a way of being ripped apart once outsiders move into an area. Those in the advance are always more selfish, greedy, and determined.

Now, wait. Try not to simplify or prejudge. Each culture has its own worth. Never forget that. We need to find ways to understand your culture and appreciate its place in the world. Let's work on that together, me with my skills as a researcher and you with yours as an elder-philosopher. We just have to make sure we stay focused on its overall integrity. Your job is to keep me honest, true to the letter and the spirit of the facts from a native perspective. We already know the European slant only too well. Any servant has to know the whims of the

master.

That is the most overlooked concern of scholarship. We are taught to take things apart, to dissect and examine all the pieces, but, having done that, we almost never put everything back together. I can see why people get angry with a researcher when they see the final product, a published analysis, derived from what knowledge they have shared, but devoid of any vitality. We work more like butchers than like surgeons, hacking off pieces instead of looking at overall health.

With analysis should come understanding, a better integration of material with more insight into facts. I can seek and examine, but both of us have to work at these connection to achieve insight and understanding.

* OK, but where do we start? In the sagas of our tribes we always begin to learn about the world when someone starts naming off things.

That's exactly right. I've thought about this. You know how everyone uses the term Indiens to refer to the natives of the Americans because of the mistake Columbus made. That name doesn't help at all, and it is confusing for anthropology to have the same name for people on two different continents. Younger people are insisting on the term Native American or just Native, but that is not all that helpful because people seem to think that it means only to be born in a place and to disparage, yet again, that native claims are much better than their own to be truly native.

My current idea is to use different spellings for these names like the French. That is the way it's often done in Europe. So, the people who live on the subcontinent of India would have their name spelled with "a" (Indiens), while those of the Americas, because Columbus named them in the West Indies would be spelled with "e" (Indiens).

* That's one possibility, but there should be variety. No one ever has only one name, even if they just call themselves "human being." Lord knows it's a problem we never had until Europeans started arriving and taking over. We always just had a name for ourselves and for close, friendly neighbors that meant "humans, people" and that shaded off into other kinds of people who were less and less like our kind of humans.

I already know what you're thinking. Yes, at base, everything is human or humanlike. All the animals, plants, clouds, and forces in the world have humanlike forms when they are at home. They only dress up when they go outside to do whatever they were created to do. They take on that guise that makes them unique, special, and distinctive as a separate creation or species. As your Shakespeare said, although women can take exception, "The measure of all things is Man." But that isn't because the human is on top of the heap and can do whatever he or she pleases, as most of the modern world seems to believe. It's because humans are the pivot, the focus and nexus, of the whole webbing of the so-called chain of beings. Since we are in contact with everything in the world, communication has to pass through us.

That is profoundly different from the Judeo-Christian notion that humans are the superior species, the apex, except for God and the angels, of the universe. That is, of course, until the Martians land.

* You're right. It is different. We natives believe that all of us are of and from the very land itself. We must learn from and take care of the land because it is our friend, sustainer, and teacher. It is, flat out, our life.

Many tribes call it Mother, believing she is alive, thinking and feeling. She knows what we do to and for her. She also knows when we do harm. She can help, punish, or withhold. These are truly the deeds of a Mother, but there is more than just the land.

There is also Father Sun, the sky, and the layers above and below the earth. All of these have spirits − that's not the best word for them, let's call them immortals − because they have always been, since even before the beginning. They are like transmitters for passing on information, potency, and wellbeing. They are nodes with special intelligence − together with compassion, concern, and justice − that make intercommunication possible and worthwhile in the universe. For many tribes, the universe is structured like a spider's web, composed of pulsating rays and circles moving out from the center and then back from the edges to the nexus. Rippling along these rays and rings is powha (energy = force = power = charged flow) unifying the cosmos. In the moment when memory began, at that instant when some Creator took moral responsibility for sharing existence, Mind originated and permeated the universe to institute time, space, and culture. It is the immortals who channel this powha and decide to share it with particular novelties of things or humans or families or places. These are the pivots at the intersections of the webbing, nodes providing this internal framework of and for the universe.

You mean guardian spirits and deities, as they are called in the literature. Sometimes, they are considered like angels, or patron saints, or, according to some tribes, the "bosses" of their species.

* Well, that is one way to look at it. They are immortals, each charged with amounts of energy. They have human emotions, harnessed by primordial wisdom. Mind is more important than anything else. As memory, as will, and as intelligence, it is shared by everything, even if they do not seem alive to us. I know of rocks that have powha, some were legendary characters petrified forever and some are just special stones, cause for particular human attention.

You know, many Americans believe that God Is Love, but it sounds like you believe that God is Mindful.

* Yes, I do, and now that I have recalled all that, I must explain the source of names. The difficulty with those distorted names that have been given to our tribes by Europeans is that they are taken from the outside. These are false names because they did not grow or come from the place where that language belonged. It is fine to use English names for things in England and German names in Germany. That is where they belong. Because there was no name in use for all the different tribes across the continent, one had to be imposed. But it came from the outside. Repeated use of a name over a long time does make it hallowed to some extent, but it remains alien. Just because names are old, doesn't mean they are appropriate. Sometimes they need to be changed to emphasize dignity and purpose. Knowing the correct name is the secret of tolerance and courtesy.

Yes, I can understand why it is not a good idea to reuse a term like "skraelling" (shrunken, shriveled) taken from the Norse records to indicate the people already here when early Viking colonies were sent to North America. The same applies to "indios" from the Spanish.

* Not quite, because, you see, "indios" has a certain attraction to us since it can be written as "in dios (in God)." This is indeed what all natives tried very hard to be: in tune and in touch with God or some version of the deity: male, female, neither, both, remote, or close. Such deified thought was a Mystery at the focus, if not the apex, of our great chain of beings. In many of our native languages, the word used for the Creator really means the thoughtful because to think is to create.

But how is thought expressed? The immortals seem to use telepathy, but biological life forms certainly have other means of communicating.

* Thought is linked with language. Every place has its own language associated with the local immortals tending it. It had to be spoken so it could be shared. Of course, the immortals

also have a language of their own, used among themselves. Telepathy also worked among many living things, but often it gets muddled up with lusts and greeds. It's like it used to be in ancient Europe, thousands of years before things got jumbled up by constant warfare, invading hordes, and refugees fleeing all over the place. Then, every region had its own local language, because communities tended to be isolated and fearful. Important people used Latin to conduct international affairs, so they were able to move freely all over because they could converse with others of the native elite.

We understand because we can think. Our ancients knew that the language used among the immortals was pure thought; they did not need speech to communicate among themselves. Rather, speech only became necessary in order to communicate across species and locales. This spoken word came into existence so neighbor living things could talk to each other and develop common cause. Because speech can not be heard over long distances, many languages had to be developed to cover all of the regions of the world.

\# Is that because all of the world is related?

* Indeed. Related but respectful of their many differences as individuals and as communities.

Members of each species already knew and understood each other. Thus, when it came time for names to be spoken, each species and other entities supplied the self-designation it had been using all along. These were true names, they came from within and reflected a particular sense of place and purpose in the universe. This is what all names must be: Direct, descriptive, and rooted in a sense of time, space, and process.

Because of these considerations, only a few terms really satisfy the requirements of true names. The names that have come to me to refer to the two races who confronted each other here in the Americas are derived from their distant lands. I call my own people, the ones who were here, the Ochers, after the red pigment from the land used so much for protection and decoration because it was believed to be symbolic of blood and life. We have recognized this link for eons in the sacred use of pipestone from quarries in Minnesota.

\# Yes, I can see the advantages of organic instead of descriptive names. For example, some tribes, such as the Pomo of California and the Mesquaki (or Fox) of Iowa, believed that they were created from the local red ocher and so called themselves red earth people. Sauks named themselves after their own yellow earth. Europeans, however, originally used the term Red Man to refer to a group of Beothuks from Newfoundland who had coated their bodies with red ocher as a decoration and a warm weather defense against pesky insects.

* There were many different kinds of Europeans here, but the ones who stayed on and took over were the English, arrogant islanders. We could say that this was ordained because of some advantage they had over the others, an advantage that derived from their relations with the immortal, and, thus, with their sense of place. Of course, it did help that they regarded their rightful place as masters of a world empire. "Whiteman's burden, stiff upper lip, and all that, you know." Their name could also be used to include all of the other European settlers, much as they eventually did by conquest. From what I heard during World War II, the place that meant a lot to the English and all of their allies was the white cliffs of Dover, which they tell me are made of chalk. Therefore, I think that those who came after and took control should be called Chalks.

Ochers and Chalks are what I mean by useful names coming from the land. They're short words, growing out of their sense of place.

\# Ochers and Chalks. Not bad, when you understand where they come from and what they represent. But it's still best to use self-provided terms to refer to each of them as individuals and larger groupings.

Of course, in Europe these groupings were much more cohesive because there were so many displacements, migrations, invasions, and military takeovers that survivors had to band closer together to protect and defend themselves. What can't be helped is that people will always make judgements about how they are better than almost everybody else. This is ethnocentrism, a self-superiority in the oldest of human traditions. Of course, if you happen to conquer or run rough shod over someone, then you Europeans assume you can tell them what to do. Some will follow directions and organize into work parties; others will balk and develop a system of their own to counteract, quietly or loudly, that of these so-called "masters."

* So, here we are back to colonialism. It's become such a topic of late among our educated Indiens that they've taken to calling it the civ / sav distinction. Somehow, that makes it seem innocuous, but it really wasn't and still isn't, at all. It hurts. It's unfair. It's wrong. We are all the same, even allowing for our many differences.

Yeah, I know. It's bleak, but also ironic. It reminds me of a marvelous quote from Elspeth Huxley (1959: 114), writing about her own girlhood in Kenya – when it was part of the British Empire. I bring it up here because she also mentions woad, the blue earth-coloring favored by the ancient Britons, as other nations used ocher. She's along with adult colonists making a visit to the local native leader before they have a picnic. An Englishman and colonist complains that the native men allow the women to do most of the really hard work, and make no effort to excel on their own, emphasing their trouble is that they "have no discipline." His wife replies to blunt this criticism. "I suppose we were all like that once, going about in woad and making human sacrifices, until the Romans came. It seems odd to think that we were civilized by Italians."

The European invasion of the Americas, regrettably, was in this ancient tradition of bringing civilization to the "savages" at the point of a sword, spear, gun, or battalion, as long ago described by Tacitus (see Chapter VII). The resulting order that comes after the chaos of conquest makes for increasingly more precise levels of organization.

Toward the end of the book, she (H59: 264)) also gives a nice account of the learning theory favored by societies still in touch with their environments. Observation is the best teacher because firing off a question is like shooting a loud gun that scares everything under cover. Instead, by being patient and quiet, knowledge will come close to you.

> The best way to find out things, if you come to think of it, is not to ask questions at all. If you fire off a question, it is like firing off a gun; bang it goes, and everything takes flight and runs for shelter. But if you sit quite still and pretend not to be looking, all the little facts will come and peck round your feet, situations will venture forth from thickets and intentions will creep out and sun themselves on a stone; and if you are very patient, you will see and understand a great deal more than a man with a gun.

Clearly, it is best to observe life quietly in its totality, to seek a culture in its overall environment. To do so, however, we must also know the limitations involved. Different families will have valid variant traditions, which must be respected, while also allowing for the possibility of unintended mistakes and sometimes being wrong.

* Right. We are ourselves, engendered of the land, imbued with all-embracing powha, and akin to the universe in word, deed, gesture, and, especially, thought.

I.
SHELTERED BY THE LAND:
An Overview of Native North America

Puwha

Pulsing throughout the Americas, informed natives believe, is a cosmic flowing of potency force energy vitality power that can be called *powha*, combining its names in Numic (*puha*) and Algic (*pow-*) languages, as the interconnection of and for everything in these diversified universes. Via these linkages, everyone has personal, kin, and community based ties to special places, often the holy homes of immortals (local spirit patrons, engendered totems), regarded as the "real land owners," dispensing and apportioning vital jolts of various intensities. Powha of itself is animating though neutral, as are most immortals – men, women, both, neither – between those always good or always bad at the extremes. Noteworthy landmarks identified as such holy homes were sites indicating intense motion or dangerous access, such as landslides, rock falls, roiling water, geysers, whirlpools, water falls, dangerous eddies, high mountains, hot springs, and distinctively eroded elevations.

Web

While powha was thinly diffused everywhere, like water vapor, its flow concentrated into circuitry that is weblike with rings and rays around a multidimensional nexus – anagramed as tysic for time, space, center with vowels indicating directions up and down. As source and summary in the flow of powha, the tysic is often embodied and/or deified as the mind of a culture-specific creator, identified as either a man, woman, both, or neither. Similarly, each of the intersections of curve and line provide increased jolts of powha appropriate for the locations of immortals and their holy homes. Not surprisingly, icons and images for powha and spirits often involve combinations of arc and dash to capture this powerful union, as in the Pawnee representation of their high god Tirawahat, Expanse of Heavens, as ∩. Webbing images provide cross-cultural significance to Spider, ranging from an all-wise Grandmother among Pueblos to the creative trickster Iktomi of Lakota, and to Turtle, who carries the earth upon his (her?) shell arranged in weblike plates, as among Delaware, who call him grandfather.

Immortals

By their very nature, immortals were shape-shifters, shimmering in form between their human, species, spatial, and spirit aspects. Often they are described as nacreous, glistening with the iridescence of mother of pearl or abalone. Indeed, the Tsimshian of the Canadian Pacific coast inlaid such shells into their heraldic artifacts to convey immortals they know as *naxnox*, some of whom were "shining youths" who descended from heaven. Christian angels, of course, also have this shimmering property, as Tsimshian fully recognize.

Even in the arid Basin, among the Chemehuevi, this quality is associated with a duck, probably the mallard, whose plumage was described in this Numic language as "water-purple" and "rainbow shimmer."[2] Among the Modoc of northern California, flecks of blue, gold, and green on salmon and glints of red, violet, green, and gold in haliotis (ear shells) inspire a similar

2. Carobeth Laird, The Chemehuevis 1976, 1980: 82.

pearly luster evoked in the telling of epics.[3] Most widespread of all, however, is the link between spirits, iridescence, and quartz crystals, which are universally present in shaman's medical bags (doctor kits). Ruth Underhill, a famous Boasian anthropologist, assigned such crystals, along with girl's puberty and first food rites, to the most ancient strata of native American beliefs.[4] Like everything else, crystals are male and female, visiting their owner in dreams and diagnosing an ailment during cures. They are never regarded by natives as just inert rocks.

Indeed, everything was in constant motion, slow, moderate, fast, as each response called for a reply and so on, in ever on-going returns. Foremost in concern and content was knowledge of powha that serves as the basis for knowledge, tradition, continuities, and, particularly, culture among informed leaders.

Four increasing degrees in the intensities of these exchanges for providing links to powha are dreams, visions, bundles, and shrines. Dreams are fleeting connections between a human and an immortal conveying limited information, often a warning or premonition. Visions establish permanent partnership between mortal and immortal, confirmed by assembling appropriate items into bundles, also called medicine or power packs, as dictated by the initial contact. Most bundles are buried or dispersed at the death of their assembler, though some become magnified into tribal or national palladia, as among the Pawnee, Crow, and other Plains tribes. Shrines, often the hallowed hollows inside peaks and mounds, are fixed on the landscape and regarded as eternal transmitters and receivers of powha.

To live healthy, productive, and successful lives people needed to maintain proper access to powha and immortals by observing certain procedures. Most significant was constant mental awareness as a member of a close, caring, sharing, and tolerant cosmos; including the avoiding, as specified by taboos, of actions that could disconnect, short circuit, pollute, or unduly surge conduits to powha.

Once established in partnership, a person became adept at whatever "gift" was associated with his or her immortal. This expertise had to be shared with others because selfishness was a major aspect of sorcery, the ultimate anti-social act. Such sharing usually took the form of acting as the short-term, informal (as needed) leader (siger) of some focused special interest group (sig) in which individuals joined together only long enough to accomplish some end, ranging from story telling, taboo warning, berry picking, basket making, or house building, to the public enactment of a complex calendrical ritual.

Since native life was intensely communal, individuals rarely acted alone. Proper people were conjoined within kin, rank, class, and position according to age and gender.

Luther Standing Bear, a Sioux writer, called these three classes the high, the good, and the weak.[5] "Old" high families were rooted in a particular locale because of hereditary access to its spiritual owners and guardians, encouraging their children to excel in the interests of communal welfare. Mid-range were the "good" contented majority, active folk who enjoyed a good life of economic, social, and religious security. At the bottom were those few "weak" families who could not "get it together," and generally made little or no efforts to try. In some culture areas, moreover, there was an "underclass" of ahuman hereditary slaves, as along the North Pacific coast, and war captives, as in the Northeast and Plains, who did onerous tasks like

3. Claude Levi-Strauss, <u>The Naked Man</u> 1981: 66, 77, 85.
4. Ruth Underhill, <u>Red Man's Religion</u> 1965: 83.
5. Luther Standing Bear, <u>Land of the Spotted Eagle</u> 1978: 130.

sheltered

keeping the family supplied with water, firewood, and labor intensive foodstuffs.[6]

Sigers graded into formal official leaders, for most of whom a simple, quiet, respectful, inherited dignity served to indicate their position, rather than obvious wealth, clothes, or houses. Like the "high people" on the Micronesian island of Pohnpei, they lacked crowns, jewels, or fancy cars. Instead, they sat in honored places, received fine food at feasts, and spoke in "clever and sumptuous" styles.[7] Throughout the Americas, four officials are known as chief, captain, shaman, and matron. Chief or captain (war chief) led their community during, respectively, times of peace or warfare, serving as head of civil or of military stances. The matron, often the daughter and wife of a chief, supervised the activities of the women of the community. Shamans saw to the emotional, medical, and spiritual needs of their family and community.

Any place where people gathered served to concentrate potency there, while entrances to holy homes – through caves, gaps, lakes, springs, or fissures – provided added access to anyone who had ritually prepared by fasting, bathing, and meditating before his or her quest.

Because the earth existed in interactive equipoise, humans could not acquire food, particularly meat, unless shamans had arranged with spirit masters for plants and animals to forfeit their bodies (but not their souls) for human consumption. Such shamans in trance visited these communal lodges to arrange for an exchange of souls, those of local animals to be hunted in return for those of humans from distant groups. Only during periods of great stress would a shaman be forced to negotiate with a "master Of animals" (generic boss or spirit of species) using souls from his (sometimes her) own human community. Such a belief made people self-conscious enough to make every effort to live in harmony with nature and interspecies neighbors, at the risk of having all foods disappear and their lives forfeited.

Control of powha provided knowledge, authority, wellbeing, and long life so the greater the age of a person, the more likely he or she was to have a strong partnership with a commanding immortal. In a few cases, however, a suspect elder lived long by siphoning off the lives and powha of others as a sorcerer. Though generally tolerated in the interest of enriching diversity; during extreme hardships, such sorcerers were publicly accused, tried, punished, and killed.

Gender

Because powha lives, it is engendered, sustained by women and directed by men. Indeed, words for "man" or "woman" in native languages include all males or all females of any shape, species, and demeanor. Mediating between these genders are key attributes of powha conceptualized as <u>mind</u>, particularly as deified in the creator of the cosmos. While these triple relationships can be expressed as

<u>Man / Woman</u>
Mind

it obscures many complexities involved.

6. See Leland Donald, <u>Aboriginal Slavery on the Northwest Coast of North America</u> 1997.
7. Martha C. Ward, <u>Nest in the Wind</u> 1989: 54.

All human languages cluster words and meanings into nested series technically known to linguists as "markedness." At each end of a logical series are words that are marked = specific, closed, or that are unmarked = generic, open. Questions ask with the unmarked, as in "How long?, How old?" because 'long' includes the marked 'short' within the series of 'length' and 'old' includes marked 'young' in the series for 'age'.

Moreover, connectedness, interlinkage, and integration involve a third term mediating between these polar oppositions by sharing qualities of both along with something uniquely its own to form a triple <u>matrix</u>.

Matrix

A matrix is a three way, internested, proportional, meaningful series defined by specific / generic opposites bridged by a categoric. Because these are cultural, not linguistic, designations, they are distinguished as <u>exclusive</u> / <u>inclusive</u> + <u>inclosive</u> linking that matrix into the fullest articulation by the <u>echo</u>, an all-pervading series whose symbolic tension informs all aspects of a total culture.

Exclusive members are specific, delimited, segregated, definite, and closed; while those that are inclusive are generic, unlimited, aggregated, indefinite, and open. The inclosive third shares properties with these other two, but also with related mediators. In the logic of any culture, each of the relations consists of instances which can substitute for each other (the paradigmatic), while the three together form a serial sequence (the syntagmatic) from the most to the least restricted.

Standard examples are clothing outfits where a wearer can select from a variety of hats, depending on what else is worn from head to feet. Fur, top, baseball, homburg, and so forth can substitute according to what shirt, pants, and shoes complete the overall sequence. Of course, this is male apparel, usually inclusive, as distinct from that of women, often exclusive, except when transvestitism makes it inclosive.

Within each culture, society, and community; three useful components can be distinguished as sensory, relating to the individual; interpersonal, involving institutions; and cosmic, applying to that universe as culturally defined. Despite the wide variety of ways in which these units have been expressed in Native America, typical patterns can be cast into sharper relief by occasional (deliberate) exceptions, which in turn highlight overall flexibility. For each type, a particular tension stands out as especially helpful for clarifying that culture's echo. For sensory, it is right/left; for interpersonal, it is man/woman; and for cosmic, it is night/day. In terms of the matrix, those categories on the right side of the stroke are inclusive (I) and those on the left are exclusive (E).

Person = membranes, tracts
<u>right / left</u>   <u>head I / feet E</u>
heart   heart O
House = flues, windows, openings
<u>man / woman</u>   <u>old I / young E</u>
hearth   hearth O
Cosmos = caves, waterways, tunnels
<u>day / night</u>   <u>summer I / winter E</u>
sun-moon   solstice O

Underneath, the inclosive (O) mediator for the sensory is the heart, that for the interpersonal is fire, and that for the cosmic is the sun. Heart represents the warm center of the body, balanced between right and left sides (although anatomists know it is left of center). Fire, particularly as the hearth where products from male effort are cooked by women to become family fare, symbolizes the unity of the couple, family, and home. For the larger community and tribe, there may also be a sacred fire burning in a town hall, plaza, or temple, as an outward sign of their shared corporate identity.

While sun and moon are distinguished in European languages, only a single orb is often named in Amerindian ones. If moon has to be specified, it is called something like 'night sun.' Before Europeans arrived, it is likely that the sun was the most obvious manifestation of deity for the Americas, worshipped for its light and warmth, but dreaded as a cannibal, fed by battle-slain warriors, victims of drought or fever, and sacrificed prisoners.

The sun was often the outward sign of the highest powha = a deified Mind, human-like intelligence, or consciousness pervading the universe, sending ripple-like thoughts throughout the cosmos while serving both as source and summary for their flowings.

Across the Americas, usual linkages were right, men, animals, black, and day (sun) within the inclusive; or left, women, red, plants, and night (moon) of the exclusive. In terms of artifacts, these associations extend to tools (building, carving, farming, and hunting weapons like knives, axes, dibbles, arrows, spears, bows) for men and containers (baskets, pots, bowls, bags, mortars) for women.

But, as noted below, there are obvious exceptions, which best make sense as deliberate decisions to reverse established patterns and to institute a distinct identity. Foremost among these are those few tribes (such as Delawares and Keres Pueblos) who attribute priority to the left, associating left with men and night.

For the Delaware, this left priority can be attributed to the teachings of the 1760s Ohio prophet named Neolin who reorganized Delaware beliefs in contrast to those of other tribes and Christian missionaries preaching about Christ sitting at the right hand of God. In New Mexico, the Keres example relates to a thousand years of close contact between themselves and neighboring Tewa Pueblos. Between these Pueblos, many sequences are reversed. Thus, by reversed exception, Keres link left and men with the exclusive, in contrast to the inclusive of right and women. For the Tewa, right, men, and winter are inclusive, while left, women, and summer are exclusive. Speakers of that language urge a male onward saying "Be a man, be a woman," while a female is only coaxed "Be a woman."[8]

Echo

These and other variations on the gender theme indicate its importance for the Americas, as indicated by the very title The Cosmic Zygote (fertilized egg) for a study of Amazonian cosmology.

$$\text{ECHO} = \frac{\text{Man / Woman}}{\text{MIND}} \quad \frac{\text{(male I / female E)}}{\text{intellect O}}$$

8. Alfonso Ortiz, The Tewa World 1969: 36.

For all North America, varying by region, this continental echo (pervasive system) consisted of the opposed categories of Man/Woman mediated by a concept of Mind. While these were, of course, biological givens for human and other complex species, they must be receive cultural definitions to become meaningful. For Native North America, culture adepts worked with the prosaic obvious to make it increasingly abstract, taking features of biology and landscape to create cosmic gender and deity. They used the seen to convey and represent the unseen. In contrast, complex societies worked with the abstract, probably because they had so many more disparate people, ideas, and elements to integrate and, in consequence, found vast abstractions useful.

For comparison, before turning to Native America, the culture of modern industrial, capitalist America has an echo with a mediating category called Love, common currency in all media, and an axiomatic tension expressed as Worthless / Worthy + Love [E / I + O].

These relationships are important concerns of and for American culture, enabling a lawyer or doctor to hold high status because of substantial income, but also permitting an impoverish scholar to undertake research straining funds because "It's worth it," or someone might say "It's worth it to me because I love it." Thus, worth can mean both quantitative measures of value, such as a paycheck, as well as qualitative ones based on Love. Of course, in modern America, this matrix also impinges on that of gender since it is often the case that men are worth more than women in terms of income levels, although, in compensation, women are believed to have greater reserves of Love, balancing out the overall system.

While modern American masculine ideals emphasize separation, females focus on attachment so "men express their autonomy (and are overthreatened by intimacy), whereas women tend to see the world in terms of connectedness (and are overthreatened by isolation)."[9]

In keeping with cultural concern for the obvious as a metaphor for the abstract, however, Native North Americans relied on such tangible expressions of life as the symbolism of hands, genders, trails, and time, though these symbolic tensions might be defused, as in the case of some tysic immortals, such as the Aztec deity Ometeotl, Lord of the Outside, who was both androgynous (transgendered man + woman) and vastly wise. Thus, even when the genders were combined, specialized knowledge remained vital.

As the American mediator is Love, Native American cultures were pervaded by the concept of Mind, as both first cause and unifying symbol. Thus, Christians who say that God is Love would be answered by natives that God is Mind. But just what constituted this notion of mind?

Primarily it was a matter of memory sustained as a weblike flow pulsing through the universe, composed of a central source at an intersecting nexus (tysic), connected by rays and rings rippling to the outer limits of the cosmos and returning. Both source and summary of energized flow, manifested as a throbbing jolt of powh
a, its nodes were located upon the landscape by storied events, either fixed at unusual rock formations or created in sacred spaces as shrines and medicine bundles. Knowing where and how to find and use these nodes came from immortals, themselves situated within an overall web. Transformed immortals − into rocks, springs, stars, and more − figure in legend to be remembered across generations.

9. Carol Gilligan of the Harvard School of Education, quoted on pages 204-205 by Bobette Perrone, "Talking and Listening," Medicine Women, *Curanderas*, and Women Doctors, Bobette Perrone, H. Henrietta Stockel, and Victoria Krueger 1989: 199-211, Chapter 17.

In addition to each of the matrices exemplifying the components of a culture, various openings also served to allow passage from one context to another. Indeed, all culture seems to be primarily concerned with boundaries and passages,[10] particularly during rituals of renewal, revival, return, and reproduction. For example, while the skin was the border between self and other, openings in the head and body, together with their out-products (such as tears, urine, wax), received ritual attention as points of transformation moving out from a tysic at heart, hearth, or sun.

Since culture was and is the singularly human adaptation, a characteristic of Homo sapiens, it was shared by all societies, both close and complex. Among those complex, however, culture has come to have an increasingly universal meaning, distinguished by nation-state impositions rather than indigenous traditions. But culture should not be confused with politics and society. All humans have cultures of equal value and sophistication, although they differ in how they are expressed in terms of social forms. A hunting and gathering band of 30 members living close to nature will, in consequence, be less elaborately organized than a city-state of thousands or a nation of millions. Yet culture will be the same for both, a system of meaning for providing order to the universe in terms of meaningful genders, tysics, and humanity.

Pipe

Among the most potent examples of this matrix series providing an Echo are carved tobacco pipes revered throughout the Americas, with particularly elaborated ones along the Mississippi drainage.

Each pipe has 3 parts, only joined together at the time and place for smoking, often during a ritual. The rounded bowl is womanly and exclusive, the drilled and decorated wooden stem is male and inclusive, and the tobacco, providing the divine offering, is mindfully inclosive. Assembled, each pipe was a universe composed of stone, wood, plants, animals, people, spirits, and complex beauty.

Each material in personified and engendered. Sacred pipe bowls are often made of deep red soapstone from the famous Pipestone Quarry in southwest Minnesota. In one version, this deposit is the body and blood of a monster transformed to good purpose. Today, saved as a national monument, Santee Dakota retain the right to extract it with hand tools and carve it for sale, much as their ancestors did for the vaste prehistoric trade.

The stem, a straight wooden shaft skillfully pierced through to make a breathing tube or windpipe, was decorated with all aspects of nature, often a prepared hide covering adorned with colored porcupine quills, stone beads, copper pendants, and long feathers, particularly from eagle wings and tails. Paired stems, manly and womanly, known as calumets (Norman French for wand) were the key emblems of the intertribal adoption rite known variously as Hako and Hunka.

Tobacco was often believed to be a thoughtful gift from a creator to sustain or regain his, her, one's goodwill. The first appearance of the plant was associated with men, either from semen among Yuchi or as a replacement for a lost son. Its transformation into a universal

10. See Ann Fienup-Riordan, <u>Boundaries and Passages</u>, Rule and Ritual in Yup'ik Eskimo Oral Tradition 1994.

offering as fragrant smoke was through the medium of fire, the inclosive mediator most linked with illuminating thought.

A functioning pipe represented sexual intercourse, so the pieces had to be stored apart in the same bundle. When smoked, the pipe interlinked the triple culture components represented by a personal smoker (sensory), a ring of people passing it around (institutional), and the potent forces (cosmic), including the creator, invoked to enjoy this aromatic offering and spread goodwill.

Watchfully Aware ~ Eternal Vigilance

All of Native America in traditional times was alive, aware, and interconnected by thought, senses, and emotions. The comfort, health, and wellbeing of everything depended on the conscious goodwill of everyone else. Closest ties were with kinspeople, then with fellow members of the band, tribe, and culture. Stress and pressures from daily life were directed toward outsiders, either enemies or unknowns.

Each day, therefore, involves decisions and negotiations to stay fed, warm, and content. A good person works hard to hunt, farm, fish, or harvest whatever foods are available, thanking each and every one for their kind gift. But some people are lazy, and steal food, or crippled, and have to be fed. Sometimes all the hard work ends up spoiled or moldy because supplies got wet. Sometimes the crops shrivel up and die before harvest, sometime fish do not come.

A good person prays for things to improve, learns from mistakes, moves to someplace better, or does all of these and more. Sometimes, neighbors with plenty are visited, threatened, or attacked to get food.

But no one in the Americas can get food without access to powha, a gift from an immortal. Therefore, it is even more important to get powha than to get food, since food follows automatically from powha but not the reverse. Where powha is concerned, however, access could be good or bad.

Good means of attracting and holding powha involve fasting, praying, enduring pain, and promising to help others. Bad ways involve selfishness and theft, siphoning it off from others – like pilfering food, killing those who already had it, or contaminating its source to drive it into another refuge easier to control.

Native life, therefore, is defensive and necessarily suspicious, since attacks could be spiritual, emotional, or physical. Everything from spoiled food to malevolent influences has be accounted for and dealt with. Responsibility, therefore, is often oblique, circumspect, and diffuse so as not to attract undue attention.

Imagine, if possible, living in a house where great but potentially harmful powha could be unleashed unknowingly by a misstep or wrong action, living in a world where fierce and venomous beasts can do both their own will and that of ill-intentioned others, and living in an environment where flood, drought, earthquake, and enemy attack loomed large.

Whatever is done effects others, and has long range consequences over time and space. Rituals and thanksgivings involving many participants always contribute to the greater good, while sorcery and theft done in secret evoke the bad. All intelligences in whatever form who are just then nearby are well aware of what is happening, but only their leaders can sit in judgement, well aware that the more severe the punishment, the more pain will be inflicted on the whole world.

Therefore, people go through life making the least amount of "waves," leading calm, contented, and composed lives which have the least impact on others. Yet, not everyone is the same, with the same modest needs, so constant vigilance of the seen and unseen is the price of sharing the world with other intelligent life forms, most of them content and similarly inclined, though a few are insidious, ready to infect, divert, or deflect benefits toward their own selfish ends.

Knowledge

Throughout the Americas, there was a standard equation that knowledge = powha = life = success. At the Pueblo of Zuni, a native priest dictated his knowledge of sacred texts to Ruth Bunzel, telling her, "I have given you all my religion and I have no way to protect myself".[11] He died two days later.

Vital knowledge was provided by immortals, either directly during a quest for supernatural aid or indirectly through a succession of human mentors, the first of whom benefitted from such an encounter. Long life was proof of this equation, but it was not without danger. An elder could thrive on the reserves of powha that he or she had acquired legitimately, but the aged could also grow old by siphoning off the knowledge and lives of weaker people. In the former case, they were religious adepts, but in the latter they were sorcerers. Yet, though the first was better than the second for community wellbeing, both were believed necessary for overall harmony. This tolerance was a distinctly Native American attitude. Everything in the world participated in a complex interplay of relations, all different and all necessary for the whole.

This interplay was an aspect of creation as a process, which began when the universe "came to" (became mentally alert, aware). Throughout the Americas, natives still use this same idiom to refer to their earliest recollections, dating them from the time when they "came to" as conscious beings with childhood memories. Since in standard English this phrase has the clinical meaning of regaining consciousness, some explanation of the native expression is necessary. Both individuals and the universe are said to have "come to" in native languages, but the person is simply an instance of the cosmological event.

Usually it was the tribal divinity, either male or female (Man, Woman, or both), who instituted creation by realizing the significance of memory. Prior to this, He or She had merely existed outside space and time, but, at that instant, memory began and with it the processes of time and the definitions of space focusing on the tysic (time space center).

Creations

The various tribal sketches which follow include their origin sagas, but for comparative purposes we will also look at the range of such epics for North America. All of the general types, however, build upon that memory instant.

The most widespread account, circumpolar across Siberia and the Baltic, used the motif called "earth diver," although it sometimes functions as an account of the recreation of the world after a flood. Beginning with only water, aquatic animals "come to" and decide, often at the instigation of a deity, that one of them should dive to the sea bottom and bring up some dirt so that the earth can be made. Generally, the last animal (the fourth, often an amphibian) to try is successful, and this allows the earth to be created by mystically expanding that muddy speck (see

11. Ruth Bunzel, Introduction to Zuni Ceremonialism 1932: 494, # 20.

Yuchi section).

In the Northeast, among Iroquoians, the earth was created on the back of a turtle to provide a home for a pregnant woman who fell out of the sky. She died giving birth to twins, Sapling and Flint, who finished the world by willfully making either beneficial or harmful things, such as butterflies or mosquitos.

In native southern California, the world was created by the union of Sky Father and Earth Mother, a belief also found among the Japanese and Pacific islanders. These met, bonded, and remembered each other as the wife gave birth to inhabitants and artifacts important for this region.

In Southwestern and some Plains tribes, people lived in an underworld oblivious to their surroundings. Eventually, they moved or were lured to the earth's surface to begin life in time and space, passing on remembered knowledge to form rituals which serve to record and sanctify their uses of a homeland.

Sporadically through western North America, particularly the Basin, there are accounts of creation by Spider, who wove the world's foundation as a weblike tracery. Though Shoshoni provide the most explicit regional statement of this belief, spider and web provide the template for powha flow implicit in beliefs across the continent.

While most but not all creators were male, in the southern Great Basin, Ocean Woman made the world, aided by Wolf, Coyote, and Cougar. She sprinkled particles of her skin over the primal ocean to create a speck of earth, then, through prayerful thought, she had it expand into a huge flat disk. The center from which she worked survives as Charleston Peak in the Spring Mountains just west of Las Vegas, Nevada. Even now, she lies on a side promontory called Mummy Peak, her own work done.

Others finished her labors. Humans were created by the union of Coyote as father and Louse as mother, placed in a basket, and intended for careful array over the landscape. Often Coyote assumed the form of a water spider. However, curiosity got the better of him and he prematurely opened the basket lid before he got to the center of the world, the logical starting point for this apportioning. In consequence, humans jumped out and ran all over the earth like lice, remaining imperfect forever.

Among tribes of the Northwest, along with the Ainu of Japan, the world was finished by a transformer, called Raven, who wandered over the land, tricking sole proprietors out of various resources and necessary elements − such as salmon, sun, moon, tides, and fire − to make these available to humans.

Sagas with more limited distributions mention the creation of the world from the body of an immortal, or through the efforts of heroic twins, who sometimes staged contests to prove which of them was wiser.[12]

While knowledge and wisdom are often mentioned in these accounts, any tribal divinity is not, leading scholars to regard such a high god as an import from Christianity. As these sagas make clear, however, it is not the idea of a godhead which is important, but rather His or Her or Its position as a deified Mind as the tysic of the cosmos. This tysic is made clearest by looking at the native language terms for such a divinity. The Delaware refer to "The One Who Created Us By Thought," the Keres Pueblos to Consciousness Deity, and the Basin Numic to "Ocean Old Woman." As variously expressed, thought, will, and memory are their gift to their intelligent

12. Anna Birgetta Rooth, Creation Myths of Native North Indians 1957; Jay Miller, Earthmaker 1992.

creations.

While these varieties of epics describe how the world was made or modified into the way it is today, not surprisingly, neighboring tribes will often have very different accounts of creation, as if to confirm their own separate and distinct identities.

Yet they all share a basic structure of the world as a flat disk, distinguished by mountains and rivers, with at least one level above it as the sky and another below it as the underworld. Overall, the world is a ball, with the earth disk in the middle, an air-filled sky dome above, and a water-filled bowl below. A central tree (sometimes, a pole or pillar) links these three domains, along with other mediators such as fire, water, and caves to allow passage between the layers. Certain beings, such as birds and snakes, also had the inherent ability to travel across these divisions. As Peter Roe, a South American archaeologist, has shown, this world layer cake inside a ball pierced by the world tree was also the cosmic model for lowland Amazonian South America and elsewhere. Indeed, the very title of his book The Cosmic Zygote (fertilized egg with female and male components), indicates the great importance of gender also for South America.

For the whole of North America, interlinked by regional high families, the universal metaphor of the cross inside a circle θ was given geographical form by the confluences of the Ohio and Missouri Rivers entering the Mississippi near modern St. Louis. As confirmation of this belief, the huge Mississippian ceremonial center, now called Cahokia, thrived there, marked by Monk's Mound, the largest human-made earth platform north of Mexico. Surrounding it were sacred spaces and scattered settlements presided over by high chiefs and priests involved in a vast complex of trade and ritual relations. In addition to such built sacred centers, all of the Americas were marked by numerous and widely scattered holy sites indicated by rock art or portable bundles.

Americanists

The history of Americanist research is tortuous, growing out of a colonialist desire to learn enough about native languages and cultures to "reform" or eradicate them. Rarely, if ever, were native cultures accepted in their own right. Knowledge improved as scholars learned to listen better and more closely to what natives were trying to tell them. In the best of cases, of course, as among literate Aztec Christian scribes, the natives themselves were doing the writing in their own voices. Much information, however, was biased and slanted by the presumptions of Europeans that there was only their own ways of doing, knowing, and understanding. Dictionaries were set up with the assumption that each Spanish or French word had an exact native equivalent.

In a few cases, learned and sympathetic partnerships developed between native adepts and foreign scholars, and continue to this day providing better understanding about particular traditions. Among the most famous examples are Alice Fletcher and Frances La Flesche for Omaha, Franz Boas and George Hunt for Kwakwaka'wakw, Marius Barbeau and William Beynon for Tsimshian, Alfred Kroeber and Robert Spott for Yurok. Again and again, over generations, learning continued and a record, either oral or written, was passed down with particular topics newly clarified.

A recent instance is Cibecue (Western Apache) contributions to the explication of thought, speaking, and wisdom.[13]

---

13. Keith Basso, Wisdom Sits in Places 1996: 84-85, 130.

Apache think in images seen in the mind, and spoken out loud to convey them as pictures, which hearers hold up for their own viewing. Conversation colors, textures, and details these projections as each speaker adds to, piles on, and rounds up these visualizations so all hearers can share them in common. Talking together is always voluntary and highly respectful, using spare phrasings, cordially affable tones, and much restraint so others can freely and imaginatively express personal creativity with regard to these depictions. Speaking forcefully, loudly, and at length with many qualifiers smothers and blocks other minds. Instead, above all, differences, nuances, variations, and individuality are encouraged. Earned with great effort, wisdom consists of heightened mental capacity to predict and avoid harmful events because of enhanced smoothness, resilience, and steadiness of mind (called <u>bini</u> in Athapaskan languages) consciously cultivated throughout life by learning about places, beings, fates, and events through informative epics.

In this fashion, on-going scholarship serves to check, recheck, and refine information about human diversity, especially in the past. The desire to salvage as much as possible about aboriginal lives and languages motivated much of early academic research. Guiding much of this early 1600-1800s work was a larger theory that saw other traditions as degenerated expressions of the civilization given by God in the Garden of Eden and sustained by Europe. Later, after Charles Darwin proposed evolution, each tradition was ranked along a scale from savagery to barbarism to civilization. Thus, in addition to describing a particular culture in detail, its place on that scale was also considered. The purpose of such larger theories, of course, is to organize data and research in ways which formulate more general questions and provide information that can be compared. Alone among emerging scholarly professions, anthropology always had a keen interest in all of humanity, both men and, uniquely for a considerable time, women.

Published in 1894 and dedicated "To all Good Women," the book that underscored the importance of women in the anthropological study of human "progress" was <u>Woman's Share in Primitive Culture</u> by Otis T. Mason, a curator at the US National Museum who set up the exhibit of "primitive" feminine industries in the Women's Building at Chicago's World Columbian Exposition of 1892, although it did not open until the next year.

Intending to show the debts of human society to women, the book devoted separate chapters to the roles of women as food bringer, weaver, skin dresser, potter, beast of burden, jack of all trades, artist, linguist, founder of society, and patron of religion.

Each chapter expanded on these tasks. For example, for native California, a woman preparing food served variously as harvester, storage facility builder, hauler, sorter, miller, and stone mason making her own grinding tools. In other regions, she also farmed, harvested, stored, and processed the crops from her fields. Among hunting peoples, she butchered, dried, cooked, and served the meat. For a quick energy food, she pulverized the dried meat and mixed it with grease and berries to make pemmican. She had to find and prepare all of the basic ingredients and tools needed in her kitchen, everything from salt and herbs to string.

Using only a pointed bone awl and her teeth, a woman wove flexible materials into baskets, basic for all storage, serving, and eating. Likely sources were forest bark and slats, marsh tule reeds, and plains grasses. Similarly, to weave blankets and cloth, she used the spindle and, sometimes, the loom. Available materials were used ingeniously, whether fur, feathers, fibers, or grasses. With a wooden gauge to set the hole size and crocheting, she made nets long

sheltered

enough to close off the mouth of a canyon during mass drives for rabbit, deer, or other game.

In each chapter, Mason treated another activity to show how female effort worked with local resources and basic tools to create necessities and works of art that glorified human ingenuity and patience. By setting the stage in terms of these "women primeval," the "fair readers" of a latter time could more keenly appreciate what woman had wrought to make the world a better place. Drawing upon a range of accounts – by travelers, some of them Victorian ladies, missionaries, and early anthropologists, sometimes too judgmental to receive that title – examples, incidents, and anecdotes from all over the world were used to illustrate these vital inventions. Looking closer, however, proves that these examples were drawn from only the dark skinned world, including Italy and the Mediterranean, but never from Nordic or English regions, where identical activities occurred.

The implication, of course, was that while the world owed a great debt to all these foreign women, "true" (white) women lived in vastly superior luxury. This presumption was regrettable because the past century has shown that those who have continued to live close to the land – as tribals, peasants, and dropouts – have generally done less to imperil world conditions than their "fair haired sisters" pushing the engines of industry.

By the turn of the twentieth century, however, early government and museum-sponsored research was replaced by the Boasian program of academic, university-based anthropology. In place of classification and scaling, Boas insisted on texts in the native languages, rather then schedules of words, like that used by the Bureau of American Ethnology for its language classifications.

Natives like George Hunt and William Beynon provided these texts in natural languages within cultural settings, which provided more and better ways for native voices to be heard, even though some of this effort was initially "in vain" since Boas in the US and Marius Barbeau in Canada both missed the sense of native chronology embedded in these writings.

With the growth of academia, anthropologists began to specialize as linguists, archaeologists, human biologists, or ethnographers. Originally, Boas sent an advanced student to concentrate not on a tribe or region, but on a language stock, as Alexander Lesser and Gene Weltfish researched Caddoan and Mary Haas did Muskoghean.

Rechecking and refining soon included cross-disciplinary research as ethnographies were compared with historical documents, archaeological remains, and legal testimony.

Concerned that Americanist research overlooked the "no" or negative response, Alfred Kroeber and Stanislaw Klimek, a Polish statistical anthropologist, devised the Culture Element Distribution lists, which allowed a researcher to mark a range of responses (yes, no, maybe, unknown) for separate traits extracted piecemeal from regional institutions.

Most recently, a reflexive argument has entered scholarship, focusing more on the researcher than the researched in the characterization of "self/ other." While much of this enterprise is self-serving and myopic, greater clarification of cultural biases is always to be encouraged. An irony of modern theory building, however, is the repeated assertion that all viewpoints are equally valid and, particularly in native literature, all efforts, even those obviously substandard, must be exalted as expressing a native voice.

Yet a check with native reality proves that all tribes and languages have rigorous standards for judging behavior, both in the positive and in the negative. Just as "the other" makes judgements and sets standards, so scholars must evaluate all sources to improve knowledge in detail, by comparison, and by abstract modelings that expand on the full sweep of the record.

More recently, against this background of increased understanding, more pressing concerns have increased in importance. Now, lawyers rather than scholars have become the closest allies of reservation peoples. In the past, anthropologists and lawyers have worked together in cases involving native religious freedom, such as the Native American Church and its use of peyote as a sacrament (before the 1972 federal Native American Religious Freedom Act) and on land claims and water rights. Since the American legal system is adversarial, however, anthropological participation is constrained by the context of the law. Open discussions and evaluation of information, the lifeblood of academia, are muted in court.

Yet the proven advantages of winning and self-interested concerns of federally recognized tribes are best represented by lawyers, who are, by definition, very much a part of the establishment. Anthropologists, because they bridge cultures, maintain a marginal role, compounded by the distrust many people feel toward academics generally. Those without benefit of a college education regard academia as a mixed blessing with too many occult overtones.

In addition, some natives safeguard their integrity and sense of self by denigrating the work of outsiders, whom they regard as incapable of understanding or accurately reporting on their cherished cultural traditions. Standard ethnographies are often called "comic books." Indeed, while distortion is a hapless aspect of any colonial record, generations of natives and scholars have worked to correct and minimize it.

Another group of scholars more problematic in the endeavor are historians, who rely preponderantly on the written record as "documents" of change and process. Given that these records are, by and large, written by colonial officials for other Americans, bias and distortion are rampant. Further, many early historians were themselves wealthy, white, patrician men, serving as apologists for American glory and imperialism. As upholders of American rectitude and presumption, native peoples were further maligned by their writings.

Recently, however, efforts have improved because of a greater ethnic and gender diversity among trained historians, and the growth of "ethnohistory," an attempt to blend written and oral history with anthropology to "read between the lines" of documents to present a more balanced and well-rounded interpretation, which, after all, should be the intended goal of all multicultural understanding. Indeed, the more sources and opinions in print, the better will be our understanding. Autobiography and biography add the personal element often missing from generalized, often dry, accounts because poetry, imagination, and outlook are best conveyed from a personal rather than an impersonal perspective.

For example, Robert Lowie,[14] a famous anthropologist well known for his work among the Crow (Absoroka) of Montana, merely wrote that "the dead live in a camp of their own. However, the hereafter seems to have interested the Crow very little."

In contrast, Two Leggings, a boastful war leader, recounted his own belief, taught to Crows by twin boy spirits, that beyond this ordinary world there is another, called the Other Side Camp − variously spirits, ghosts, and ancestors − who are collectively called the Without Fires. This parallel universe to that of living Crow, mirroring its rivers, peaks, and praire, is divided in halves.

One, led by Old Man Coyote, comprised all that moved − such as animals (land and water), the sun, moon, stars (except comets), thunders, dwarfs, and the souls of the dead themselves − which could be seen as dust-devils moving over the plains.

The other, led by wind, fire, water, and the earth as our mother, consisted of all the fixed

14. Robert Lowie, The Crow Indians 1965: 69.

sheltered

parts of the earth – such as plants, trees, flowers, and rocks. All of these beings and things were divided into various clans. Gaining a spirit in a vision also conferred membership into its clan among the Without Fires. A series of visions by one person created a special "medicine clan" of interrelated humans and their helpers. Those helpers who were more powerful selected some of the weaker ones to be included in a human's medicine bundle.

The over-all deity was known as First Worker. Other beings ranked by degrees of powha below him, although each was aided by particular allies and clansmembers. For example, Eagle was helper to the Sun and Owl to the Moon. Most visionaries preferred to be visited by the Moon rather than the Sun because, while solar spirit was powerful, he was a poor gambler, but the Moon, though weaker, rarely lost at gambling.

In both worlds, gambling is a favorite pastime, but the stakes among the Without Fires are human lives. When a spirit loses, its human partner is said to become a "child eaten by the other side." This forfeit is how Crow explain human deaths. A warrior who died in battle, however, received special honors by the "spirit father" who had won him in gambling and he joined the Without Fires in glory.

While the fate of a human life often depended on the luck and skill of its patron, humans could themselves shorten their own lives by failing to observe the various instructions, restrictions, taboos, and requirements imposed on them at the time of a successful vision. Such a lapse, though human error, denied the person any help or protection from the Without Fires, and thus ended his or her life prematurely.

The logistics of arranging for the battles resulting in such loss of life and for leading the souls to their winners is the duty of a being in giant human form with pine trees growing out of the lower lids of his eyes. Yet his plans do not always come out as he intended because other spirits and lucky conditions might intervene, forcing him to return home tired and discouraged. Such were the contingencies of fate among the Crow that belief blends with accident and intent during any event.

In a more personal and humorous vein, Two Leggings told about his brief career as the chief of a bison hunt. This position indicated great trust by the camp and was earned only after someone had come to realize that the needs of the community were more important than those of the self. Indeed, Two Leggings had previously been sneaking off to raid and take horses without proper community sanction either through participation in public rituals or the possession of a medicine bundle. He was chosen to lead the hunt because he realized "I had been selfish and had not thought of our hungry women and children."[15]

As hunt leader, he had virtual control over the lives in the camp. To be successful, all their efforts had to be coordinated so that the herd would not stampede, frustrating the hunters' purpose. Everything depended on his dignity and abilities because he was the mystical bond holding together everyone's efforts. Yet when Two Leggings charged alone into the herd to make the first kill, he somersaulted into the air when his horse stepped into a badger hole. His horse then fled so he had to hunt on foot, listening to everyone talking about this spiritual guide who killed bison without a horse.

To say the least, he was humiliated, but, as a warrior, he bluffed his way though the day and even withstood the silent rebuke of his own wife when he returned with little meat. Rather than crumple from the experience, he vowed to purchase, as soon as possible, the proper medicine bundle to guarantee future hunting luck. By doing what the community expected, he

15. Two Leggings 1967: 156.

sheltered

reaffirmed their pledge of goodwill.

Environment

Landscape is the abode of both species and memories expressive of powha. For this reason, America still belongs to the natives who first experienced its wonders and passed this remembered knowledge on to each generation. Delaware (Lenape) families in Oklahoma whose ancestors left New Jersey two centuries ago still know details about the Atlantic coast, a poignant example of their strong love for their homeland. Yet home was only incidentally the soil of a land, since it was really water that held people together.

Marian Smith,[16] relying on her fieldwork with the Coast Salishan Puyallup and Nisqually near Seattle, devised a generalized model for describing how native peoples of the Americas related to their watersheds. Based on increasing levels of integration, she explicitly recognized that greatest allegiance and loyalty coincided with an entire drainage system. The major nodes in this overall system were cedar plank houses built along the shore near rich resources that often included a clam bed, salmon stream, berry patch, and hunting ground.

Within a watershed, group affiliations became more expansive in terms of (a) hearth mates or commensal families sharing a fire, (b) coresidents of households, (c) birthright locals - those born there in contrast to inlaws, visitors, and foreigners, (d) towns, settlements, and seasonal sites, (e) community networks clustering as hamlets and towns, (f) side tributaries, and (g) the entire drainage.

In terms of crucial cultural concerns, this series extended from the person (the combination of body, mind, and soul with spirit allies), the house (including hearth family, locals, and distant kin), and the land (as seasonal camps, sacred sites, and towns), to the world (the drainage linked to more remote people, places, and deities through marriage, trade, and ritual).

Moreover, the Americas were occupied by people who made their living as tenders or tillers. Those who tended their landscape practiced the more ancient economy: a mixture of hunting, gathering, and fishing that varied by gender, age, season, and terrain. Such activities were counterpoised by traditions adhering to necessary commandments established by a local deity. Foods and other resources were harvested with respect, guided by religious specialists who regulated these efforts by omens, prayers, and rituals serving to moderate and space out any ecological impact.

The same orderliness applied to the tillers who occupied the warmer southern portion of Native America, below the frost line allowing 100 growing days, farming indigenous domesticates like sunflowers and Mexican imports like the trinity of maize, beans, and squash. Tillers were also tenders, but their farming provided a steady surplus that enabled them to maintain larger, more sedentary communities, regulated by sigers, both political and religious, who conducted more elaborate rituals timed by the growth of their crops. Stages from planting to harvesting were marked by prayer, ceremony, and thanksgiving.

All motivations, abilities, and institutions were sanctioned by appeals to the immortals. An individual or family was gifted during encounters with particular immortals, who directed

---

16. Marian Smith, The Puyallup~Nisqually 1940. Smith (1941) revised this model to include pasture meadows so important for Nisqually horses, but this need does not reflect aboriginal conditions. As George Gibbs (1877: 169) sagely noted Nisqually fondness for horses created "an exception to the otherwise universal aquatic life of the coast region."

sheltered

each to a career, status, or success for the common good. These encounters forged partnerships providing access to a primordial powha intended to enhance general wellbeing. Having a mostly neutral valence and no self-motivation, such powha could also be used selfishly for individual ends. Such anti-social behavior was classified as sorcery or witchcraft. Unlike Euro-African intolerance of witches, however, sorcerers were accepted for their difference until a major catastrophe indicated that the world was out of balance. Then, sorcerers were put on trial by the community or its leaders and, if found guilty, killed. The assumption was that witches could not help being as they were. Often their abilities were attributed to physiology. Some Pueblos called witches "two-hearts" because they were believed to be born with a good and a bad one.

The crime of sorcery, in native belief, was greed, selfishness, and excess. People were supposed to take only what they needed, and often less. Major activities, particularly ceremonies, were scheduled for times of seasonal abundance to feed a large gathering.

Ecological differences were explained by divine interventions and sanctions. Animals had to be hunted in a particular manner within an area; plants gathered in specific ways; fish taken by either a net, trap, or leister at specific fisheries; and crops planted in breast-like mounds of even number because all of these customs were instituted at the beginning of the modern social order. Precedent set patterns for all time, unless someone, such as a prophet, received a revelation to make a change.

Hardships tested mettle, scarce foodstuffs encouraged sharing (not hoarding), and interacting biological communities lived in harmony. People could go without, or, at least, use resources sparingly so that famine would not be such a stark contrast to times of plenty. Those tribes which lived almost entirely by hunting, however, more often alternated between famine and feast, gorging themselves after a successful kill, then tightening their belts again.

Availability of a particular staple was signaled by a first food rite, a meal of thanksgiving celebrated in honor of the yearly return of a fresh supply of plants, berries, nuts, fish, or game. Often, these were family gatherings at camps near that resource. Some were community or tribal rites, such as the Green Corn Festival among tillers, celebrated just before the harvest, while the crop lived, to consecrate new storage of maize for the upcoming winter, when it was augmented with fresh game.

Such ritual regulation of food exchanges between humans and other species of people (plant, animal, fish, spirit) helped to make America a Holy Land, pervaded by powha.

Further, the land itself included reservoirs, nodes in a web-like pattern of concentric rings and rays pulsing with the flow of powha. Any place where people gathered served to concentrate potency there. Moreover, there were the fixed abodes and landmarks identified in legend as "holy homes" = hollow hills, deep pools, peculiar features inhabited by a community of immortals. Entrances to these domains were through caves, lakes, springs, or fissures, provided that an individual had ritually prepared by fasting, bathing, and meditating before his or her quest. These holy homes were communal lodges where shamans visited in trace to arrange for the exchange of souls, those of local animals for those of humans from distant groups.

Because the earth existed in interactive poise, humans could not acquire food, particularly meat, unless shamans had arranged with spirit masters for plants and animals to forfeit their bodies (but not their souls) for human consumption. Only during periods of great stress would a shaman be forced to negotiate with a "master of animals" (a generic boss or spirit species siger) using souls from his (sometimes her) own human community. Such a belief made people self-conscious enough to work to live in harmony with nature and intespecies neighbors, at the risk of having all foods disappear and their lives forfeit.

sheltered

Noteworthy landmarks identified as such holy homes included whirlpools, water falls, dangerous eddies, high mountains, hot springs, and distinctively eroded elevations. Generally, these locales were sites indicating intense motion, such as landslides, rock falls, roiling water, and geysers. Their location was connected with tribal heritage through a narrative of events involving legendary ancestors or historical figures. For example, a famous example from the Coast Tsimshian tells the story of a man named Asdiwal who married among inland and coastal human families before becoming petrified at the top of a mountain. To this day, the name-title of Asdiwal continues to be inherited by prominent men (sometimes women) who thereby acquire rights to hunt and fish in these same areas where their ancestor married and prospered.

Throughout Native America, religion was characteristically linked with locale, as the term "nature worship" implies. When tribes were dislocated, disoriented, and removed far from their homeland by Euro-American avarice and hostility, survivors often merged with other native communities. A tribe like the Delaware, forced halfway across the continent from the Atlantic, was graced with prophets who preached an annual worship set in their community hall, giving the tribe a renewed orientation toward a future.[17]

Those tribes fortunate enough to stay "grounded" in their homeland benefitted from a continuous reverence for place. Navahos and other Athapaskan colonies, who have moved into their present lands in recent centuries, developed a sense of place consistent with that of tribes long indigenous to a region like the Southwest. Shiprock, a giant stone landmark in northwestern New Mexico, is described by Navaho as the tail of a huge bird who followed them south and anchored itself (and them) in this new territory by diving head-first into desert sands.[18]

These saint-like immortals who "own" and control the land, renewing their relations with the human communities in each generation, along with the dead, buried ancestors dissolving into the earth, are the only permanent residents. Humans moved over the area on regular treks among fixed camp sites near resources, as each of these ripened in season. Major towns were located at the junctions of rivers and streams. Farmers, with their stored crops, occupied such towns during the winter. Foragers, however, had to scatter during the cold, then congregate when natural harvests were abundant. The singular exception was the North Pacific Coast, where annual salmon runs, halibut banks, and dense vegetation enabled foragers to live in luxury, surrounded by fine woodworking made from the western red cedar, especially the heraldic art on houses and artifacts owned by local aristocracies.

Throughout the Americas, the conduit between immortals in their lodges and humans in their homes was the succession of local leaders, the tysics of the community. As on other continents, people occupied their territory by virtue of a divine right to do so bestowed by the immortals who first inhabited the land. As the Japanese emperor descended from a Sun goddess, some Plains chiefs were Stars who came to earth and founded leading families. It is this bond among spirits, people, and land which constitutes a tribe. Sometimes, legends are even more explicit and say that human languages are different because each tribe acquired its speech from the spirits who dwell in that place. Similarly, Hebrew was anciently believed to be the language of God and of the Judeo-Christian holyland.

Ironically, as tribes are now moving towards greater political autonomy under treaty

---

17. Jay Miller, Old Religion among the Delawares 1997.
18. This bird shape is geological in that the standing tail of Shiprock was the plug of a volcano with two lava dikes leading off at angles like the outer wing edges of a bird that plunged head first into the ground.

guarantees, scholars are mumbling about giving up the term "tribe" because, they argue, it is "a fiction." They assert that "tribes" were a creation of the colonial situation, after loose aggregates of towns, racked by disease and death, consolidated into new groupings with leaders who collaborated with the colonialists. While there was great death, destruction, and displacement, such tribes were only one aspect of their aftermath. Such academic debate, however, ignores obvious European bias that, while tribes as merely political units were indeed a product of colonialism, ancient tribes were first and foremost religious congregations. Thus, the answer, of course, is that those who look for the meaning of a tribe in terms of politics or mere territoriality are missing the essence of its real spiritual and moral nature, as articulated by the parameters of its waterway and neighbors.

Over eons, the spiritual bond between native peoples and their lands grew stronger to fill out the landscape with many more dimensions than just the geographical and the biological ones. Often, at onset, the land itself had to be created from nothing and shaped to meet the needs of all life forms, not just humans but all the other "people" who came to live on the land.

Each tribal land was its own world, defined as sacred space by a combination of terrain (depths, rocks, trees, outcrops), belief, and stories filled with memories of experiences gained by generations living in that same place.

During Medieval times, Europeans, at least educated ones, knew a similar sacred map of the world. Jerusalem was at its center, at the eastern end of the Mediterranean Sea. Its directions were marked by colors, attributed to waters in these quarters still known as the Red Sea, Black Sea, and others. The tysic at the very center was the hill called Golgotha, the place of skulls, where Christ was crucified, redeeming the prior world from the original sin of Adam and Eve. Indeed, theologians taught that the grave of Adam was directly under Jesus's cross where his blood washed over the skull of Adam to redeem him and his descendants.

The Renaissance shattered these tightly interwoven beliefs and the beginnings of scientific inquiry further denied their validity. Critical tests and questioning confounded such logical but unprovable cosmologies.

Throughout the Americas, however, natives continue to live on the landscapes of their foreparents, or, if far removed from them by historical forces, to visit them frequently enough to keep their topography fresh in the minds of tribal members. Compelled by an on-going belief in a vital bond with the land, this continuity is an amazing feat, but a crucial one for keeping the sense of tribal identity with the land which is a defining characteristic of life in the Americas. Indeed, many modern natives see their unique place in the world as being ever-responsible stewards of the earth.

Archaeology

While each and every local native community held beliefs about how and where their ancestors were uniquely created in their homelands, a more global perspective requires that the bodies of these ancestral humans had to come through Asia by way of Siberia and the Bering Strait. These were not natives, nor were they Americans as such. Instead, they were the ancestors of the tribes who adapted to the Americas and made these continents their very own through millennia of personal interactions with the spirits and spaces of their special places.

It is unclear when humans first arrived. Certainly, after the split of the great single continent of Gonwandaland, many mammalian life forms, particularly monkeys, evolved in both the old and new worlds. But (here is the catch), there were no other primates, close relatives of humans, in the Americas. Horses, with a 45 million-year old fossil record in Wyoming, evolved in the Plains and, seven million years ago, drifted across the Bering Straits to grasslands of Central Asia, but, except for some tribal stories about a tiny breed of horse, these equine species became extinct in its homeland about 8,000 years ago. Similarly, the growing popularity of the large, hairy, smelly primate called Bigfoot or Sasquatch (derived from one of its Salish names) finds some support among natives who regard it as a New World ape, though none exist in the scientific record.

The archaeological record is vague about human beginnings in the Americas. Tens of thousands of years ago, these people would have lived as hunters of big game animals (megafauna), such as mammoth, mastodon, and huge bison. Following such herds, they needed to be mobile and so lived in skin tents, wore leather clothing, and made hide sacks and containers. This Paleo-Indien way of life survived for generations as people scattered thinly over the northern and central Americas.

An obviously continuous ancestral tradition, however, does not stand out until about 12,000 years ago when the Clovis mastodon hunters left behind distinctive spear points. By 10,000 year ago, beautifully made spear points − with a channel flute down the middle to funnel blood from wounded bison − mark the complex known as Folsom. Then, after that, things get complicated as Paleo-Indiens diversified their economy to cope with environmental changes. The tradition of big game hunting survived only in the Arctic and Plains, where modern, smaller bison lived until Euro-Americans slaughtered them off in the 1880s.[19]

Over time, many of these specialized hunters became generalized foragers, living off the land, moving by seasons to harvest available foods, whether fresh greens, small game, berries, seeds, or fish. During this Archaic period, camps were widely scattered over a region to make effective use of its resources as these became available. In some cases, the largest sites indicate a central homebase from which families left to harvest at regular seasonal camps. To assist storage needs, cache pits and basketry were developed by women. In the Southeast of five thousand years ago, a porous pottery was also invented probably to transport shellfish.

Because of their generalized efficiency, Archaic peoples lived on a rich variety of foods and developed a thorough knowledge of their landscape, including its spiritual aspects. Highlands, caves, and springs became foci of ritual attention since they symbolized passages into and through the earth. Foragers identified more intensely with a place and so self-created themselves therein through the agency of an immortal who became their Creator, whether man, woman, both, or neither. Indeed, people, especially well aware shamans, began to systematize beliefs, sometimes to the extent of deliberately reversing or otherwise manipulating general beliefs to make them unique to their own society. For example, if most towns in a region had round houses, one group set itself apart by building square homes. If most houses were rectangular, towns varied by aligning the long axis north to south, east to west, or along the shoreline. Thus, among the Iroquois Five Nations, four aligned their longhouses east to west, while the Onondaga, the hub, set theirs north to south.

More abstractly, where one community regarded Man as the unmarked generic form, including both males and females as American English once did; the next tribe down the river, speaking another language and observing another ancestral tradition, defined Man as the marked category, the specific in contrast to a generic Woman, as between Iroquois and Delawares, or Keres and Tewa Pueblos.

19. By great irony, we have more evidence for extinct mammoths and mastodons than for these millions of slain bison because their bones were shipped east, ground up, and sold as fertilizer.

Over 3,000 years ago, Late Archaic people began to specialize again, farming local crops like sunflowers and various seed plants before embracing the corn-beans-squash trinity from central Mexico, getting these seeds from overland trade and learning the necessary crop rituals, which were even more important, from intertribal prophets. Holy goodwill assured success, not mere human effort.

Farming often provided a steady food surplus stored in towns, composed of thatched homes dug into the ground (called pithouses), along with pottery, though it was breakable and did not transport as well as baskets and skin bags. Families still moved with the seasons to take advantage of local produce, but they stored it back at the town for winter use, rather than in camps or pits near the harvest area. Local populations increased and became more dense, encouraging organizational elaborations. Therefore, with farming towns came complex kinship systems based on unilineal descent into various clans, each of which was associated with a special place where its ancestors began as spirits, plants, animals, rocks, or heros of some sort.

As previous periods were characterized by reliance on stone for tools, weapons, and necessities (finely made both to be diagnostic of its function and its maker's identity); with farming surplus, creativity focused on pottery, the hallmark of recent centuries.

Needless to say, each prior adaptation continued somewhere in the Americas (as detailed in the next section on culture areas). Big game hunters thrived on the bison (buffalo) herds of the Plains. Archaic foraging developed into a sophisticated tending of the landscape, with fall burnings to clear the terrain and selective scattering of seeds to guarantee another local harvest. Such tenders lived throughout the West and North of North America and some still do. Farmers or tillers lived in the East and South, usually with women doing most of the farm work while men continued to hunt in season. Only the Southwestern Pueblos assigned the field work to men, although women did have kitchen gardens.

Each of these lifeways was adapted to regional climates and, moreover, fed into the vast trade network that exchanged the meat and furs of hunters for the crops and crafts of farmers. Particular local treasures, such as copper ore, turquoise, shells, minerals, and mica also figured in the trade as exotic goods, often to indicate elite ranks.

A curious aspect of this intensifying localization by people − who were truly becoming native Americans − was a corresponding differentiation between ordinary folk and leading families, who traced their own ancestry to other remote peoples, places, and worlds. Not uncommonly, a leading family described itself as founded by a Star or sky being who came to earth with special powha. Or, their ancestor emerged from the sea or a lake to assume prominence. Sometimes, the human ancestor married a resident spirit to establish the family. In all cases, leaders were therefore believed to be different, more enhanced than other members of the community, tribe, or region. Of course, they sought intermarriage within the regional elite, perpetuating chiefly families who provided stability and security until some natural or social cataclysm demanded a re-sorting of their ranks.

Ultimately, the disaster of European arrival de-stabilized the cultures of these continents, although, with great irony, some of these leading families survived because alien conquerors deliberately married important native women to entrench their own claims to their new homes, as illustrated by the life of Gacilaso de la Vega, who called himself El Inka (Chapter VII).

A similar irony of contemporary scholarship, noted above, is that many scholars have been attracted to Native American Studies because of the wealth of documentary evidence that exists, ranging from annual and serial reports for all reservations and enrolled members to full scale ethnographies, histories, and popular reports. Yet in many cases, especially in government

sheltered

and missionary works, the documents convey Indiens as white officialdom wanted them to be, but they never, in fact, were. In consequence, the officials get their revenge by criticizing or creating, in writing, Indiens who conformed to pressures of American culture. We have individuals where we should have communities, and we have material success where there should be spiritual fulfillment. Throughout, we face denials and glimpse distortions, as noted in the opening dialogue.

Modern American growth was part of the world-wide colonial enterprise, in which distortion worked its insidious way into all aspects of the encounter. As a reverse strategy, aspects of these falsehoods were used by the colonialized as a way of manipulating situations. Thus, love of nature and deep spirituality have become THE native traits, simplifying a much more complex dynamic. At first, newcomers wanted food, goods, and services, particularly (ironically named) goods, gold, slaves, furs, crops, and minerals – along with novelties like tobacco, hammocks, and canoes. With European settlement, native middlemen brought resources from hinterlands to the traders. Such was the incentive for Iroquois and Osage and Chinook ascendancy.

Motivating settlement was land hunger, stifled in Europe by the landed elite. Thus, land loomed large in the recent history of the Americas. While conquest played its part in beating natives into submission, trailing behind disease and discouragement, the actual loss was only made legal by treaties. But most "reserved" to natives a toehold of their former territory as reservations in the United States and reserves in Canada. This was land kept by the Indiens themselves, with the rest exchanged for goods, money, gifts, and services like health care, needed because of European diseases, promised by the national government.

After the loss of natural resources, most of the land, and much of their communal integrity, natives were left with their labor to exchange, just like any other citizen. In addition, of course, they also had whatever "valuables" were left on their reserves. While these often appeared barren and desolate in the West, hidden reserves of oil, gas, minerals, and gems were sometimes included. Thus, the very few wealthy tribes (Quapaw zinc, Osage oil, Navaho coal, Laguna uranium) receive more mention than their numbers would merit, either to highlight a missed opportunity on the part of American business ("If we had only known, those Indiens would have never been allowed to keep that land.") or the divine land right of natives ("The Great Spirit put that oil there to help us poor Indien people"). Even so, the capitalist world market has found ways of exploiting every and all of known resources.

Rock Art

All over the world, humans see painted, pecked, and sculpted markings on smooth rock surfaces and attribute them to powerful causes, sometimes spiritual, sometimes ancestral, sometimes both. No better example of human reverential relations with the land can be found than such "rock art," which is best described as a system of notation for showing special relations with the land in all of its dimensions.

Unlike graffiti, done anywhere by anyone, these markings resulted from special privilege. In native belief, after the world was made, a changer (or a group of transformers) went through the landscape preparing the way for humans. Sometimes these changes were deliberate, and sometimes they were inadvertent, depending on the characters involved. Two-way rivers and abundant foods become restricted so that humans would be challenged and not have life too easy. In other cases, brambles were given berries and trees sustain fire so that humans would benefit.

In the process, the most dangerous inhabitants of the earth – variously called monsters, cannibals, and demons – were reformed, modified, or petrified. For example, whenever a changer met monsters, he variously sent them into the earth under a hill, dismembered the body and flung the pieces in various directions, petrified the body on the spot, or turned the giant into something harmless. Thus, Mosquito was once a huge blood-sucking killer until a changer killed and burned its body. From the ashes, however, arose tiny suckers that continue to plague the world, although now as a nuisance rather than a menace.

To mark each of these sites of transformation, particularly to remind humans of acts done for their benefit, rock markings appeared, usually at river rapids, springs, trails, and mountain peaks. Often, these markings indicate the type of being fixed there to become available as a spirit partner. When a boy or girl had such a successful encounter during a vigil, they marked clothing and other artifacts with a sign of their partner and powha. Shamans, however, did even more and marked details of their vision on outcrops near the site where it happened. Because shamans dealt with great reserves of powha, their marks served to substantiate and harness these flowings. Using red iron oxide, black carbon, and, rarely, white glaze, the source and direction of the powha was vaguely indicated, as a reminder to the shaman and others who came after him or her that powha flowed from that spot. Yet the pictographic representations were never explicit because that would reveal too much and make the powha both too accessible and too ordinary.

Like an icon painter in the Orthodox tradition, the shaman became a channel for the flow of powha. Thus, he or she could also apply marks to other locations to spread powerful influence. In this way, approaches to the town or camp were the shaman lived were marked with signs of his or her powha as protection against enemies or hostile thoughts. More than boundary markers, these paintings served as warning signs, legal claims, and military challenges to outsiders venturing too near that community.

In general, rock art research indicates the great disparity between chalk and ocher perspectives. While researchers, both amateur and academic, have concentrated on the placement of these markings near springs and game trails, supposedly to indicate the location of likely hunting places, natives emphasize that such markings – whether on rocks, debarked trees, or caves – really communicate between these spirits, species, and humans of that place. Like a carved totem pole, which grew out of this same tradition, the marks were a "deed" or "covenant" between place and people in all forms and intelligences. More than "signs from the ancestors," rock art was aboriginal writing, preserved at a place which was simultaneously a university, cathedral, library, and eden used to instruct later generations of well-trained questers who were fasting in proximity to such murals to gain a successful career of benefit to themselves and their people, human and otherwise.

Planting Arc

An imaginary arc bending westward from the mouth of the St. Lawrence River to the mouth of the Colorado divided those native Americans who farmed from those who harvested the natural bounty of their lands.

Along the south and east, inhabiting the drainages of the Atlantic coast and the Mississippi River were the tillers of the soil raising corn, beans, squash, sunflowers, tobacco, and a host of other plants domesticated in North America. In the west and north, also according to water flows, were people who fished, gathered plants and fruits, and hunted for a living. Both economies depended on a close and careful relationship with the environment, but each had different social expressions.

By virtue of living in these lands for tens of thousands of years, natives developed a loving regard for the other species sharing their time and space. In a real sense, these millennia made humans the tenders of their landscapes. Just because one half tilled their fields according to time honored cycles of planting and harvesting did not mean that the other half was not intimately involved with their own local environmental cycles. Indeed, regular spring burning over of the landscape, transplanting wild foods and resource materials to more convenient locations, and sorting for better plantings were practiced throughout the Americas.

After thousand of years, although most foreigners failed to see these efforts, natives had groomed the Americas without doing violence to the local ecologies, as happened worldwide with the Industrial Revolution. For example, throughout the entire Micronesian island of Pohnpei, every place has a name, an owner, and epics about its immortals and genealogical history detailing its "gardens, boundaries, and a complex system of land tenure" which look to an outsider as jungle.[20] Collectively called tiaken sapw, "the law of the land," the Americas had much the same, where the distinction between tillers and tenders meant that the farmers had a more reliable surplus of foods to sustain them in more permanent towns. Tenders relied on the bounty of nature, helped along by their own efforts at natural selection, and were involved in an annual round of seasonal migrations to age-old camps sites at weirs, traps, and harvesting locations for fish, meat, shoots, seeds, fruits, nuts, and roots.

Farming supported large populations living in towns, whose members also dispersed with the seasons to gather the bounty made available by nature, which supplemented their stored crops during the winter. Larger populations in more settled abodes needed more complex social and political organizations than did mobile peoples. While families recognized bonds of kinship with all other forms of life, tillers often emphasized one side of their family for tracing descent. Most often this was the mother because women were believed to have a special bond with the land, crops, and life via birthing.

While the southern peoples traced kinship through the mother, northern farmers traced through the father. The major difference between these matrilineal and patrilineal descent systems involves male succession to official positions. In patrilineal systems, authority passed from fathers and brothers to sons, while in matrilineal ones, descent passed from mother to daughter but the positions succeeded from uncle to nephew, specifically from mother's brother to sister's son. Men were important because of who their mothers and sisters were, not their fathers, and all significant links were through females.

Kinship

Among all human societies, social units with distinct identities depended on the size and density of the population, which itself depended on the local economy and available foods. Larger kinship networks engulfing families (married pairs and their children, mostly as an abstracted analytical unit) included three well-known types – unilineal, bilateral, and ambilateral.

Unilateral (one sided) kinship occurred in more complicated and populous societies where it was traced only through the father, only through the mother, or through each parent for different purposes. In these cases, family households were submerged within lineages, transgenerational linkages through fathers and sons or through mothers and daughters within larger institutions. But patrilineages and matrilineages were not mirror images of each other

20. Martha C. Ward, Nest in the Wind 1989: 30, 58.

sheltered

because men always took the public community positions of leadership in both. In other words, while men were both leaders and kinsmen because of who their fathers were in a patrilineage, for a matrilineage based community, kinship depended on mothers but leadership passed from brothers to nephews through the common link of a woman who was sister to the office holder and mother to the inheritor, as described for the Iroquois and Hopi since the 1600s.

Lineages are, in turn, components of larger groupings such as <u>clans</u>, phratries, and, sometimes, moieties. While lineages rarely have a name apart from the oldest living grandparent, all of these larger clanship units are named formally. Whether a patriclan or a matriclan, real or metaphorical kinship was traced among all clan members, so they can never marry.[21] For example, when a member of the Turtle clan travels, he or she will receive a warm welcome and open hospitality in any Turtle clan household, even of another tribe. The virtues of this mystical bond of clanship, therefore, are readily apparent because of the wide range of kin, mutual caring, and supportive protection which are automatically assumed among clanspeople. If a member is hurt, injured, or killed, men of the same clan as the victim are obligated to take revenge or otherwise seek justice.

Clans, in turn, gather into <u>phratries</u>, often on the basis of some logical parallel that forbids intermarriage. Thus, clans called Crane, Frog, Sand, and Willow would belong to a Water phratry. Among Hopi, phratries protect rituals owned by clans from extinction so that its last official will teach its rite to a man in another clan within that same phratry so it can then inherit the necessary fetish and take over hosting that rite.

<u>Moieties</u>, whether composed of phratries or only of basic households, divide a community into two halves, bisecting the universe into sky or earth, land or water, right or left, and any other likely opposition. Along the southern United States, moieties called Red or White, symbolic of War or Peace, were characteristic of the sophisticated farmers known as the Mississippians, the ancestors of tribes who later emerged as Creeks, Cherokees, Choctaws, and so forth. Along the upper Mississippi and Missouri River, various Siouian peoples had Earth or Sky moieties, each composed of a number of clans aligned into land, water, and air phratries. Among the Pueblos of the Southwest, Summer or Winter, also known as Squash and Turquoise, were characteristic halves (see below).

Bilateral (both sided) systems included only about three generations focused around a set of individuals forming a <u>kindred</u>, a unit also know as "extended family" in modern American society. Members of a kindred were traced through both the mother and the father as far as acceptable memory allowed. During a life time, each member was the center of a <u>personal</u> kindred of all known relative, while a <u>prestige</u> kindred involved all those who traced kinship to someone famous, wealthy, or honored. Among tribes, therefore, such kindreds were huge. In practice, however, kindreds functioned in terms of significant individuals who guided and directed the membership. Most commonly, a <u>nodal</u> kindred formed around the node of a married couple, and, after their death, around a cluster of their children, siblings (brothers and sisters) with their wives and children. A typical example is the *tiospaye* of the Lakota, larger than a married couple for protection but smaller than a tribe to be easily fed. In cases where an office or fetish was inherited, successors formed the descent line of a <u>stem</u> kindred, as with the transmission of certain sacred bundles among towns of the Skidi Pawnee confederacy.

Ambilateral (chosen sides) descent can be traced through both parents, with the resulting

21. In some cases, since clansmembers can not marry, boys and girls not closely related teach each
     other about sex.

sheltered

discrete units called <u>septs</u>, though actual residence determines which of the possible septs someone belongs to at that moment. Where special rules, such as primogeniture, are vital, high ranks trace membership in a <u>ramage</u> composed only of privileged links such as that from first born son to first born son, who in turn marry only first born daughters, important in the proper inheritance of high or chiefly rank, as among Wakashans of central British Columbia.

Arrow Releases

Native Americans, in all things, wanted to be precise, as defined by village, district, drainage, and tribal customs. A particularly apt example was the manner in which men released their arrows. This simple and vital task involved many cultural differences that distinguish neighboring communities from each other. The four basic variables were the hand, the bowstring, the arrow, and the bow, whose various combinations formed five named patterns.[22]

"Primary" used the thumb and bent index finger to pull on the arrow, as in the Northeast, Southwest, and California among Penobscot, Miqmaq, Navaho, Maidu, and Luiseño; along with parts of Africa.

"Secondary" used the same grip to pull on both the string and the arrow, as in the Great Lakes and Southwest among the Seneca, Ottawa, and Zuni.

"Tertiary" plucked the string between the thumb and extended index finger, particularly on the upper Mississippi River among Siouians, along with Menomini, Blackfeet, and sections of Africa and Southeast Asia.

"Mediterranean" was thumbless, pulling the string between the index and middle fingers, as in Southern Europe and among the Eskimo and Seri. Luiseño learned the technique at their Spanish missions.

"Mongolian" involved a leather or iron ring around the thumb to pull the string and was used by specialized archers in Siberia, China, Turkey, and the Californian Yahi, as demonstrated by Ishi, the last Yahi whose final haven was the museum at the University of California in Berkeley.

Bows could be held vertical straight up along a standing body, as among the Welsh, or horizontal crosswise. Along coastal flyways of Brazil, huge bows were drawn with the legs to shoot down migrating waterfowl.

Across North America, the patterning of these releasing distributions was Tertiary in the center, Secondary around that, Primary around the outer edges, and Mediterranean in the North.

All other basic techniques – such as fire making, house building, pottery shaping and decorating, and clothing – also required precise techniques both to accomplish the task and to indicate various social identities, ranging from that of the village to that of the wider culture area.

Languages

Intended to be the most precise of all expressions were languages and rituals, where an aesthetic of perfection was expected. Words and phrases were chosen with the utmost care, to convey exact shades of nuance and meaning. The grammars of most native languages required the speaker to specify automatically whether or not the information was the result of direct

22. Alfred Kroeber, Arrow Release Distributions 1927.

sheltered

experience or vicarious hearsay. Referents were marked with verbal tags, such as the Algonkian obviative which specified the "other (B) guy" in a sentence like "I gave him (A) to him (B)."

For a speaker of the English language, the diversity and complexity of Native America speech comes as a surprise. Befitting their long residence in Americas, many varied tongues evolved here. There never was "The Indien Language." Rather, in North America alone, over half a dozen major language stocks divided into hundreds of mutually unintelligible languages.

Distinctive and intriguing features of these languages will be contrasted from the perspective of English grammar. Speakers of other languages would be perplexed by slightly different forms. While no detail is absolutely unique to Native American languages, some do have a very limited distribution in the world.

By comparison with English, Native American sound systems (phonetic inventories) include few vowels but many consonants, often "harsh sounding" when produced at the back of the mouth and in the throat. In particular, these include glottalized consonants made by closing off the windpipe. The Pacific Northwest area has one of the most complex consonant systems in the world, often stringing several consonants together without any intervening vowels. In some sound systems, the length of time that vowels are pronounced or that tones change the meaning of the word. Keresan even has sounds and whole syllables that are whispered, suggesting they are slowly passing out of usage.

Linguists trained in Amerindian linguistics learn to be sensitive to these and other possibilities, using written characters developed from the International Phonetic Alphabet (IPA) by Franz Boas (1916), Edward Sapir, and others to transcribe them.

Native speakers who learn several languages modify the sound systems of each to conform to a generalized pattern. Thus, as in the past when leaders spoke many languages, grammars have continued to be modified through the historic period as natives have also learned to speak English. In even more diluting fashion, American speakers have filtered many native place names through the English sound system so they have lost all but vestiges of their original pronunciations.

Native languages are grammatically complex because, where English would use different words or sentences to convey different shades of meanings or ideas, these languages either add a sound cluster or a particle (lexical) to express nuance. The addition might sound unlike any other full words meaning the same thing, or be formed by a standardized contraction of the whole word.

Other grammatical features unfamiliar to English speakers include inflecting (if the language has verbs) for aspect rather than for tense. Aspect expresses types of actions: inceptive (starting), instantaneous, durative, continuative, cessative (ending), and so forth. Verbs can also express different modes (modalities): indicative, imperative, negative, and so forth.

In all native languages, verbs distinguish between transitive and intransitive forms, although not all of them take accusative objects. Languages such as Tsimshian are ergative, meaning they "work" differently because what look like intransitive subjects and transitive objects are treated as the same.

In some languages, speakers automatically or inherently, without conscious deliberation, add lexical affixes that specify (like English prepostions) exact locations (beside, near, far, on the water, in the house, upward through the air, etc.), position (left, right, front, back, above, below, etc.), and shape.

sheltered

For example, Navaho[23] has over a dozen inherent shape classifiers of round-compact, animal-animate, long-slender-rigid, separate objects, contained substances, packed-consolidated material, fabric-like, parallel objects, bulky objects, bunched-together objects, granular masses, fluffy-vaporous-uncompact substances, long-flexible objects, amorphous-mushy substances, and so forth. Navahos delight in word games in which a bizarre shape class is applied. In a famous example, a hunchback referred to himself as "round-compact" instead of "human."

Instrumentals are affixes which indicate if something is done by hand, by foot, by mouth, by canoe, with a certain tool, etc. Other affixes might specify whether someone/thing was directly or vicariously experienced, was directly visible or not, and has ever been living or not.

Some languages have different counting or number systems for enumerating shapes – such as boxes, canoes, balls, people, animals, or tools – and concepts, such as offices and duties. As the great traders of the Pacific Northwest, Tsimshian used seven different ways of counting, either all-purpose or for humans, long objects, canoes, humans aboard canoes, volume unit measures (cups), linear unit measures (spans), and animals, including flat objects like hides.

Some languages do not have the English form of plurality, but rather recognize the singular, dual (pairs, as pants), distributive ("each their own"), and collective ("all their"). A frequent feature is two forms of the first person plural pronoun: the `exclusive we' (first and third pronouns, s/he and I, not you) and the `inclusive we' (all pronouns, s/he, you, and I).

Another widespread grammatical process is reduplication: patterned repetition of certain sounds or words. English uses reduplication in so-called `baby talk' as an affectionate diminutive in forms such as John-John and lovey-dovey. Many native languages use it to bolster their grammatical richness. In Lushootseed (Puget Salish), different reduplications express different meanings. An example is the word for "American," which is derived from the word "Boston" as filtered through the Chinook trade pidgin: Boston = pastad; Americans all over = paspastad, American (pejorative) = papastad, American child or Caucasian friend = papstad, and American children = papapstad.

Socio-linguistics studies the social contexts of languages, particularly what are called registers, which range from personal to informal to poetic and eloquent. Usages also include argots and pidgins. An argot (also called a social dialect) is a speech difference recognized within a community, usually associated with particular roles or careers. Examples might be the distinction of the speech of men from women, old from young, and sacred from mundane.

A pidgin (sometimes popularly called a jargon) is a trading vocabulary and minimal grammar used by people of various linguistic and cultural backgrounds. Pidgins must have occurred prehistorically, but the ones we know best have blossomed and proliferated, if not originated, during the era of the fur trade and European goods. The best known spoken pidgins were associated with a major river that served as a trade route: the Delawarean, Mobilian, and Chinookan.

The Delawarean pidgin was spoken along the Delaware River, blending Delaware and Dutch with some Swedish and English. Some Delaware words that were borrowed into English were filtered through this pidgin: wigwam from /wikwam/ `house,' corn pone from /ahpon/ `bread,' and moccasin from /maksin/ 'shoe.'

The Mobilian pidgin was spoken from the mouth of the Mississippi River throughout the Southeast. Like Creole Cajun cooking, it blended Choctaw, French, and other languages, including some from Africa. Folktales of Uncle Remus and Brair Rabbit using Southeastern,

23. Gladys Reichard 1951: 339ff.

African, and European motifs filtered through Mobilian.

The Chinookan pidgin was spoken along the Columbia River and throughout the Plateau and Pacific Northwest, blending Chinookan, Nootkan, French, English, and some localized forms from Spanish and Russian.

In addition to these spoken pidgins, the Plains sign language of gestures was ancient enough to have northern and southern dialects.[24]

More than half of the 2000 Native American languages estimated to have been spoken at contact have disappeared. This does not always mean their speakers died because some communities have merely shifted to English or to another native language. These shifts in language preference reflect indigenous processes, reported from all over the world.

Western Subarctic and Plateau peoples who lived along rivers which empty into the Pacific have long been shifting to coastal languages and cultural patterns, which became successively adopted upstream, village by village, until, to use an English suffix, they "-ized," as, for example, aboriginal Athapaskan Subarctic communities have been "Tlingitized" and "Tsimshianized" over the past century or so.

Our understanding of the underlying semantics of these languages remains inadequate, but is being addressed. Especially helpful in this undertaking is a small group of linguistically trained PhD native speakers who are providing remarkable insights into their languages. Navaho, Nootkan, and Tohono O'otam Papago.

Understanding is growing about the profundity of semantic dimensions for some languages and stocks. For the Salishan family, a pervasive grammatical distinction indicates whether or not the speaker was in control or careful of a situation. Puget Salish lexicals which express control (-t) or the lack of it (-du') provide one example: /uk^walt/ = someone poured it, /uk^waldu'/ = someone spilled it.

Athapaskan and Algonkian grammars include an "animacy hierarchy" based on the degree of mental discipline and willfulness of beings. According to this scale, humans have more deliberateness in their actions than horses, which have more than bugs. Significantly, while all share minds, some beings have more mindfulness than others, but this does not mean that those with more can or should dominate those with less. For example, animacy makes it impossible to say "The horse kicked the man." Instead, it has to be said as "The man allowed the horse to kick him" because he was not paying attention.

For Algic (Algonkian) languages, grammars inherently distinguish two qualities, named animate or inanimate. But this does not seem to be a clear-cut living/non-living distinction. Charles Hockett[25] pointed out that in a Cree story, the word for the skull of a witch, which chased and spoke to children, had an animate ending. He argued that the key features of the animate was the ability to communicate. But other data does not support his argument. In Ojibwa, `airplane' is animate, as is `knee' in Delaware, but both do not usually communicate. Building on the work of Mary Black and others, Miller[26] proposed that the key feature of the Algonquian animate is the ability to move, the property of self-propulsion or self-motivation.

Recently, scholarly attention has turned to ways in which English is spoken by native peoples, leading to the study of so-called Red or Indien English. Of interest, these dialects of English include grammatical features of the original native language spoken by that community.

24. Brenda Farrell, Do You See What I Mean 1995.
25. Charles Hockett 1966: 62, note 10.
26. Jay Miller, Delaware Alternative Classifications 1975.

Politeness, constructions of indirection, and expressions emphasizing process enable these speakers to modify English in ways appropriate to prior native contexts.

In general, native languages are much more concerned with verbs than with nouns, with process rather than product. Indeed, they often rely on "pronoun arguments," assuming that a listener is fully aware of what they refer to. In this regard, native pronoun systems are highly complex, incorporating some very specific forms that allow for "switch referencing" so that a hearer will always know which of the several males called "he" is the current topic.

Survival

If pressed to explain their present situation to outsiders, modern elders will often say that they have to maintain their culture because their children are too busy just surviving, staying alive, to devote much time to upholding their own traditions.

Though a severe statement, it is a truthful one. Indeed, survival is what native people have to do to keep themselves and their families in food, gas, clothing, and other necessities. They usually need money to do this, earned from unskilled and semi-skilled jobs involving resources such as forestry, fish, and crops. Often, people have to stay away from their native community for long periods and so lack the time to participate in on-going social and ceremonial events.

On the other hand, ritual leaders and ceremonialists are often too busy with their sacred responsibilities to earn an income and so have to rely on gifts and payments from employed tribal members to have ready cash. Though this delicate interaction, those with incomes learn that their emotional survival requires the continuing support of those elders and leading families who were and are the core sustainers of tradition.

Survival means that children are not encouraged to learn native languages and traditions in the mistaken belief that this will interfere with their education in American schools. Well-meaning elders hope that by denying these traditions, their children will profit from the perceived advantages of white Americans. Usually, this does not happen unless elders also provide a strong sense of direction and self-confidence for finding a way through the social and emotional morass of the modern world. Too often, they have simply bought into the distortions of colonialism, or the intolerance of grade-based education.

In consequence, elders have had to point out that culture, a satisfying life, is not the same as survival, earning a living. Often, for them, the two are incompatible. Both require vast amounts of time. Any ritual requires commitment and effort during its preparations and performance. Special materials have to be gathered from nature, certain clothes must be made, and the setting for the rite must be cleaned and readied. Any job, particularly when a time clock has to be punched, conflicts with these needs. So does caring for family members, who are often quite numerous. As a result, not surprisingly, elders, grandparents and older, do the work of keeping a culture alive.

Nor is this a new solution. In ancient times, grandparents were the baby sitters and the teachers of tradition because parents were too busy hunting, fishing, farming, or gathering. It was easier to leave young children at home with elders and to allow the able-bodied to harvest available foods.

In many languages, this closeness between alternating generations, grandparents and grandchildren, was indicated by their use of exactly the same kinship term for each other. By skipping a generation, these reciprocal terms indicated the bonds of culture uniting the old and the young. Because of this training, after their own time as parents engaged in survival, older

sheltered

adults could recall the knowledge they needed to be good grandparents.

During visits home, parents are re-exposed to aspects of their culture at summer pow-wows and tribal gatherings. During such occasions, elders speak in public to instill values, attitudes, and practices that were once commonplace.

Primary among these traditions was sharing, with humans and with the world, as vital to the intermeshed community of life. When the late Martin Sampson, a Swinomish leader, was asked by Vi Hilbert, his relative, to define native culture, he said "culture is learning from the land."

With great insight, Sampson captured the essential difference between culture and survival. Culture involves keen attention, receptivity, and reciprocity within the entire community of sentient, sensitive, and sensory life. Survival merely consists of a disinterested utilization of some obvious, but less important, features of this unity. As with beliefs about salmon giving their blanket of flesh willingly, the superficial covering of something needed for survival is less significant than its immortal essence.

Culture is a dynamic, interactive, and receptive process of learning and sharing, while survival involves a drudgery, mechanical and uninformative, that is both lonely and soul wearying. The first recognizes the primacy of the spirit and spiritual; the second ignores them for mundane reasons of practicality until such time as conditions become so wrong that they require a ritual to restore proper relations. Tribes such as the Navaho have specific "sings" that must be performed when a family member returns home from being away to remove any taint that comes from living with other Americans and non-Navahos.

In the greatest sense, culture is more than sharing, which was itself but an expression of the connectedness of all things. Many of the "omens and portents," termed superstitions by early missionaries, were also reflections of these connections.

For example, in Chicago, a native couple who had been born and raised in the city and had only the vaguest of ties with their ancestral cultures, nevertheless understood this overall unity. Once they came home to find that a bird had gotten into their apartment, itself a portent that things were out of order. In trying to catch the bird to put it outside, the boy, who had been drinking, fumbled his catch and bent the bird's wing. Even after the bird was safely outside, he felt bad about hurting the bird. A few days later, the boy was picked up by the police and had his shoulder joint wrenched when the officers twisted his arm backward. Though he was released with only a warning, the couple remain convinced that his hurt shoulder was a direct consequence of his inadvertent treatment of that bird. They too knew that if life is to continue, every living thing deserves to be treated with respect.

Natives invest most of their time and energy in people and places, not in things. While the first impression most Americans have of an Indien reservation confirms a sense of the poverty and despair they associate with a ghetto, that perception is fed by their own preconceptions about the value of possessions over greater human concerns. While a popular bumper sticker proclaims "The one who dies with the most toys wins," natives deplore that attitude. Their stance is personal, moral, and good, but never that of the mainstream.

Reservation yards are littered with derelict cars, keeping spare parts handy. Houses are unpainted and neglected because, in addition to lack of money, time is better spent with fellow humans. Moreover, painting and keeping up a house will make neighbors look bad. While other Americans delight in one-upping their neighbors, natives do not, as a rule, challenge other people to competitive yard work or house keeping. It is not the native way to confront or to embarrass anyone, except enemies.

sheltered

When natives speak to each other, they do not mention income, clothes, houses, or investments. Instead, they mention travel, relatives, and gatherings. They delight in visits, gifts, and food acquired by hard effort.

Even their use of space is different. All rooms serve many purposes. Food is prepared in the kitchen and served in the dining room, but, more often than not, fish, game, herbs, and berries are also prepared wherever space is available. During winter, for example, deer are best butchered in the bathtub before the joints are taken outside to freeze. Housing, traditionally, was just a shelter from the elements for both people, pets, and stored food. The same practice continues in manufactured homes where people still spend most of their time outside.

No space is wasted. Extra supplies, whether food, cloth, yarn, feathers, hides, or beads, are piled around the edges of rooms or behind chairs. While the inside might look cluttered, everything is arranged and stored with an eye to the future. Sofas, as many as possible, are used instead of chairs because they can seat more people, hold more bundles, and offer more space.

Native homes, whether on the reservation or in a city, will be arranged in much this same way. Time has proven its effectiveness. The major difference is that there is more to store and stack on reservations because this is where people belong. These lands, even if they were not originally ancestral territory, have now become tribal homelands, places where families are rooted and where, after a career in a city or corporation, elders retire to be buried. For most natives, time in the cities is only temporary, even when it spans forty years, most of a lifetime. Cities are places with jobs, wages, and excitement, among other "urban Indiens," but they are also places of discrimination, repression, depression, and social pathologies, most of which also occur on reservations though relief is much nearer.

For "traditional" natives, however, cities are places for drugs, unsafe sex, alcohol, abuse, despair, and a host of problems. But for those people for whom a reservation is mostly wasted time because they do not belong to the right family or are not old enough to take on ceremonial responsibilities, life in the city gives them an outlet to avoid drinking or living alone.

Yet, for all the problems and disease in the city, natives remain adept at ignoring the worst things and highlighting whatever they like best, such as relatives living close by, handy shopping, and many more out-of-town visitors dropping in. As most urban elders repeat, "There is just more to do in the city than back home." Unfortunately, not all of these doings are beneficial.

Are there native perspectives on other facets of life and appearances? Indeed there are. One example, setting this contrast into relief, is missing teeth. Dentists have enabled most Americans to have exemplary teeth, even if they are artificial implants. People who are missing teeth do not go to dentists, probably because they are poor. Of course, they might be afraid, but that is never given serious consideration. Usually, when Americans see lost or decaying teeth, they think poverty and ignorance.

Yet many natives with gaps in their teeth recite harrowing stories of how they extracted their own painful teeth with great personal bravery. Instead of indicating poverty, therefore, missing teeth indicate native values of bravery, fortitude, and self-reliance. Many could have gone to dentists (and may go eventually), but instead chose to take care of their own problems in their own way.

Modern Americans, wanting everyone to be the same as they are, have a difficult time with natives, who love the nuances and subtleties of differences. How do natives cope with all these offers to do good and interfere? They ignore them until the do-gooders go away or learn to behave. Much as orthodox Jews avoid the world to espouse their own beliefs, so most elders and

sheltered

other traditionalists ignore or avoid contact with representatives of the modern world. This strategy is well proven.

Native America shared a network of kinship obligations, social concerns, and valued kindnesses. All natives understood these needs and participated in endless reciprocations. It was only with the arrival of Europeans − with their set notions of submission, obedience, taxes, prices, and rewards − that the system underwent strain and breakdown. Natives continued to share with each other, and, after a fashion, with Europeans, Americans, Canadians, and Mexicans during the pressures of treaty councils or revenue payments, but otherwise they kept their distance. As time has shown, the best recourse for natives facing nation states has been to avoid them as much as possible. Indeed, history has proved them right. As one elder said, "We are still here, but the governments of Spain, France, England, and Holland went back where they belong. Given time, our land will triumph again."

II
CULTURE MODEL

Because every culture seeks coherence, members must have some sort of model in their heads, not hard and fast but a flexible template, based on an overall tension and its ramifications through its own logic of connections between basic units as building blocks. An approximation of this model is the struckon, which consists of a series of meanings arranged in terms of a triple nested series called a matrix, and an apical echoing tension ordering the overall system.

Each and every matrix has a set of threeway relationships in which opposed categories were either specific (segregating, exclusive) or generic (aggregating, inclusive), with the span between them provided by a mediating (congregating, inclosive) categoric member linking that matrix into other of the culture whole as another expression of the crucial tension informing the totality.

This reverberating echo and its emanations match the matrices with increasingly more expansive exclusive, inclusive, and inclosive examples. Exclusive members are specific, limited, definite, and closed; while those that are inclusive are generic, unlimited, indefinite, and open.

The inclosive serves to combine both of the opposites to integrate them into the larger whole. Within each culture, three components stand out: the sensory, relating to an individual (personhood); the interpersonal, involving institutions; and the cosmic, applying to the universe as culturally defined. Each component has a particular tension that is useful for clarifying the overall echo. For the sensory, it is right/left; for the interpersonal, it is man/woman; and for the cosmic, it is night/day.

Across the Americas, usual linkages were right, men, animals, black, and night within the inclusive; or left, women, red, plants, and day of the exclusive. In terms of artifacts, these associations extend to tools (building, carving, farming, and hunting weapons like knives, axes, dibbles, arrows, spears, bows) for men and containers (baskets, pots, bags, mortars) for women. The inclosive mediator for the sensory is the heart, that for the interpersonal is fire, and that for the cosmic is the sun.

Sensory Expressions

Although some cultures may recognize that a person has more than just the senses associated with the eyes, ears, nose, mouth, and skin; our discussion will be limited to these five, considering, in turn, representative emanations of the visual, auditory, olfactory, oral, and tactile sensations. Because of their use in body symbolism these sensory emanations also encode gender. In addition, a few of the sensory emanations reflective of Mind will be presented at the end of this discussion.

As four of the five senses are located in the head, we begin at the top of the body and work downward. Among the Delaware, the living are careful to put grease in their hair because the dead are always buried with their hair ungreased. To leave the hair ungreased is to evoke death. This equation of living / dead with greased / ungreased also expresses the relationship of Man / Woman since men kill the animal that supplies the grease and women render it. Unlike the usual association of men with death, for the Delaware, women are responsible for the human dead and for all other life cycle rites. Among the Delaware, Man is inclusive and Woman exclusive, as living and greased are inclusive and the dead and ungreased are exclusive. Among the Lakota, hair is a symbol of vitality (because hair seems to grow after death) so that the scalps of slain enemies were taken to increase the life-essence in the group. Sometimes, for a year, Lakota parents will adopt a lock of hair from their deceased child in a Spirit Keeping Rite.

Among visual images, colors are the most striking examples of coded information. All tribes associate men or women with specific colors. Keres Pueblos use grue (green-blue) for men and yellow for women, linking each with turquoise or maize to imply hard/soft and smooth/lumpy textural differences. Keres express this color symbolism when painting their bodies or various offerings such as prayer-sticks. Among the Delaware, black is for Man and red is for Woman. This association of red with women is widespread, due to the association of women with birth, life, menstrual blood, and animal butchering. For example, some tribes believe that a child is conceived by the conjoining of semen and blood, white and red, which respectively produce the bone and flesh of the fetus. In some tribes, it is not the relationship between colors but a particular color that is emphasized, serving as a tribal emblem as one shade of purple does for all the Kickapoo.

Ears themselves were singled out for attention. Among the Inka of Peru and other nations, the nobility were called "big ears" to indicate that they were willing to listen and knew a great deal. Among the Adena and other archaeological complexes (BP 3000), polished ear spools of stone or wood served as badges of such leaders. Indeed, listening was a more important characteristic of taskers than giving directions. Similarly, one of the greatest insults in native languages is calling someone "no ears," implying that they do not listen, pay attention, or talk about anything worth knowing. Needless to say, this term is now frequently applied to bureaucrats.

Auditory emanations can include various sounds, songs, musical instruments, and periods of silence. Some native languages have different vocabularies for men and for women. Among the Californian Yana, the language of men had longer words spoken more deliberately than that of women with shorter words spoken haltingly.[27] Throughout the Southeast, many of the Gulf languages recognized different male and female social dialects.*

Universally, men and women also use different songs and musical styles. Amerind men predominate in the use of wind and percussion instruments. Men used flutes for courting, whistles for religious events, and drums or rattles for a wide range of activities, both social and sacred. At Creek dances, a few men use gourd hand rattles and several women strap turtle shell rattles on their leg calves. Among the Hopi, when men dress to impersonate the masked deities called Katsina (Kachina), they use gourd hand rattles as male katsina or rasps played on inverted calabash halves as females.

Native Americans also plucked instruments with one or two strings, particularly the musical bow. There is some controversy over the origin of the Apache fiddle of the Southwest for, although it is of native manufacture from thick yucca stalks, the likelihood is that it is inspired by Spanish or Mexican fiddles.

Each of the culture areas has its own distinctive song and musical style. In lieu of a discussion of their complexities, I will note that they are summarized by Driver (1965) and Nettl (1954).

Any treatment should also include mention of the contributions of ethnomusicology to Americanist research. The invention of the phonograph provided a permanent record of many songs and styles over the past century, as among the Numipu (Nez Perce). Songs or music was recorded by Alice Fletcher from the Omaha in 1884, by Franz Boas from the Inuit in 1883-4, by

27. Theodora Kroeber 1961: 30.

Jesse Walter Fewkes from the Passamaquoddy in 1890, and by James and Charles Mooney from southern Plains tribes in 1894. More recent recording and analysis has been done by Francis Densmore, George Herzog, Willard Rhodes, David McAllister, Gertrude Kurath, Alan Lomax, and many others.

While much research has been done on music, comparatively little has been done on acoustical features of silence and laughter,though both are particularly well developed in Native America. Silence is full of complex meanings.[28]

Ochers have learned to sit quite comfortably for long periods in silence, simply enjoying the physical presence of another person. Obversely, among the Tsimshian, if the audience greets someone's formal speech with stony silence, whatever that person said or claimed is immediately invalidated. Among Plains tribes, someone wanting to be alone in a lodge full of people has only to turn facing the wall and remain silent for his or her privacy to be respected while bustle continues in the lodge.

Laughter, joking, and fun remain important aspects of Native life, prime ingredients in their survival. People are constantly joking, sometimes innocently and sometimes obscenely if a formal joking relationship exists between inlaws. In addition, laughter and ridicule remain the most effective forms of social control in all tribes. Physical punishment was rare and the high regard for personal autonomy kept people from ordering things done. Therefore, people were shamed or ridiculed into following social norms as they grew up or backslid.

The one aspect of laughter that has received considerable attention is the institution of the sacred clown or ritual buffoon.[29] Professional interest in these figures started because they are so very alien to the pattern of extreme seriousness expected during Judeo-Christian rituals. Throughout the Americas, there was and is a belief in a dynamic balance of the cosmos, where everything exists in harmony. Ergo, even the most serious rituals need to be broken by comic relief and buffoonery. In most cases, this comic relief is extremely ribald. In the past, scholarly descriptions of this portion of a ritual were either printed in Latin or Greek, laundered, or omitted. George Catlin published the sexual parts of the Mandan Okeepa in a Latin appendix, while Washington Mathews left out the sexual joking during a Navaho Mountain Chant until sufficiently criticized by colleagues to publish that section for private circulation. Although sacred clowns are invariably men, they act the roles of either men, women, or both.

Olfactory emanations include a wider range of impressions than is usually recognized by our modern scrubbed society, where odors are unwelcome and all refuse immediately removed. Among some tribes the stench of a camp was proportional with the esteem of a hunter. Some Anglos found Gosiute camps unsanitary and littered with human waste. These and other odors are totally unacceptable to modern Americans, but natives were equally aware of them, except that they had learned to either regard them favorably or studiously ignore them. Nuuchahnulth (Nootkans, West Coast people) mention the overwhelming stench released when a whale is butchered to expose a stomach full of several tons of rotting material. Yet no one ever showed any offense for fear that the whale's spirit would be insulted and inform other whales to avoid these humans thereafter. Whaling was the ultimate Nootkan career, entirely reserved for chiefs of the highest rank. The whale is more than a large mammal, it is anthropomorphized with the honorific title "noble lady". Similarly, the Tlingit and Tsimshian allow their olachen catch to rot

28. A resounding work on silence is that of Keith Basso for the Cibecue among the Western Apache.
29. Julian Steward 1931.

so it can be rendered more easily for oil. The resulting odor is never mentioned out of respect for the olachen and fear that any insult would prevent future runs of these candlefish.

At the other extreme from these strong smells are the aromatic aromas of various perfumes, incenses, and sachets. Everywhere except the Arctic and Subarctic, one of twelve species of tobacco was raised or collected for smoking, chewing, and offerings. Usually smoking was a ritual act in and of itself, closely associated with men and old age.* Among the Pueblos, old men continue to frown on tobacco use by the young. Often, native tobaccos are so strong tasting that various other plants, bark, and leaves are mixed together to "cut its bite." In the Pacific Northwest and California, tobacco was usually eaten or chewed rather than smoked. Among the stricter rules instituted by prophets, such as John Slocum of the Shaker Church, was that converts give up smoking because traditionally men inhaled to the point of stupification rather than as a light recreation. Among Coast Salish, such delirium was used by shamans to help them enter the trance state.

Other incenses include the use of sage, sweetgrass, maize meal or pollen, and red cedar needles. Among the Delaware, tobacco is inclusive, used to open channels of spiritual communication, and within the category of Man; while red cedar is exclusive, used for exorcism, and within the category of Woman. The Omaha accord great emphasis to smell in that they use the term "bathon" to mean both smell and powha.[30]

Oral sensations are closely related to food preferences in all societies. Food is always among the most conservative features of any cultural tradition. Thus, ethnic Italian-Americans continue to value pasta even if they have no other linguistic or cultural ties to Italy. Exact parallels to this can be found among ethnic Creek, Modoc, Pawnee, and so forth. Each of the staples of a Culture Area continues to evoke strong emotional ties among modern descendants. For example, although a series of dams prevent salmon from migrating into the upper Columbia River, Sanpoils continue to truck in fish for their First Salmon Rite. Every human group also recognizes only a limited number of ways for preparing food that is acceptable. Among these Sanpoil, women baked roots in pit ovens, while men roasted meat on grills. Similarly, throughout the world, men are associated with animal foods as hunters and women are associated with plant foods through their own labor as harvesters.

Seasonings also enter into the realm of taste. Salt was one of the most important items in the precontact trade and had great symbolic value. One of the ways a Tohono O'odam Papago could become a "ripe man" was to journey to the Pacific several times as a "salt pilgrim." Elsewhere, interior peoples traded for salt from coastal traders if there were no local salt deposits. Among Delawares, the word for salt also means penis, indicating its strong association with Man. Accordingly, salt is never used in food that Delawares intend for the dead or memorial feasts, since death is exclusive and womanly, as noted previously. Moreover, many elders alive today lament that individuals salt their own individual plates of food. In the old days, everyone ate from a large, common bowl because people believed that eating together from the same pot gave all of them "the same mind."

The tactile sense includes touch textures, body decoration, and clothing styles, all involving the hands. One of the reasons sometimes given for why animals are human under their skin cloaks is that they need human hands to function effectively in the world. The uniqueness of the human hand is widely known and appreciated throughout the Americas. A Californian tale explains that a contest was held between a lizard and a mammal to determine the form of this

30. Reo Fortune 1932.

hand. Fortunately, the lizard won so humans have digits instead of paws for greater dexterity. This story, moreover, illustrates the close kinship between all animate life in an anthropocentric world. Humans, lizards, and mammals are all closely interconnected so that the acts of one effects them all. Indeed, Naive America was pervaded by a sense of "oblique responsibility," meaning that a person was more obliged to others than to self. The welfare of the group came before that of the individual, particularly among elite families.

Almost universally, humans give priority to the right over the left.[31] For example, words for "right" usually have pleasant or valued connotations, while those of the left are undesirable. In Latin, right is dextra and left is sinistra, from which English derives dexterous and sinister. In French, left is gauche. In English, right also means proper and correct, as holds true in most native languages, where right is usually the inclusive and left the exclusive. Among the few exceptions are Keres and Delaware.[32] In some languages, the term "hand" encompasses the lower arm and hand from the elbow down, not just the palm and fingers as in English. Hands are so distinctively human and the right one is so often accorded priority that bears were and are believed to be left-handed.

This emphasis on laterality or handedness, as a natural way to represent both similarity and difference via body symbolism, conveys complex right and left meanings in all cultures. Usually, men have priority to women as right has priority to left. Since the Christian God is male, his right hand is valued. By analogy, if God were female, her left hand would receive the attention. Among several reformist native religious movements, adherents were taught to give priority to their left hands in order to distinguish themselves from Christians. Thus, in the Delaware Big House Rite and the Ojibwa Midewiwin, left is emphasized, with the explanation that it is closer to the heart.

Similarly, as pagans proudly distinguish themselves from Christians by reversing hand polarities, so several cultures placing primary emphasis on anthropomorphism, and thus concerned with the boundary between real and metaphoric humanity, solved the ambiguity by regarding ever-dangerous bears as left handed. A cultural rule was created to distinguish a discontinuity in Nature, albeit an anthropocentric nature.

Having discussed the extreme pairs of the sensory emanations, we will turn now to three common mediators expressive of the inclosive Mind. First is the significance of the number "3," second are various combinations of line and curve, and third is the symbolism of the heart, alluded to above.

All cultures use pattern numbers to give the impression of an ordered world. The most frequent pattern number in Native America is 4, redundantly expressed as the four directions, four seasons, and so forth, until it reaches the elaboration it has in Lakota cosmology. Other numbers such as 5, 6, 7, and 12 are also common, but all these pattern numbers require a base number of 3.

In mathematics, three points are necessary to define a plane. In any cultural system, three units are required to achieve closure. Thus, there are three elements: land, water, and air in every cosmology. Similarly, triads often collapse into dyads (pairs), with the missing inclosive or mediating third member assumed. For example, the world is usually described as a sky dome over an earth disk. In this conjoining of curved sky and flat earth, a closed semi-circle is created to represent the mediation of the curvi-linear and the linear. Three points are needed to create

31. Rodney Needham 1973.
32. Jay Miller 1972.

this form: the two end points of the earth and the peak of the sky.

In similar fashion, the form of the world is often represented as a cross inside a circle, combining lines and curves to express an integrated unity. Most directly, Keresans use a D-shape for sacred precincts. Among Pawnee, the design used to express Tirawahat, their high god, is a horizontal curve with a line down the middle, like a curved E with the barbs pointing down.

As the senses represent the interaction between the body and the external world, and the hands represent the boundary between self and other, so the heart represents the nexus of the internal world of the body, a microcosm. While modern industrial cultures have a centripetal orientation, always reaching outward, tribal cultures have a centrifugal orientation, focusing inward toward a logical central tysic. In terms of the societal macrocosm, this center can be a tribal shrine, leader, mystic bundle, pyre, or community lodge. For the microcosm, it is the heart, located in the middle of the body and often considered the locus of both thought and emotions. Natives fondly say that they think with their hearts and not with their heads, which is fully supported by linguistic and cultural evidence. In Delawaran, Tsimshian, and Salishan, the heart and the mind are equated. Among Numic people of the Basin, the liver fulfills the function of the heart as mind and among the Pawnee it is the throat, yet each of these is a tysic located in the torso of the body. Nor is this phenomenon unique to the Americas. Some Indo-Europeanists have argued that the heart and Mind were equated when ancestral Europeans lived in tribal societies.[33] In all of these cases, the vital significance of such crucial pivots is that they permeate and enclose personal and societal worlds.

Interpersonal Expressions

The basic universals for all human societies are gender and age, which provide both biological and cultural limits. Every member of a society has different roles and functions depending upon whether they are male, female, young, adult, or aged. In tribal societies, these differences are usually imperceptible in terms of dress or housing because, most commonly, social rank derived from control of knowledge and skills.

Often this knowledge was specific to various careers, such as prediction of prey behavior learned by hunters or sense of plant cycles shared among women. More esoteric data was restricted to magico-religious leaders such as shamans and priests. Usually, in the course of a life time, children began ignorant of valued information, but, as they mature into men or women, they acquired data appropriate to their gender and career. Children gained knowledge and maturity as they outgrew their tasks as baby sitters, messengers, errand runners, and helpers.

Among Winnebago, children were sent onto quaking bogs to gather cranberries because of their lighter body weight. The Quinault had children frolic on the beach so clams would spout bubbles to identify their locations for diggers. Sometimes, particular children, especially those from better families, specialized in a domain of information quite early, fulfilling the expectations of their family or kin group.

The most frequent pattern in Native America for tracing descent was bilaterality. Accordingly, kindreds, bands, and tribes, increasing in size, were the most common social groupings.

The other, unilineal, pattern traced descent either matrilineally through the mother or

33. Jay Miller 1977.

patrilineally through the father. In terms of increasing size, the unilineal groupings were lineages, clans, phratries, moieties, and tribes.

In some areas, tribes were bound together in loose confederacies under a ceremonial leader living at a religious center, capital, or mecca where a sacred fire burned. Within this larger system, individuals gave primary loyalty to their settlement, both residential and genealogical, where they had the strongest emotional ties.

While families were by and large socially submerged, a few elite families did play a crucial role in an overall community because the most important information was transferred within their household. Significant knowledge and positions were passed down through residents who consistently proved that they belonged to the better families.

Most communities recognized social ranks, but social classes were nascent, if present at all, in Native America. These ranks consisted of the high families who persistently produced hard-working, exemplary, generous, and thoughtful men and women. Distanced from them were other ranks held by individuals by virtue of personal achievement or pretensions. At the margins were ranks held by default.

Ideally, everyone had the option of advancing, accepting, or rejecting his or her natal destiny because all tribes accorded high value to personal autonomy, spiritual directives, and individual preferences. These better families were able to entrench their position by continually filling leadership roles in civil, military, religious, and shamanic tasks.

Each of these three leadership types required the possession of proper credentials, such as personality attributes, generous attitude, lifelong training, motivation, ability, and proper supernatural sanction from spirit partners.

A recurrent insignia of civil leadership, irrespective of other trappings, was a name-title attached to that office and passed on in perpetuity, for naming things made people distinctly human, charged with potentials and concerns culturally significant to all humans since they related to the order and meaning of the universe.

Examples of such hereditary name-titles were the 50 names of Royaner (Iroquois League Chiefs), chiefly names endemic to all Pacific Northwest Coast tribes, and the name Soktchum ("scratched") maintained through eight generations of Luiseño leaders in southern California.[34]

Since the Colonial period, Delaware have called each Governor of Pennsylvania by the name "Miquon," a word meaning feather, a pun on the last name of William Penn at a time when quill pens were used.[35]

At a more practical level, better families were able to maintain control of these names and civil positions because each leader produced a dozen or so children, who guaranteed a sizeable constituency during his or her lifetime and, afterwards, provided a stock of ancestors and spirits.

Military positions were held often by young and able men who earned respect because of their proven bravery, war records, trophies, plunder, and the safe return of all members of their war parties. Any fatalities within their recruits had be compensated for with gifts or the adoption of captives to "take the place" of the deceased.

Later in life, when an active military career was no longer feasible, a war leader might assume a civil position, as among the Cheyenne. A few tribes, like the Iroquois, had old men plan strategy and conduct war magic to steal away the souls of the enemies before any engagements. In many tribes, such mystical aspects of warfare were under the care of shamans.

34. Raymond White 1963: 97.
35. The Iroquois called Penn "Onas," with the same meaning.

Shamanism was among the very oldest of human specializations, practiced by the Asiatic ancestors who entered the New World. By and large, shamans were men, but for northern California, Nova Scotia Miqmaq,[36] or other areas that suffered severe population loss, female shamans predominated. While they might be biologically women, however, these shamans were often conceptualized as "men".

Such female replacement also occurred in Russia after the 1917 Revolution when women became doctors or took over high prestige job because men were scarce. In America during World War II, women who assumed many jobs formerly held by men became personified as "Rosy the Riveter." After men returned from the war, they again filled these jobs. In most cases, however, women were restricted to quasi-medical, care taker careers such as those of midwife, herbalist, or massage therapist.

Despite the male chauvinism of this resupplanting, it does serve to illustrate how universally the division of labor associates men with activities external to the home and women with duties that are domestic. For this reason, the most frequent native American pattern was for men to be inclusive and women to be exclusive.

This same external/internal distinction also applied universally to shamanistic techniques. In general, these medico-religious specialists were divided into brushing or sucking shamans, using varying curing procedures respectively for external or for internal treatments of diseases.

On the whole, aboriginal medicine was technically naive, emphasizing sweat baths, herbs, and psychological cures particularly for soul loss and sorcery. Cures were effective because shamans did not have to contend with epidemic diseases until these were introduced from Europe.

The Bering Strait "cold screen" and lack of domesticated herds to provide hosts for germs kept virulent diseases out of the Americas. Except for the Aleut (Unangan) and a few other groups who allowed for medical curiosity in terms of autopsies, anatomical knowledge was vague. Surgical sophistication was limited to setting broken bones, lancing wounds, trephaning skulls, cosmetic incisions for wearing ornaments, filing of teeth to points, and, sometimes, deliberate mummification.

Native medicine has a very different orientation than does modern (allopathic) medicine with its focus on curing the symptoms of a disease rather than the disease itself. By contrast, native medicine focused on the patient, in keeping with their more humanistic orientation. During a cure, varieties of song, dance, drama, and sleight-of-hand were used to divert the attention of patient, kin, and audience away from the symptoms so as to encourage a spontaneous recovery.

As many reports attest, these cures were every bit as effective as those of allopathic physicians. Since outsiders often scoffed at the use of legerdemain, it is important to note that, in the native view, simulation was done "not as a trick as we understand the term, but as a solemn representation of an unseen reality, as a dramatization of immaterial influences, as a miracle, and an efficient curing technique."[37]

Similarly, native law was based on providing compensation to pay for a crime instead of the more Biblical notion of direct retribution or punishment, except in extreme cases. Both medicine and law were eminently successful in their traditional settings, perhaps more so than modern medicine and law because the entire community was involved in these actions,

36. Frank Speck 1919: 246, #2.
37. Reo Fortune 1932: 34.

contributing to the psychological well-being of everyone, rather than just a single patient or victim.

This more communal, humanistic attention to individual and community naturally had patently beneficial results as a community maintained its solidarity and continuity during the succeeding life cycles of its members.

While life cycles are detailed in the five tribal configurations (Chapter V on language isolates zzz), we need to consider more closely the phenomenon of death – the most serious internal threat to social continuity.

Each society had its own means for providing cultural recognition of the biological fact of death. Usually these were rituals of mourning, burial, and bereavement, followed by those of memorial, name perpetuation, soul release and readoption, or of reincarnation. As death was a paramount cultural concern, significant cultural categories can often be seen most clearly in rituals for the dead.

In all societies, men and women carry their gender roles into the grave. Funerals were different for men or for women, and their graves were often distinctively marked. In modern America, grave stones, like the people they mark, have sex-specific names, if not also different styles of decoration. Delaware graves lacked names, but those of men were marked by a pole and those of women by a cross.

Some tribes held a series of funerals for a dead person at different stages of the decomposition process, as Chinese still do. In the proto-contact Northeast, individual graves were opened every decade or so for a Feast of the Dead. Bones were cleaned and wrapped so these bundles could serve as rattles during a night-long dance before all of these packs were buried together in a common ossuary. On the Plains, remains from a scaffold or tree grave were gathered up and buried at the same spot. In the Northwest, some buildings were used as charnel houses. Among Tillamook of coastal Oregon, the last members of a family line were placed together in their ancestral home. Among the Wishram, grave houses were used for generations, so older burials were periodically gathered and deposited in the Columbia River to provide room for new corpses.

As we have seen, among Delaware, human dead were associated with women, who dug the graves and prepared the feasts. Among the Keres, only men attend to the dead, dig the grave, and take the body to the cemetery. Because death was a boundary, provoking anxiety, between ghosts and the living, those who handled corpses were regarded with ambivalence, requiring that they bathe and purify themselves for a set time afterward.

These funeral specialists could be men, women, or both. Twana of Washington State recognized two men whose guardian spirit powha enabled them safely to handle the dead. Among the Choctaw, special old women grew long fingernails so they could clean off any flesh lingering on human bones before these were reburied in specially made basket caskets.

In addition to these religious considerations, graves also had an important political function by providing a permanent claim to a place. Given the frequent seasonal shifts of communities, the only people who could be considered permanent occupants of a place were the dead who were buried there. Because of tribal differences in grave markers and care, residents could argue forcefully for their claims to an area by pointing out these graves of their own ancestors.

When communities moved to new homes, they took their dead to establish new claims. When Tuscarora survivors moved from the Carolinas to New York State in 1712, they carried along the bone and flesh remains of ancestors and buried them near Niagara Falls. When

Puyallup-Nisqually of Puget Sound moved a winter village, they exhumed some ancestral remains to rebury them at the new site. According to the Jesuit Relations, when a fire broke out in a Huron town, the people rushed first to the cemetery, protecting their exposed dead before themselves.

Moreover, such reburials might be used to elevate the status of a particular individual or kin group. A Coast Salishan seeking to claim high rank might exhume a close relative and have the remains reburied with an elaborate memorial feast. He or she and their family could claim thereby that since the deceased merited such treatment, then so too did they.

In addition to such interpersonal emanations relating to gender and age, others related to the mediating powha of Mind, specifically the berdache (modern two spirit gays) role, games, and the symbolism of fluids.

The term "berdache" came from French to refer to a transvestite "man-woman," a biological male who adopted the clothing and gender of women. In rarer instances, a few women assumed male clothing and sex roles, becoming female berdaches. Often this role reversal involved only transvestism, vesting oneself in the clothing of the opposite sex, together with either celibacy or heterosexual relations. Among some tribes, most notably the Mohave and Lakota, berdaches were homosexual. Of interest was the tolerance if not acceptance given to such "gender benders."

Some scholars have argued that becoming a berdache was an alternative for those boys with neither the ability nor the personality to become Plains warriors, but some of the Plains berdache were fierce, earning many war honors. A more likely explanation of berdache was either an innate sexual ambivalence, an over-protective mother creating a strong cross-sex identification,[38] or evidence of both sets of genitals.

Such variation on gender and sexual themes made berdaches important mediators in anthropocentric cultures. They were often accorded high status because they possessed many abilities and had a powerful supernatural sanction. Tribes like the Apache are intolerant of berdache, although they do not prevent someone from assuming this role. Other tribes like the Cheyenne accorded them elite status. In many tribes, berdache were also shaman, combining two ambiguous roles to achieve greater powha. Among the Sioux, the berdache (called *winkte*) were considered *wakan*, thereby equated with the cosmic intelligence of Wakan Tanka (mysteriousness greatness).

As a whole, the Plains culture area recognized at least six gender roles. Aside from "natural, normal" men and women, there were the berdache, the contrary (a super warrior who did everything backwards), the amazon, and the virgin (who had a revered role in ritual).

Games also served as social mediators. They were universally used as a means for maintaining societal solidarity by defusing conflicting tensions. Among Tewa Pueblos, if the tension between the Summer and Winter moieties became too dangerous, native priests ordered an intra-town game with teams selected from the north or south sides of the pueblo or married men played against bachelors. In this way, moiety memberships were jumbled so that Summer and Winter members would have to play on the same team. Such enforced cooperation during a game regarded as holy and necessary generally was successful at disarming any further conflict.

Throughout the Southeast, the two stick ball game was played with Red side against White side. Among the Creek, if a White town lost four games in a row to the same Red town, it had to extinguish its town fire and rekindle it from a Red capitol (mother) town. For its violent

38. See Judith Suchowski ms.

intensity, the ball game was often called "the younger brother to war," though encouraging a more peaceful cooperation among tribal towns. Among Creeks, old men who controlled both the Busk world renewal rite and the ball game were called "the minds," indicating an equation of age, ritual, sport, and mental awareness.* [Parsons]

Among the Kwakwaka'wakw (Kwakiutl), the potlatch historically became a substitute for warfare much like the ball game. Accordingly, they say they no longer attack with weapons, but instead fight with property.

At a more general level, this all-pervading quality of Mind was symbolized throughout Native America by fluids. As discussed above, bones were not the only traces left by a person. Consciousness or life-essence was represented variously by breath, clear body fluids like spit and sweat, blood, and flesh, in addition to bones, hair, or several intangible souls, shades, shadows, ghosts, or spirits. Cherokee recognized that each of these substances decomposes at different times and they accordingly treated each span as a further release of the life essence.[39]

Data from elsewhere in the continent also suggest such timed releasing. Pawnee regarded a pipestem as "symbolic of the human windpipe and the breath was considered the essence of life itself."[40] The powha of a Tohono O'otam Papago shaman resided in quartz crystals primordially formed from the solidified spit of one of their creators, Elder Brother I'itoy.[41]

Throughout the Americas, quartz crystals were the most usual insignia of a shaman, suggesting that, regardless of locale or language affiliations, this association of shamans, crystals, and clear fluids was an ancient one. A Kootenay hunter spit on his arrow to make it fly true,[42] implying that his goodwill and respect for the game animal was given in return for its death.

Blood seems to be regarded differently than these clear fluids.* Traditional Delaware were utterly opposed to embalming their dead since it drained all blood, preventing it from becoming a spherical spirit in its own right. Today, all blood extracted from the corpse is kept in a special bag and buried with a respected Delaware elder.

The flesh of the dead was also treated separately. Makah ghosts repeatedly return to a corpse so as to remove all of its flesh in order to reconstitute their bodies in the afterlife.[43] Among Navaho, the body substance was considered an outer form (a symbolic Woman) and the spirit was an inner form (a Man).[44] Several other types of spirits also are relevant here, but they will be discussed in the next section on cosmic dyads.

Of all liquids, water had the greatest symbolic elaboration. Throughout Native America, water courses bound together all the lifeforms of a region. Traditionally, waterways were not regarded as boundaries, as they are now for American states and counties, but, instead, closest neighbors were those who shared the same drainage system, or traveled along the same river. In many locales, the phrase "we drink from the same water" was the equivalent of saying "we share the same mind, outlook, or identity."

The type of inhabitable locations along a waterway exerted a direct influence on the size of settlements, amount of inter-communication, degree of trade, kind of travel, strength of political integration, and nature of seasonal fluctuations in population size and residence.

39. According to Raymond Fogelson, eminent Cherokeeist.
40. Gene Weltfish 1971: 475.
41. Ruth Underhill 1948: 271.
42. Claude Schaeffer 1966: 13, 48 note 6.
43. James Swan 1870: 84.
44. Gary Witherspoon 1977: 142.

Common occupation of the same river system creates some unlikely alliances, such as that among the Karuk, Yurok, and Hupa along the Klamath River of northern California. Because waterways united many settlement and cultures, they were sometimes believed to be personified as water spirits. In common belief, all bodies of water are interconnected by a complex labyrinth within the earth. Thus, their spirits travel freely all over the globe.

In terms of anthropomorphization, waterways have been equated with Man, Woman, and Mind. Hidatsa believed that the Missouri River was the transformed, snake-like body of a personage named Spring Boy or Black Medicine at different times of his life. The Haida believed that each stream had its source with a particular Creek Woman. When White-Man-Chief of the Skidi Pawnee first saw the Atlantic, he said it was like God. By the term God he meant Tirawahat, the Pawnee deification of Mind translated as "this expanse" with reference to its all-pervading powha.[45]

Thus, in many ways and guises, genders of Man and Woman, along with gradations of various sorts, typify the social, political, and economic life of the Americas.

Cosmic Expressions

As the interpersonal parameters are gender and age, so the cosmic ones are time and space, populated by numerous creatures, spirits, deities, demi-gods, mortals, and immortals.

One aspect of the anthropomorphization of nature is that the humanoid souls of animals, fish, and plants are held to be immortal so they could surrender repeatedly their "worthless blanket of flesh" as food, as long as their remains were treated with respect and then ritually deposited in shrines, water, or fire. This repetition of death and rebirth implies a cyclicity of time involving human reincarnation.

Gitksan Tsimshians believe each of them is the reincarnation of a maternal grandparent of the same sex. Those with a strong will, when approaching death, might seek to influence their subsequent rebirth. One old Gitksan woman threatened her relatives, who were neglecting her, by asserting that she would be reborn as an Anglo-Canadian if they were not more respectful, thus depriving her matrilineage of a descendent.

Delawares believe that only a few babies are reincarnations, as determined by a visit from several old ladies who watch the infant for adult-like behaviors, general disposition, and physical features distinctive of some deceased person. For example, they look for dents in the earlobes where earrings were once worn, a mature disposition, and birthmarks in the same location as prior wounds.

Eskimos believe each of them has four kinds of souls: a soul of existence, a name soul providing personality and character, a breath soul of life, and other souls specifically fixed at each joint in the body. Name souls, at least, are distinctively identified as male or female, regardless of the body housing them, which can suddenly switch gender at the moment of birth. For Keres Pueblos, each person has a breath soul supplied by the father and a heart soul from the mother.

In addition to the cyclical concept of time with its recurrent deaths and rebirths, some tribes hold beliefs in either an instantaneous change or an incremental improvement in the cosmos. Puget Salish believe the Animal People (of Myth Age) ended when the Transformer

45. Preston Holder 1970: 43.

finished his work and the world "capsized" to assume its present form. Among the culture areas with modifying origin epics, Coyote or another Transformer created a series of gradual changes to tame the world of the Myth Age and slowly usher in the modern period.

Throughout the continent, there is the redundant belief in what Irving Goldman[46] calls "human consubstantiality," a belief that the underlying substance of the animate world is anthropomorphic.

The particular pantheon of spirits, deities, and monsters found in a culture mirrors its concerns and anxieties, as expressed through what is available and appropriate in the local ecology. In terms of the process of cultural projection onto nature, riverine people often place symbolic emphasis on turtles and frogs as amphibious mediators, boreal inhabitants do the same with humanoid bears, and desert dwellers use insects like ants or spiders to express their cultural tensions.

A few species (such as coyote, rabbit, bear, wolverine, dog, raven, and lizard) play the role of culture hero over a wide area. Usually these animals receive attention because of their impressive cunning, successful competition with humans for some valued food, or morphological similarity to humans.

Among Subarctic Chipewayan, in some contexts, the dog as a domesticate is equated with Woman and Culture, while the wolf as a feral sibling is associated with Man and Nature. Yet, at another level, wolf is Nature in opposition to Culture, which is maintained by men. In this context, dog serves as a mediator between these two perspectives by virtue of its movement between camp and bush pulling a sled.[47]

Thus far, all of these associations are congruent with American apperceptions of the natural order, but this is not always the case. Delaware divide all living things into "Man" and "Woman" members of each species, depending upon whether or not they produce offspring. Women of each species are identified therefore by flowers, eggs, or young, as Americans would expect.

When, however, the Interior Salishans add their terms for "Man" or "Woman" to the words for herbs, trees, bushes, animals, birds, or fish, they reverse what Americans would expect for plants. Man plants are those with flowers, seeds, fruit, and straight stems; while Woman plants are bushy, leafy, and crooked. While this seemed to imply that fecundity is a masculine trait, Salishan herbalists explain that Man plants have flowers that grow on a stalk. What the Salishans recognize are not the flowers themselves, but rather the stalks, which they regard as phallic. In addition, this recognition is strengthened further by cultural practice. Among the Salishans, men are the fancy dressers, wearing more colorful and detailed clothing. This ostentation is in keeping with the high value Sanpoil and other Salishans place on attractiveness, especially for males. As a logical anthropomorphization from the cultural to the natural worlds, this practice extends to biota with stalks because attractive plants with straight stalks are considered doubly "men."

Aside from these transformations in relationships, there are also a few features which seem to hold constant across the continent. Among these is the division of the universe into three elements: land, water, and air. Sometimes these elements are also divided into levels or tiers. Acoma Pueblo recognizes four tiers in the sky and four underground. The Delaware have 12 heavenly tiers, and some Great Lakes tribes have seven sky tiers and seven earthly ones.

46. Irving Goldman 1975: 200.
47. Henry Sharp 1976.

Some tribes also add fire as a fourth element, like the system used in Medieval alchemy – earth, fire, water, and air. Among Siouians, the halves of Earth (both land and water) or Sky encompass all other elements.

Another logical organization opposes land to water and sky, since the sky is reflected in water, thereby suggesting their equation. Among the widespread avatars of these elements is the belief in the perpetual antagonism between sky beings associated with thunder and lightning or their serpentine water-being adversaries. In the Pacific Northwest, these beings are called Thunderbirds and Whale, while in the Northeast, they are Thunderers and Underwater Panther.

Among Hidatsa, the process of making a clay pot is considered to be a recreation of the antagonism between sky and water, so potters worked in a darkened earthlodge to prevent the Thunder beings from causing lightning-like cracks in the vessels.[48]

Usually, as the aggressive hunters, Thunders are in the category Man while Water Monster is womanly, exclusive of the water since the moment any portion of it protrudes above the water, a Thunder being attacks it.

At the more prosaic level of the seasons, all societies have a round of economic and religious activities in which one of the genders predominates. Often, summer is the economic season of women for farming or gathering plants, while winter is the religious season of men and rituals. The spring and fall are transitional zones in which women collect greens or men hunt. Usually these seasons are tied into a directional symbolism such that winter is often personified as a fierce man living in the north and summer by a woman living in the south. The other directions are associated variously with men, women, or both living in the east, west, above, below, and center of the world.

Having reached the directional limits of the universe, we can reflect on how far we have come. MacCannel (1976) argues that the proper image for our time is not that of the industrial age, or men in quest of fame and fortune, or workers enslaved to money, but rather, the tourist in search of "authentic" experience. After all, everyone in the labor force works toward time off, leisure, and retirement, often for a chance to travel. In this regard, anthropologists might be considered as the ultimate in trained, professional tourists, intent on going further, probing deeper, and trying to communicate more articulately their authenticated experiences.

In areas of the world such as Native America, where this authenticated experience can involve tribes who are socially extinct, preserved only in memory, notebooks, or artifacts rather than via lived behaviors; researchers can nevertheless use these traces to recover for the human record further evidence of generosity, personal autonomy, unilineal descent, kinship terminology, indigenous or syncretistic rituals, cultural categories, and complex vocabulary.

Templates which continue to exist in the Minds (hearts) of Native Americans fortunate enough to share in an on-going tradition reflect their common appreciation of land base, language, sense of community, and shared long term experiences.

In addition to these cultural differences specific to Native Americans, general contrasts and similarities of Native America relate to the apical or near apical categories of gender (a paideuma variously called anthropocentric, Man/Woman, Precopernican, metaphorically human, or humanoid consubstantial). Yet none of these facts or features is unique to Native America. Only the particular concatenation of the relationships involved is singular by virtue of ecological factors, demographic trends, and cultural reactions, both to internal tensions and to external pressures on the community, society, region, province, culture area, or continent.

48. Alfred Bowers 1965: 374.

Uniting these disparities, however, has been an all-pervading concern with the images and concepts of Man, of Woman, and of Mind.

Most people have enough trouble with their own minds without bothering to find out if other minds work in the same way or not. Hopefully, by journeying through Native North America, guided by an appreciation of anthropocentrism, we can understand why the Iroquois speak of Man Great Beings and Man-Woman Great Beings, the Pawnee planted an even number of maize hills, the Chipewayan equated men with wolves and women with dogs, guardian spirit partners appeared in human form, and much more.

In doing so, we learn that human minds work in many different ways, but all are nonetheless understandable as resonating, via all these messages, that, to paraphrase Shakespeare, "The Measure Of All Things Is Human."

Summary

The various signs (concrete representations of concepts, categories, and values) used by a culture are drawn first from local surroundings and then from personal historical events. They are specific to that place and time, but select from past and future expectations to achieve coherence.

Still, there are some which are so general and obvious that they can be treated as American universals (particularly those relating to gender), allowing for a certain manipulation of their interrelationships into reversals or into expansive / constrictive patterns, as illustrated by examples given below, assuming that Woman is exclusive and that Man is inclusive.

Aspects of culture that relate to the senses include

Sensory	inclosive	inclusive	exclusive
touch	heart	right	left
shape	⊕	line |	curve)
taste	baking	roasting	boiling
sight	white	black	red
smell	offerings	smoking	cooking
hearing	silence	speech	laughter
thought	heart	brain	belly

For the interpersonal or institutional aspects of a culture, the divisions − though interconnected and strongly influenced by factors of gender, age, and social cohesion − are distinguished here for reasons of analysis as

Interpersonal	inclosive	inclusive	exclusive
technology	houses	tools	bags
economy	fishing	hunting	harvesting
polity	chief	captain	matron
	shaman	shamen	shamaness
kinship	hearth	fathers	mothers
religion	return	protect	nurture
language	holy	men's	women's

For the cosmic aspects of a culture, which tend to be the most specific, as explained in details of origin saga and religious practices, useful units are terrain, cycles (days and seasons), and some version of a network of immortals.

Cosmic	inclosive	inclusive	exclusive
terrain	water	air	land
day	noon	night	day
seasons	return	winter	summer
creatures	bosses	animals	plants
immortals	creator	males	females
	changers	spirits	humans

Of special note within the network of beings were the Transformers, who made the world as it is today. These beings were simultaneously spirits, animals, humans, and places. Across the continent, various species have these attributes. For the East it is Hare, for the West - Coyote, for some of the Plains - Spider, and for the Northwest - Raven.

In addition to each of the matrices exemplifying the components of a culture, various openings also served to allow passage from one context to another. Indeed, culture seems to be primarily concerned with boundaries and passages,[49] particularly during rituals of renewal, revival, return, and reproduction. For example, while the skin was the border between self and other, openings in the head and body, together with their out-products (such as tears, urine, wax), received ritual attention as points of transformation moving out from a tysic at heart, hearth, or sun.

Person = membranes, tracts

right / left	head / feet
heart	heart

House = flues, windows, openings

man / woman	old / young
hearth	hearth

Cosmos = caves, waterways, tunnels

day / night	summer / winter
sun-moon	solstice

49. See particularly, Ann Fienup-Riordan, Boundaries and Passages, Rule and Ritual in Yup'ik Eskimo Oral Tradition 1994.

III.
TRIBAL LANGUAGE ISOLATES
quileute, kootenay, keres, yuki, yuchi

Discussion for each of those tribes speaking a language isolate properly begins with a recounting of their origin saga to provide a sense of being and belonging at their special place. Then we consider housing since it best represents this unique relationship to a particular environment. Forests mean trees for house posts and planks, marshes supply cattails for mat covering, arid conditions lead to the use of adobe or stone, and frequent movements encourage the use of skin tents. Moreover, houses mirrored the contours of the world. Not surprisingly, people who live in round houses regarded the universe as round, while those who live in square homes spoke of a world with four corners.

The dimension of time – of successive movements matching those of the sun, seasons, succeeding generations, and outside forces – is considered in terms of a day, a year, a life, and local history. In doing so, the symbolic importance of often doing things by fours is also recognized.

The coming together of space, time, people, and spirits into some kind of perfection is expressed by the rituals that provide a sense of identity and belonging to those in the same tribal congregation. More than any other feature, native memberships were defined by participation in rituals, formerly aboriginal and now a mixture of native, Christian, and truly ecumenical.

For example, Shiuchi Nagata, an anthropologist from Japan, tells the wonderful story of being at Moenkopi, an Arizona Hopi town on Third Mesa, during World Peace Day when he had the delicate task of remaining neutral while a Chinese Buddhist monk, through his Japanese translator, both of whom had been invited by the local Eskimo Bahai missionary, made a speech that simultaneously lauded Bahai beliefs and denounced the duly elected governments of the United States and the Hopi Tribe.

Lastly, we consider how and what we know about this particular culture and its people from a variety of sources.

Among the topics deferred until this section are life cycle events and rituals, which can now be discussed within an integrated ethnographic context. Since no one tribe is ever that typical or atypical in terms of its Culture Area, except in a statistical sense, serious consideration was given to finding a fairly consistent way of selecting tribes for coherent sketches.

The decision to limit the discussion to the surviving linguistic isolates has meant that the more homogeneous Plains, Arctic, and Subarctic are not represented, yet these cases proved a good choice because these tribes have generally underscored their linguistic distinctiveness by having more formal, articulated political and social organizations than those of surrounding tribes. One integrative consequence of this articulation was that these isolates had a singular Creator who made their world, legitimized their leaders, and instituted their major integrative rituals.

66

QUILEUTE of the North Pacific Coast

Creation

Kwati changed things long ago so that they became as they are now. There are many versions of how he did this. According to one, he made humans from parts of the salmon, native from the brown portion of livers, Europeans from light colored glands, and Africans from the veins. In another, he went all over improving things by slaying monsters and settling tribes in specific places, then instructed them in proper behavior.

In his travels, he met the humanoid prototypes of various animal species, with diverse results. Once, he encountered a man sharpening a knife. Kwati asked who he was and what he was doing. The man said, "I am Beaver and I am getting ready to kill the one they call Kwati because he is going all over messing things up." Kwati asked to look at the knife and when he held it, implanted it as a tail on this being, changing him into the forerunner of all the beavers who were to come. Then he went on.

At the Hoh River, he met people walking on their hands and carrying baskets between their legs. He turned them right-side up and told them to live by fishing. At the mouth of the Quillayute River, he changed Man and Woman Wolves into the ancestors of the Quileute. He instructed them that a poor man should have one wife, and a rich man four to eight wives. At Ozette, he turned Dogs into people, who occupied a village there.[50]

During all this, the world remained in twilight or darkness. Kwati intended to change this, so he turned into a small boy to trick people who kept sunlight. He visited them and went in a canoe to gather mussels. Also in the canoe was the box holding Sun and Moon. When the people went off to gather mussels, he stole the canoe and box.

He continued on, "liberating resources," until all the world was satisfactory; then he went up into the sky to live forever.

World

Immortals populating the known world included dwarfs, stars, Raven, Kwati, ghosts, and various monsters, including a kidnapper with kelp for hair. Thunderbird snatched whales out of the ocean and ate them at its home on the Blue Glacier of Mount Olympus, on the so-called Olympic peninsula. The Universe itself was alive and addressed in prayers.

As the cedar tree provided materials for all Quileute necessities, from wood for tools and houses to roots for baskets, so the various salmon species, through the bounty of annual runs, provided the staple food.

Housing

Quileute lived in rectangular longhouses, framed in by using massive logs as four upright supports, lateral beams, and a single-slope or shed roof. The entire outside was covered with split cedar planks lashed to poles set at intervals. Side wall planks were set horizontally, while the end ones were vertical, allowing space for a door. Roof planks were troughed to carry off rainwater.

50. The Ozette village has since become an important archaeological site where woodworking and other fragile items were preserved under a mudslide about 600 years ago. These artifacts are well displayed at the Makah Tribal Museum in Neah Bay.

Inside, the floor was bare earth, excavated down a yard or so, with a row of fires along the center line. Interspersed along the sides were planks set into the ground for use as backrests. Paired families shared the same fire, living on bunks at opposite sides. A large house, sixty feet long and forty feet wide, could hold six families and three fires, but most houses were smaller and had fewer families. During winter cold spells of snow or rain, houses were drafty so families built snug skin tents over their bunks to stay warm.

Like all tribes of the Pacific Northwest, Quileute clustered in winter villages composed of such cedar plank longhouses located along waterways. A few houses were also located on inland prairies to safeguard a particular resource or sacred site. Two leaders of equal status, known by a term that meant both "primary" and "rich", directed each village. Each community also included a few people with Eagle powha, which allowed them to take anything from the wealthy that they wanted. Descent was traced bilaterally, but residence was patrilocal, giving relations a patri-emphasis.

A Day
The typical day began before dawn as the women prepared food and the household head preached to awakening children to be honest, chaste, truthful, diligent, brave, generous, and considerate. Any child who failed to conform to these standards was ridiculed in public. The rest of the household was reminded to help the old and poor, to bathe every morning, to emulate their wealthy ancestors, to avenge the murder of any kin, and to excel at fishing so their family would never want for food.

Men spent the day fishing or hunting, while women harvested plants and prepared food by sun drying, smoking, roasting, boiling, steaming, and broiling. In the evening, a household gathered for dinner, followed by entertainments of stories, games, and conversation.

A Year
Quileute recognized five seasons: winter, spring, summer, early fall, and late fall. Activities in the winter villages were largely devoted to rituals, potlatching (high status give-aways), and guild matters, but the men did some fishing for cod and sea bass.

During spring, women gathered fresh roots, such as camas, and tender shoots, along with sea gull eggs. Later in the year, they collected berries, fruits, and seaweeds. Men gathered bearberry (kinnickinnick) to add to their smoking mixture.

The pace quickened with each arrival of five species of salmon.[51] The first appearance

---

51. These five salmon species have a confusing variety of local common names, but all belong to the genus called Oncorhynchus as further designated by species.

A. O.tshawytscha (chinook, king, spring, quinnat), up to 80 pounds, spawns in large streams or rivers, sometimes with spring and fall subspecies.

B. O. kisutch (silver), usually 6-12 pounds, up to 30 pounds, runs in early fall but may not spawn until late fall, in smaller streams far from the sea.

C. O. gorbuscha (pink), 3-10 pounds, spawns early fall, smaller streams near the sea

D. O. keta (chum, dog), 8-18 pounds, spawns late fall, smaller streams near the sea, lean and smokes well.

E. O. nerka (sockeye), usually a few pounds, fattest species, spawns upriver in lakes; when landlocked, known as kokanee.

of each resources was greeted with a return foods feast.

Summer was spent fishing for salmon, steelhead, halibut, snapper, cod, trout, flounder, octopus, and other marine foods; digging for shellfish; and hunting deer, elk, beaver, seal, sea otter, ducks, geese, and whales. Men took all of these species with the help of weir, trap, net, hook, dibble, bow and arrows, spear, snare, deadfall, and harpoon. All of this technology could only be used effectively, however, after the proper ritual purification and mental conditioning had been performed.

Quileute were justly famous as seal and whale hunters, tasks requiring the most rigorous ritual preparations. Before whaling, a harpooner avoided all contact with women and bathed in the icy sea from winter until June. As the moon waxed, he bathed in the ocean nightly at his own isolated spot, swimming like a whale. When he was thoroughly numb, he went to the beach and vigorously rubbed himself with prickly hemlock branches. During the whole time, he prayed to the Universe itself to send him a whale.

The whaling crew prepared for a shorter time, singing together accompanied by a rattle. Then they dragged a line attached to human skulls along a beach, imitating a harpooned whale dragging sealskin floats. The dead could supply food for the living, so these skulls served as an appropriate focus for the ritual. A human skull cap also decorated the prow of each whaling canoe for the same reason.

A full whaling canoe had eight members; the harpooner at the bow, six paddlers paired along the sides, and the steersman in the stern. For safety, whaling crews generally joined together in a flotilla, but the harpooner with the highest rank always made the first strike. Then others moved into position and plunged their harpoons, each of them attached to a long line of inflated sealskins, which resisted attempts by the whale to submerge and so hastened its exhaustion and demise.

Once the whale was dead, a man jumped overboard, made holes in the lips, and tied the mouth shut so it could not swallow water and sink. The whale was joyously towed into the village beach and butchered according to strict rules. The first harpooner to impale the whale received the hump or saddle, the choicest piece, as his due. He also received a flipper to keep as a part of an ongoing tally recording his prowess. The whale was primarily rendered for its oil, but nothing was wasted.

A sealing crew had three men who also made special ritual preparations, but, through the years, ones analogous to those for whaling have replaced these.

A Life

During pregnancy, an expectant couple restricted their eating and other activities until two months after the birth, eight months in the case of twins. Throughout the Northwest, twins were equated with salmon, probably because the double birth represented the endless return of the salmon, believed to be the same Salmon souls with new bodies offered as food.

A mother kept track of her due date with a string knotted in eight places, untying one knot for each month. She delivered sitting up, helped by midwives. A newborn was carefully washed, than massaged with shark oil. The afterbirth was believed to represent Old Woman, the source of children, so, after wrapping it up with beads and gifts; it was

---

In addition, steelhead (Salmo gairdneri) is a sea-run rainbow trout, up to 36 pounds, that, like Atlantic salmon, spawns and returns to the sea. Pacific salmon spawn and die, nourishing local carnivores and generally poor soil (Suttles 1990: 24-25).

hidden in a salmonberry bush as an offering to her.

The cradleboard was used for a child until he or she was able to walk. Shredded cedar bark served as diapers. In leading families, a board and cedarbark cushion were added to the top of the baby carrier to put pressure on the forehead to make it slope back. When the parents ended their restrictions, their baby was laced into a cradleboard and presented at a potlatch.

Children played at adult tasks as a way of growing into later careers. The bestowal of successive names and the piercing of the ears and nose, allowing ornaments to be worn, celebrated increasing maturity. Children were taught to be clean, moderate, generous, considerate, and dexterous so they would be admired and bring honor to the family. With the onset of puberty, boys began quest training, trying, until middle age if necessary, to gain contact with an immortal. Particular partnerships conferred specific careers, as indicated by this chart:

Quileute Partnerships

Career   Partner

Shaman   =Snake, Lizard, Screech Owl, Mink
Whaler   =Whale, Seal, Porpoise, Spear, Rainbow, Lightning
Hunter   = Wolf, Owl, Elk, Deer, Horned Owl, Bow, Arrow, Elk Leg or Horn, Cougar, Robin, Two-Headed Dog, Forest Monster
Warrior = Bear, Sea Lion, Knife, Sword, Sky, Stars, Bow, Arrow
Sealer =   Otter, Kingfisher, Bird, Spear, Dragnet, Fisher, Trap, Fish, Duck, Salmon, Cormorant
Rich Man =   Wild Goose, Warbler, Surf Scudder, Grey Swan, Summer, Whitecaps, Ravens, Sun, Moon, Dentalia
Runner = Fog, Wolf
Wrestler =Bear, Forest Dwarf
Gambler =various Double-Headed creatures
Beggar = Eagle, Shark
Rich Woman   Ocean Waves, House Dirt, Salmonberry Bush, Red Huckleberry, other kinds of Berries
Canoe Maker = Axe, Wedge, Adze, Cedar Tree

At menarche, a girl was secluded in her home, abstaining from fresh and bloody foods, staying awake for five days, and using a scratching stick. While most women did not have contact with the supernatural, some girls from leading families did. As indicated by the chart, they received Wealth Powha from things that naturally occurred in vast numbers.

After puberty, children were ready for marriage, which had at least ten different forms, including levirate, sororate, and polygyny among the rich. Premarital chastity was desired, especially in high families. Parents of a boy took the initiative in negotiating a first marriage. Both sets of parents then exchanged food, gifts, and wealth; first, at the home of the bride, then, several days later, at the residence of the groom, where a feast and dance were held. Exchanges among poor families were much less elaborate. If the couple divorced after a few years, their wedding gifts were returned.

Both men and women were shamans, each possessing five or six immortal partners, but the most powerful ones had as many as 20. Each partnership was represented by a six foot pole topped with an effigy of that immortal. To sort out their relative positions in terms of differential powha, shamans held competitive displays for demonstrating their control of fire, manipulation of hot rocks, and consumption of vast quantities of whale oil.

Like other Northwest tribes, Quileute were stratified into three classes of leaders, commoners, and slaves. High families based their prestige on appropriate spiritual partnerships, generosity, and hereditary claims to "crests," legitimated by epics enumerating songs, dances, resource areas, designs, and names. A leader was also a member of one of the guilds (below), which were most active during winter.

Each of the bilateral kindreds formed a corporate unit localized into households, sharing a set of "crests" nominally under the care of the corporation sigers. These men were able to call upon the assistance of slaves, acquired by trading or raiding, and of several wives to fulfill expectations of generosity.

Around the actual leaders there was a penumbra of notables, linked to them by close ties of blood, training, access to spiritual partners, and inherited prestige. Membership in this paramount class was physically represented by high sloping foreheads, the result of being bound into a cradle with the top of the head pillowed between angled boards to shape the skull as it slowly grew and hardened.

Commoners were average people without claims or pretensions to greatness. In some cases, ordinary children could elevate their status and gain prestige by becoming successful warriors or shamans. As warriors, they had the opportunity to capture slaves, who performed extra labor to produce wealth for their owners. Shamans earned wealth, gratefully given as payment by the patient and his or her family, every time they cured successfully.

Crimes included murder, adultery, and hoarding, which were considered inhuman behavior. For murder, close kin were compensated by wergild (blood money), otherwise they led a revenge raid on the murderer, his or her family, and that household.

Everyone had an inner and an outer shade, and a soul, which left the body in stages leading to final death. A week before, the outer shade went directly to the afterworld. A few days later, the inner shade began visiting favorite places before rejoining with the outer shade. At the moment of death, the soul became a ghost, which remained with the body until the instant that the shades recombined. If the shaman could trap the inner shade while it was visiting familiar places, the outer shade would also return to the person and the illness would be cured. Otherwise the patient died for good.

Sickness resulted whenever these spiritual components of a person left the body. If they could not be retrieved by a shaman, death was inevitable. Only shamans with powha from a Dwarf could safely journey into the beyond and return with the missing shade or soul.[52]

This was an underworld, a large valley divided by a river flowing down the middle. Recent dead lived on one side and ancient dead on the other. The trip there took a soul two days and nights along a trail that led down from the surface through a resthouse and a lake. If the shades or a pursuing shaman drank from this lake, they immediately died without hope

52. Among Lushootseed of Puget Sound, similar dwarfs, called Little Earths because they are said to "own" the land, took a crew of shamans to the afterworld to retrieve the lost soul, mind, or spirit of a patient who was wasting away in winter (Jay Miller 1988).

of reviving. In general, time and conditions between the living world and the afterworld were reversed so what was summer in one was winter in the other, high tide in one was low tide in the other, and what was broken in one was whole in the other.

After death, a body was taken out of the house through a hole made into the back wall so that ghost would be confused if it ever tried to haunt the house. Wooden sculptures representing the immortal partner of the deceased were destroyed, but any designs were inherited within the family.

The wealthy were placed into canoes with many grave goods, deliberately smashed so they would be whole in the afterworld. This canoe was used to cross the river in the underworld when the person was accepted by the ancient dead. The poor were buried in logs that had been hollowed out. They crossed the river in the afterworld by walking over a communal fish weir. A dead child was put in a cedar box that was then added to the canoe containing a dead relative.

Mourners cut their hair, and a surviving spouse and children applied red ocher to the face and body. A spouse could not lie down to sleep for five days, so he or she slept huddled in a large basket. The family had to move very slowly and deliberately during this mourning period. To help them do so, they carried small black stones in their mouths and armpits to curtail their speech and movements.

The name of the dead was not mentioned for ten years. Doing so was a grave insult to the family. If anyone had the same or a similar name, mourners paid them to substitute another one. Words similar to that name were discarded in favor of circumlocutions invented by the family.

The ghost remained on the earth. Each had an elongated human shape, moss covering, long nose, round yellow eyes, and peculiar gait – constantly recrossing its legs, moving in a crooked fashion with the left foot moving to the right and the right one to the left. People knew how to avoid it because ghosts also whistled while they ambled along, warning the living.

Recombined shades stayed in the afterworld, continuing activities their body had done in life. In other sections of this underworld were the shades of whales, fish, animals, birds, plants, and so forth. Quileute and other humans visited these areas to collect food. Dead babies had a place of their own south of that occupied by grownups.

History

The Chemakuan language family includes the Quileute, Hoh, and extinct Chimakum, who once lived around Port Townsend at the northeast corner of the Olympic Peninsula.

Several hundred years ago, Klallam, Straits Salishan speakers, arrived on the north coast of this peninsula, forming a wedge between the Chimakum and the Quileute. Both of these tribes account for their separation, however, with a flood legend. At the northwest tip of the peninsula, the northern neighbors of the Quileute were five Makah villages, speakers of a Nootkan language from Vancouver Island, since resettled on a single reservation at Neah Bay. Makah also recognized Kwati as the transformer, but their relations with Quileute varied between intermarriage and the transmission of the Whaling cult to occasional battles.

All Chemakuans had the reputation of being fierce warriors. Though a tiny group, Chimakum fought off many larger tribes until decimated by epidemics and other hardships. Hoh massacred landing parties of Spanish in 1775 and English in 1787. Quileute maintained a stockaded fort on James Island near La Push as protection from retaliatory attacks. La Push, at the mouth of the Quillayute River, took its name from the Chinook Jargon term, derived from French, meaning "mouth."

Quileute signed one of the series of treaties negotiated in 1855 to legalize American title to Washington State. They attended another treaty conference at the state capitol of Olympia in 1856. At that time, they were expected to leave their ancestral lands and relocate on the neighboring Quinault Reservation. Once back home, however, they decided not to move, remaining as aliens in their own land until Grover Cleveland signed an Executive Order to create a reservation for them at La Push. The closely related Hoh were given a portion of their homeland, noted for its spectacular rain forests and coastal beaches, for a reservation in 1903.

Ritual: Guilds and Potlatching

In addition to the return foods feasts for salmon, whales, and berries, Quileute had a complex series of guilds and festive displays at potlatches.

Guilds

Much of winter was devoted to religious activities such as guild initiations, potlatching, and displays of powha. In order of their prestige, these guilds were the Warriors and Fishers (both derived from Wakashans), the Hunters (original to the Quileute), Whalers (from the Makah), and the Weather Workers (from the Quinault). Membership in these guilds could either be purchased for a child by parents hosting a potlatch or be personally acquired by encountering the necessary partner during a quest, which led to an illness whose cure was formal initiation. All members of these guilds were considered "ripe" as opposed to everyone else, who was "raw."

These five guilds followed the organizational features of the largest Warriors whose officials included two fathers, two firemen, a doorkeeper, a water carrier, and a woman face painter, who applied the color distinctive of that cult (Wolves = black with white or red highlights, Hunters = brown, Fishers = red, Whalers = dark brown, Weather = tan). This color also appeared to a shaman when he was diagnosing which guild a patient needed to join.

People who met a partner appropriate for a guild took sick and were cured by becoming special members entitled to wear its headgear and face paint, to dramatize its ritual, and to act as father, also called starter. Membership, though a less intense form, could also be purchased for children by their parents so they could share in gifts given at subsequent initiations. Ideally, membership was open to all, but, in actual practice, it was a prerogative of the elite.

The guild with the most members was the Warriors, also known as Wolves and Blackfaces, whose ritual derived from the elaborate Wolf Ritual of the Wakashan Nuuchanuulth (Nootka, Westcoasters) and Kwakwaka'wakw (Kwakiutl), some of whom claimed descent from Wolves transformed into ancestors, as Kwati did locally. Initiations went on for five days, using the songs inherited by each candidate from their family. The drama included embodied Wolves, Wild Men, and an Eagle, together with some tests of strength and stamina. Finally, two Buffoon dancers entertained the crowd.

Hunters belonged among Quileute, and its initiation enacted a quest to and from a mountain top, which for someone with a proper partner took six days, but for a purchased membership lasted only two days.

The Fishers, Whalers, and Weather Workers were more strictly occupational, performing dramatic enactments of their activities in a ritual context, such as that already described for whaling.

Potlatching

The most sweeping and integrating institution among the Quileute and other Northwest tribes was the "potlatch," a term filtered from Nootkan Wakashan through Chinook trade jargon meaning "to give." These elaborate give-aways were public displays of family pedigree held to commemorate births, namings, marriages, initiations, assumption of crest privileges, and memorials. As such they served as periodic reminders of claims to property and rank. According to legend, the first potlatch was held to give birds the colors that distinguish their many species. Ever since, these feasts have been occasions for giving and sharing.

A potlatch was given by families in the name of specific members, who usually, if old enough, had amassed gifts, contributed by family and friends, to be distributed. When the event was held, important people were specifically invited, feasted, and gifted, along with everyone else who attended. The reason for calling everyone together was stated in public and dramatized, if the family had claims to appropriate songs, dances, masks, and costumes. Then, everyone was given a gift proportional to their rank to serve as a reminder, in case any disagreements later arose these compensated witnesses testified to the legality of these proceedings.

Summary

The Quileute language marks gender by indicating female forms with a k- affix. Thus, "s" means "the (for males)" and "ks" is "the (for females)". Moreover, the term for "right" has associations of priority, men, and all of the directions except south; while "left" relates to others meaning "second hand, southward, and women's way". These and other forms of marking indicate that Man was inclusive and Woman exclusive for the Quileute.

Sources

Quileute are discussed in slim works by James Swan, Edward Curtis, Albert Reagan, Alice Ernest, and Livingston Farrand. Major sources include an ethnic history by George Pettitt (1950), several detailed articles and a manuscript by Leo Frachtenberg (1920, 1921) based on close cooperation with a shaman, and more recent linguistic and ethnographic work by Jay V. Powell (1976), including a dictionary, and Vickie Jensen done under the auspices of the tribal government. Harry Hobucket published a collection of legends from his tribe.

KOOTENAY of the Intermontane

Creation

From the beginning, this world was populated by immortals, shimmering simultaneously among the forms of spirits, humans, species, and places. For example, Chicken Hawk acted like a Man, had "chicken hawk" as his spirit partner, and was married to Grouse, who committed adultery with a water being and was killed by her husband. Regardless of their shape-shifting, all of these beings were nonetheless identified as either Man or Woman. For instance, Frog is called the Grandmother of everyone.

The leading immortal, the Supreme Spirit (<u>kwiłqa nupik'a</u>), constantly reminded others that "Humans are coming soon" and the world had to be made ready for them. While some immortals tried to prevent this, the majority planned for the impending change.

The Transformer ("The One From Down Under," because he was born in the water) wore clothes painted red and cast a red shadow. His father was White Stone, his mother Young Doe, and his nephew Duck. His job was to trick certain immortals who were hording singular resources so these could be scattered around the world to be made available for later human use.

Namer crawled over the earth on his hands and knees, leaving waterways in his wake and providing names for everything. When he finished this task, he stood up one day to stretch and stuck his head on the sky, knocking off his feathered headgear. As it fell to the ground, he uttered his last words, "The place where my hat lands will be called Ear." The long, low hill marking his last resting place can still be seen on Canal Flats, British Columbia.

When all was in readiness, the leader called a council of immortals to finally decide what forms each would take, the places they would live, and how they would regard humans. At the same moment that humans appeared, the last being decided to become Rabbit.

Of several versions of how humans arrived, all express a belief that they somehow came from water. Accordingly, humans, specifically Kootenay, are described as arriving by canoe, or genders appeared separately – men sprang from the hairs that fell off a Black Bear regurgitated by a water being, while women were found in the mountains. Or, humans emerged from the grass where Chicken Hawk wiped off the blood of water being. Or, possibly reflecting Biblical influence, the leader attempted various life forms until he finally managed to make the biped he intended all along.

Both associated with water, Kootenay and their Transformer lived together until they, in fear, killed him, and submerged his body, but he was revived by fish to take avenge on Kootenay for their bad faith. Then he went away.

World

Before Catholicism, Sun, Dawn, and Moon were worshiped as visible avatars of divinity. Their origins are explained in a legend where Sun and Moon, twin sons of Lynx, are given these roles for the benefit of humans.

During the final council, not all of the immortals were willing to help; some chose to ignore humans and others to harm them. Among these latter was the Owl Ogre, a Kootenay version of the Basket Ogress summoned throughout Western America to frighten children into behaving with threats that she (or he) will carry them away in a pack basket and eat them. Razor-sharp awls in the bottom of this basket were a Kootenay touch.

Similarly, recalling beliefs about Subarctic Windigo − giants with a heart of ice who attacked people out alone and turned them into cannibals unless killed by their own kin and burned to ashes − Kootenay feared cannibal Skeletons who once had been men. Each became so obsessed with hunger that he ate all of his own flesh, starting with his own lips, before turning on siblings, children, and friends. According to one account, a lone woman was able to kill one of them by convincing him to get into her cooking pot. Because women once spent much of their time smashing up bones to make soup, their stone hammers gave adequate protection against these Skeletons.

Divisions

The common boundary between the two tribal divisions, Lower Lake and Upper River, was Kootenay Falls, a sacred spot between present Troy and Libby, Montana, along that River. Historically, these divisions were diverging even further as Upper Kootenay were acquiring an increasingly more Plains orientation replacing Plateau traditions.

Lower Kootenay lived along the lake, formed about three bands, and maintained an aboriginal Plateau lifestyle with mat lodges, distinctive sturgeon-nosed bark canoes, rush or tule garments, coiled basketry, and a fishing economy.

The Upper Kootenay, forming about six bands living along the river, were Plainsized by the adoption of horse, tipi, buckskin clothing, feather bonnets, pottery, Sun Dance, and treks to hunt bison in the northern Plains.

Some writers have mentioned a distinct division called the Plains Kootenay but these were probably the Michele Band of Upper Kootenay who lived in Crow's Nest Pass and thus had continuous access to the plains of Alberta until none survived a 1730 smallpox epidemic.[53]

Tysic for Kootenay was Tobacco Plains on the border between Montana and British Columbia. The camp leader there was regarded as the steward of all the bison and served as the first chief among equals during the annual hunting expeditions sponsored by Upper Kootenay.

Kootenay used several terms for important individuals, but none of them was paramount. The term "leader" (nasu?kim) was an honorific applied to the band chief whose tent was at the center of the camp circle, to renowned warriors who had counted coup at least five times, to the leader of the Sun Dance, and to the heads of two guilds − the Crazy (Fey) Dogs made up of 20 fierce warriors and the Crazy Owls composed of select women who were able to prevent epidemics by praying as a group.

"Siger" (yaqasin) was used for any man with the proper supernatural sanction to take charge of communal fishing, game drives, netting of wild fowl, and camp movements. He had authority only for the duration of that task, but no longer. The camp leader called an assembly of all the men and announced the appointment of such a task leader. This assembly then accepted or rejected his choice. Different sigers led hunts for elk, or deer, or goat, or other mountain game. To be successful, a tasker had to have a powerful spiritual partner, constant ability to locate game, skill at avoiding attacks from enemies, and repeated safe returns with all members of his party.

The Upper Kootenay had the more formal organization, divided between a guide =

53. According to Claude Schaeffer, after decades of research in Alberta and British Columbia.

peace chief and a band = war chief. The Guide appointed various sigers for fishing, fowling, and hunting, subject to the approval of the male council. The band chief had as his insignia a pipe and eagle wing fan.

Housing

Kootenay mat houses were built by work parties whose members, whether related or not, were thereby entitled to live in the new home. Lodges had floors set a foot deep into the ground for warmth. Tripods of twelve foot poles were set up at each end, on the ground surface above the depression, and two crossed poles were set at intervals along the sides. Instead of a ridge pole or uprights, four rows of saplings were lashed at intervals along the sides to hold the framework together.

The entire outside was then covered with overlapping mats sewn of rushes and tules. The Lower or Lake Kootenay occupied mat tipis in the summer and mat longhouses in the winter. Their mats were sewn together with stalks of a shrub called dogbane. Often arranged as double lean-tos, such winter lodges had four fires down the center, each shared by a family on either side. Thus, a four fire lodge housed eight families.

Upper or River Kootenay used a tipi with a four pole foundation, adapted from the Plains to replace the ancient use of mat longhouses characteristic of the Plateau. About fifteen support poles were placed against this foundation and covered with eight elk or bison skins shaped, fitted, and sewn together. Four women could cut and sew a tipi cover in a day. A fire burned in the center and the floor was carpeted with fur robes in summer or by skins placed over fir boughs in winter. Finely tanned hides were set near the walls to serve as seats and beds. Family possessions were piled against the wall to provided additional insulation.

The older couple slept on the right or honorable side of the oval door, while a daughter and her husband might sleep on the left. Ideally, each married couple had its own tipi, but family poverty or space needs determined living arrangements. Children slept toward the rear. Young males only slept at home during bad weather, otherwise they acted as guards roving near the camp. Their only sleep came during naps while out hunting by day.

Lodges were arranged in a circle at various camp sites, with the home of the chiefly family in the center. Except for its location and greater size, the chief's tipi was identical with all the others.

A Day

People rose before dawn and plunged into a nearby stream to bathe. If a man were pious, he filled his pipe and sang to the dawn. A pious woman prayed, extending her right hand in turn to the east, west, and below. Later, at sunset, a man might point his pipestem to the west.

During the morning, little was eaten. Men might grab a handful of cold food from a pot as they left to go hunting, and women did the same as they went to gather plant foods. If a hunter made a kill during the day, he might cut off a snack before bringing the rest home.

At noon, everyone returned to the camp for a hearty meal of boiled or sun-dried foods. Another meal was taken after sunset. So routine were these meals that Kootenay had to overcome their initial dislike of broiled or baked food offered by early settlers. Women worked all day long, gathering food, tending children, and cooking, which included crushing bones for soup.

Unless there was pressing work, men devoted the afternoon to exercise, such as wrestling, trying to shoot arrows through a hoop, or playing ball. Between sunset and supper, they raced on foot, more recently on horseback.

After supper, children received moral instruction among the better families. Also, they were warned to stay inside. A fear of the night was instilled by stories of ghosts twisting the mouths of people they met and of the Owl Ogre carrying off youngsters in his awl-studded basket.

People went to bed soon after dark, unless there was to be an all night ritual or gambling session. Only men could kindle fires, so in the misfortune that the fire went out, a male of the family had to be summoned to light it again.

A Year

As elsewhere in the world, men were hunters, women gatherers, and fishing involved them both. The year was counted in moons, beginning at the Midwinter Ceremony when visionaries sang and danced according to the instructions of their spirit partners.

Economic activities began with spring fishing, which lasted until May. Men caught the fish; women cleaned, dressed, smoked, dried, and stored them. Fishing was more important for the Lower or Lake Kootenay because fish were their staple, taken with traps and fir pole weirs. Any catch was evenly distributed to everyone then in the camp, even casual visitors, regardless of whether they had helped or not. Withholding fish from anyone gave offense to the Salmon spirit, who had come up the river expecting to be shared. The spring was also the time when small plots of tobacco were planted.

About May, women dug up bitter root (rock rose) and camas bulbs, took them back to camp to clean, and prepared them for storage by drying or grinding.

Kootenay traders were middlemen in an extensive network. From the east came catlinite pipestone, bison horn beads, bison hides, pemmican (meat flour), and dry pigments. These were exchanged for goods from the west − dentalia (tusk shells), abalone shells, stone, pipes, eagle feathers, mountain goat horns, dressed moose hides, bows, wood, salmon flour, fish oil, bitter root, camas bulbs, woven bags, and coiled baskets.

Mid-June, River Kootenay organized at least 80 households, bolstered by some Spokan and Coeur d'Alene allies, to conduct their summer bison hunt. They needed at least this many people as protection from attacks while hunting in the Montana territory of the Siksika (Blackfoot) and Piegan. Most families hoped to return with two or three pack horses of dried meat; prominent families desired five horse loads.

Back from the Plains, women harvested serviceberries, huckleberries, and chokecherries. A siger was appointed to organize a communal duck hunt. Tobacco plots were harvested and each band made its own distinctive blend to smoke at council meeting and to trade with other bands. Lower Kootenay staged a communal deer hunt, while the Upper Kootenay went after elk. When all of this food was collected and processed, it was cached in the forks of trees in time for the River Kootenay to lead the fall bison hunt into the Plains.

Just before the first snowfall, this expedition returned and set up winter quarters in the more sheltered western portion of Kootenay territory. During winter, men repaired snowshoes to use during a short winter bison hunt. Mid-winter until spring was the religious season, devoted to ritual, prayer, and close contact with immortals.

A Life

For her first birth, a pregnant women was assisted by three midwives. Kootenay believed a baby boy took eight months to develop and a girl took nine months. After a couple had many babies die in infancy, they left the next one exposed in a tree as a sacrifice to assure future healthy children.

New mother and child were secluded for four days. Then a respected man came to name the baby after a famous deed or exploit of valor, influencing its life. If the child or mother suffered misfortune, the name was regarded as ill-chosen and a shaman selected a new one.

A child slept between his or her parents until able to whistle. Then it bedded elsewhere and the parents prepared for another baby. To make weaning less traumatic, a child was sent to visit grandparents, diverting attention from the mother and breast. Play was the means by which children learned to assume adult roles and duties. Unlike most other tribes, Kootenay sometimes resorted to spanking disobedient children, although this was considered an affront to their independence and self-esteem.

At the onset of menstruation, a girl was secluded in a hut where her movements, eating, and talking were severely restricted. Better families secluded their daughters a full seven days, but other families were not as strict.

As a boy matured, he began strenuous physical exercises in preparation for his vision quest at puberty, when his voice was changing. According to Kootenay, during a successful encounter, an immortal placed an object inside the body of the human. Later, that spirit would infuse this item when the spot where it had entered the body was touched by the visionary (or by his wife, if he had confided this information to her).

A few individuals left puberty identified with another gender. Usually, these were boys who then assumed the role of women, technically called berdache. Kootenay are somewhat unique, however, in that at least one of their women, Qanqon, with a strong personality and a larger than average body size, opted to become a man. This female berdache appeared often in the records of the early fur trade. Another woman kept her gender when she became the Sun Dance Leader, a role held by men before and since.

After puberty, a person was ready for marriage. Boys were then about 20 and girls about 15. Better families prized bridal virginity, but did not demand it as an absolute. It was only required that a girl be discrete because promiscuity could change a girl into a frog. Marriages were arranged by the parents, but they were expected to seriously consider the preferences of their children. While a son could take the initiative to negotiate his own marriage, a girl had to be demure, using an intermediary. Betrothal lasted three days, then the parents-in-law exchanged gifts.

The ideal time to hold a marriage was during the glee of a Victory (Scalp) Dance when everyone was gathered together. A feast was held for the public, and important men addressed speeches to the couple. Although kinship was traced through both sides of the family (bilaterally), the couple went to live near the parents of the bride (matrilocally).

Paupers were married by having the household of the girl find them in bed together one morning. Regardless of the type of marriage, any wife was admired who could tan hides with skill, gather dry firewood, and work cheerfully alone or with others. As a tribe, moreover, the Kootenay were justly famous for the whiteness and long fringes of their clothing.

The insignia of men in mythology, games, and rituals was the bow, and those of women were the digging stick (dibble), stone hammer, and basket. A husband provided meat, hides, and protection in return for plant foods, clothing, housekeeping, and children from his wife. While children were much desired, a barren woman was not blamed unduly for her condition, but a man might take an additional wife to assure offspring.

Monogamy was the general rule, although wealthy men were expected to support several wives, usually sisters. In addition to this polygyny, Kootenay also recall some members who practiced sister exchange, sororate, and a rare case or two of polyandry.

Adultery was a reason for divorce, but it was expected to be amiable. The only exception was a husband who had counted coup, permitting him to berate his wife and her lover in public for as long as he wanted. Actually, the lover was taking a dangerous chance because any form of sexual contact was believed to be offensive to his own immortal partner, causing his spirit to depart.

Kootenay distinguished families on the basis of ability and pedigree. The old, high, or better families consistently provided community officials, powerful visionaries, sigers, and shamans. Members were expected to be generous, so these families were often numerous so as to have enough labor to sun-dry quantities of meat as a surplus to be given to visitors, friends, and the needy.

Anciently, Kootenay kept war captives as menials until a shaman was instructed by Grizzly that this was wrong and slavery was abolished.

After horses arrived, social ranks became more clearly distinguished because better families had large herds. Thus, in addition to the intangibles of fine manners, diligence, eloquence, and distinguished ancestry, such a family had 50 wild horses or 25 tame and broken to harness. A family was considered to be comfortable if it had ten tame (broken) horses; Less, and the family was regarded as poor. Most people lived in comfort, with a few rich and a few poor families at the extremes.

Shamans had an important role among Kootenay, as they did everywhere. Each of them had two names, a personal one like everyone else and a medicine name given by their immortal.

Other specialists included female herbalists, Sun dance director, and guide shamans, who gave advice on hunting matters. Unlike most tribes, Kootenay preferred to consult a younger shaman because his powha had not been diminished by use. Older shamans, while having greater experience, had powha that weakened unless they actively renewed it.

Various shamans were ranked on the basis of the relative strengths of their spirit powha and the area of the body they treated. All shamans in a camp were nominally led by the most powerful senior one, who worked in close cooperation with the civil leaders. This type of "holy alliance" between secular and religious leaders, once common in Native America, entrenched elite families and gave communities greater stability and supernatural aid.

Recognized offenses included murder, rape, and stinginess. These and others were judged by the guide chief, not to penalize the offender, but to find a just compensation for a victim or his/her family. Anciently, the worst punishment was to be banished since this was tantamount to being executed by enemies. Directly or indirectly, missionaries had the dubious distinction of introducing flogging as punishment for some crimes.

Disease was diagnosed and treated by shamans using drums, songs, and juniper smoke cleansing. Younger shamans had the freshest powha, but older ones could undertake additional quests, acquire new partners, and thus renew their ability. Some were able to reencounter their original partner to recharge powha that had become a personal curing specialty.

According to legend, death was the result of an argument between two leaders. One thought that everyone should die twice before it became final, the other was Raven, who wanted to eat the eyes out of corpses. He therefore decreed that people would die only once. Only those souls who were able to travel to the Sun earned the right to be reincarnated in later generations.

In prehistory, the dead were placed on scaffolds held up by four corner posts. The famous Lake Kootenay leader named Three Moons received a vision that he was to be buried with his face painted red, so the people followed his wishes when he died around 1830, placing him in a shallow grave covered by a rock cairn on Pine Island. There after, all dead Kootenay were buried in the same manner until converted by Jesuits. Now they are buried in cemeteries after Catholic services, and the surviving spouse is still expected to mourn for at least a year.

Every person has an "inner" and an "outer" flesh. The inner one left with the last breath to roam the world as a ghost hoping for rebirth, but the outer one decayed with the body. Better families were more vital to the world, so when their members died, strong winds or thunder marked their passing.

If someone died inside a tipi, it had to be moved. When a man died, the lodge poles, floor covering of fir boughs, and anchoring tent pegs were destroyed. For a woman, the floor liner and outer covering were discarded. In other words, the hard, separate, and exclusive parts were associated with Man, while the soft and inclusive ones were linked to Woman.

History

Archaeologically, the Kootenay appear to have lived in the Rocky Mountain Trench for thousands of years. While their language remains unclassified, research by Lawrence Morgan indicates that Kootenay and Proto-Salishan are collateral branches of a common parent speech community.

Their territory was oriented in terms of Kootenay Lake and River centered on Tobacco Plains. They were gifted with some outstanding shaking tent shamans, particularly Three Moons (see above), a Lower Kootenay leader who correctly predicted the arrival of Father Pierre Jean de Smet and other Jesuit black robes bringing Catholicism and a "new kind of peace" in the 1840s. Kootenay became willing converts to the Christian God, whom they called "The Tasker Who Made = Owned Us" to distinguish Him from the supreme immortal of their ancient faith, their primordial font of spirits and powhas.

Rituals

Montana Kootenay are still renowned for celebrating the Blanket rite, a version of the conjuring lodge or shaking tent distributed throughout the circumpolar north. A blanket shaman had awesome clairvoyance when he went behind a blanket hung to partition off a room or crawled inside a small tent set up outside. His feet, hands, and thumbs were bound together, and he was left alone. Using a bone whistle, he summoned Owl, Giant, Woodpecker, and, particularly, the immortals called Sculpin, Sun Dance, and Sweatlodge. These flew that shaman around the world so he could see and report what was happening. His audience asked specific questions, and he relied on this travel to supply answers. When everyone was satisfied, he returned to the enclosure and emerged unbound.

Along with the Blanket rite, traditional Kootenay celebrated three major spring ceremonies – Sun Dance, Grizzly Bear, and Fir Tree. About 1900, some Kootenay adopted the Midwinter and Bluejay Dances from the neighboring Spokan and Flathead.

The Sun dance, also called medicine lodge, was held during mild weather and directed by officials who served for life. It was, of course, introduced within the past few centuries, inspired by Plains ceremonies of the same name.

Before midwinter, the Sun dance spirit appeared to a worthy person to request that the dance be held next spring. To make sure that the message was genuine, a blanket rite was held. If affirmed, then, in late January, a special leather effigy of the Sun dance spirit was made by a man and clothed by a woman. During the early spring hunts, Lower Kootenay reserved choice ribs and kidneys from the right sides of slain deer, together with limb joints and tails. Upper Kootenay saved choice bison tongues, hearts, and kidneys.

Just prior to this celebration, a fine tree was selected, cut down, and never allowed to touch the ground until it was set up within the sacred precinct as the Sun dance pole decorated with offerings of food from the poor, along with clothing and shells, now ribbon substitutes, from the rich. Crazy Dogs were sent to violently remove the covers off three lodges and bring them back to enclose the medicine lodge.

This rite lasted seven days, under the direction of the Sun dance siger, who remained in seclusion in the special lodge. Four days were devoted to preparations, followed by two days and three nights when three or four men danced, punctuating their own exertions with whistles, accompanied by drums and songs.

In early March, the Grizzly Bear rite was held at the time when bears were about to emerge from their dens. In years when bears where particularly hostile, it was also held in the fall to send them into hibernation with good feelings toward Kootenays.

During the Bear ritual, people opened their mystic bundles and renewed them, while special songs were addressed to male and female bears. Because Grizzlies were believed to be left-handed, all gestures were made with this hand.[54] The rite could last as long as three days before it was concluded with a feast of berries. Everyone present offered a pipestem to Bears, a symbol of life, breath, and the windpipe, and these were buried together at the conclusion. Bear spirits examined these pipestems to judge the sincerity of the donor, who was accordingly helped or harmed.

After a long, hard winter, spring could be a time when famine threatened so the Fir Tree or Pole rite was held if game were scarce and people suffered from stress and uncertainty. Over three days, a shaman danced, sang, and prayed inside a specially built longhouse to lure animals back onto Kootenay lands.

Summary

Among the Kootenay, Man is exclusive and Woman inclusive. Associated with males were Namer, men, bows, animals, sky, and the skeletons; and with females were transformer, women and men, dibbles, pounders, baskets, plants, the camp, Salmon woman, and Frog, the universal Grandmother. Those in the category of Man could and did act alone, not always for the public good, as with anti-social skeletons. Those associated with Woman worked collectively to benefit the greatest number, for the sake of family and greater

---

54. Throughout the Americas, bears were believed to be left handed, as discussed in the section on sensory aspects of culture (Chapter III).

harmony. For example, at death, the exclusive inner parts of a lodge were removed if a man, or the inclusive outer ones if a woman.

Sources

Kootenay materials were published by Franz Boas (1918), Alexander Chamberlain (1892), Edward Curtis (1911), Lawrence Morgan (198x) and, in most detail, Harry Turney-High (1941). The best source, however, is the unpublished notes and papers by Claude Schaeffer at the Glenbow-Alberta Institute in Calgary.

YUKI of California

Creation

Taikomol (The One Who Walks Alone) made the world and everything in it, after assuming human form. At first, a downy feather or a fleck of foam floated upon an expanse of primal water, gradually drifting north while it developed feet, calves, thighs, trunk, shoulders, arms, and face in accord with the rhythm of an all-pervading song. Finally, Taikomol looked human. When he tried to raise himself up with an elbow, however, the water gave him no support, so he decided to make land. Three times he sang to make land, but it was always too soft. By the fourth attempt, the land was solid so people learned that things need to be done four times to be finished.

According to one version, he stitched the world together as though it were a basket. Then he began to organize it, placing fresh and salt water over the surface before taking up his rattle and feather quills to add mountains, rivers, and springs. Suddenly, Coyote appeared so the Creator had him run errands, including killing and flaying four whales so Taikomol could use their skins to make the sky vault. Then the earth disk was placed upon the front paws of an enormous Mole, addressed as Grandmother, and guardians appeared at the north end of the world to work in alternation, a brother during summer and a sister during winter.

Coyote was directed to make the first rotunda, a community hall called the "Poison House." When it was finished, the Creator carefully placed sticks of different sizes around the inside before he began to sing. As his song continued, large sticks became men, small ones = women, and tiny ones = children. They were fully formed by dawn, talking and jostling with each other such as occurs at every waking since then.

Taikomol had sexual relations with a sister, but found that it was not satisfactory until he had thrown a mussel and some sand into her. Since then, everyone has learned to enjoy sex for the purpose of procreation.

He instituted a Creator cult among these first people, but the first class of young boys to be initiated died of fright when they saw the real immortals coming to visit. To prevent this from happening again, the next class to be initiated, themselves embodying the spirits, wore elaborate vision-obscuring caps with many long feathers sticking out.

Finally, Taikomol began to travel everywhere, teaching people to speak different languages, make special tools, and use particular resources he left in their regions. Singing the whole time, he made three attempts before accomplishing each goal.
Since Yuki were his favorite, he gave them his own language, much as the Biblical God gave Hebrew to his chosen people.

While the Creator was away, Coyote's son died and was buried. When he returned, he offered to restore life = health to the boy, but his father refused so death became everlasting. After a few other deeds, Taikomol went up into the sky, together with his twin sons. They live there still with Pal, a giant eagle-like bird.

Yuki know that the Creator in the sky remains interested in their welfare because thunder is his voice, wind his breath, and lightning his punishment. Particularly fond of the smoke from wild tobacco, Yuki offer it to him as often as possible.

World

The immortals of the Yuki included dwarfs two feet tall, female Deer bosses, various underwater monsters, a cannibal Owl, and Night people – ghostly forms who cause illness by fright. Grandmother Mole holds the earth on her front paws whose shifting causes an earthquake.

The sky was a male domain, the later abode of Taikomol, his twin sons, Pal, and souls. Pal chipped pieces off his block of obsidian and dropped them to earth for humans to treasure. Large blades of finely chipped obsidian were particularly valuable and fed food and drink before every meal.

Sun had control of rattlesnakes, but he was periodically devoured by Bear, resulting in an eclipse until people could rally and scare off the ursine attacker. Morning Star is a young man sent by Coyote to live in the sky.

Housing

During summer, Yuki families lived in brush shelters in the hills. During winter, they lived in single family houses, set a foot deep into the ground. Shaped like a cone, each was covered with layers, inside to outside, of poles, slabs of bark, grass, pine needles, and dirt, with that excavated from the floor banked around the outside edge to keep out drafts and rain. A smoky fire burned in the center of the house, under a smokehole at the apex. Its ashes were piled continually along the inside walls to provide a backrest and insulation. One man, sometimes with the help of a brother, could build a house in a few days that would last about two years. Winter houses were clustered at fixed locations, with the more important communities having a rotunda dance house to serve as a regional center.

Dance Houses had the same shape as homes, but were forty feet across the base and excavated five feet into the ground. Each had a center post and beams, covered with both and an outer layer of earth. Known as a roundhouse, it had a smokehole, a door at the end of a short, low, entrance tunnel, and a wall opening to pass firewood inside. Since the building also served as a sweathouse, it was located near a stream so bathers could plunge in. Serving as a social center, the building was used for public ceremonies, as well as a men's club for casual lounging, singing, doctoring, and telling stories.[55]

Men's tools consisted of arrows, sinew-backed bows, spears, clubs, slings, and other weapons used daily to hunt. Women kept their tools in their homes, primarily a slab mortar and basket hopper, used with a bulbed stone pestle to crush and grind acorns and seeds, musselshell spoons for eating, wooden mush paddles for cooking, skin scrapers, a fire drill, and a variety of stone knives and mauls. Women were adept at making coiled baskets for cooking and storage or twined baskets for use as seed beaters, sifters, and conical burden baskets.

A Day

Every dawn was met with the commotion of talking described in the origin saga. People left after a breakfast of cold leftovers. During the day, people would snack on whatever they foraged, such as berries and greens, returning home in time for a dinner at sunset. Everyone ate together out of a common basket because this promoted solidarity and sharing, using fingers or spoons of musselshell. Dinner consisted of meat, acorn mush,

55. Alfred Kroeber 1925: 175, Virginia Miller 1979: 19-20.

seasonal specialties, and a bread made from acorn meal leavened with red earth. During feasts, men ate first, then the women and children.

Men dressed lightly, usually wearing a coating of deer marrow grease and a deerskin around the hips. A deerskin cap was worn when it was cold. Women, their hair arranged in two braids, wore a two piece apron decorated with a fringe about two inches long. Both genders wore buckskin bands around the head and wrists, used combs made of fish backbones, and placed ornaments though the earlobes and nasal septum.

A Year

Seasons began in winter when people were eating their stores of ground up acorns. By the time spring arrived, frequent famines were relieved by fresh fish and fresh clover. Four plants provided fish poisons for stunning large quantities of salmon and trout. During the fishing season, men and women worked closely together. Several compatible families shared a camp for work and play. Some fish were eaten right away, and the rest were processed and stored. All bones were carefully returned to the water because these were the essence of the fish, revived in the flow to return the next year.

Spring was also spent setting fire drives for grasshoppers, gathering eggs, and collecting the sap of pines and milk weeds for chewing gum. Women kept busy gathering ripe plants, seeds, and berries.

During summer, men hunted animals and snared birds. Hunting specialists wore a disguise made from a stuffed deer head and imitated the movements of these animals so as to mingle with the herds. Thus, their kills were of the best quality. Among the religious precautions taken by every hunter were sexual chastity, rising early, sweat baths, and fasting. A hunter could gain public esteem by killing tender fawns and giving them to toothless elders. Men who were able to use a sling, which killed without leaving holes, were accorded additional prestige.

With fall, attention turned to acorns, the California staple. Much time was devoted to leaching out their tannic acid, which could be toxic, before they were ground up. This meal was left as it was or shaped into loaves, then stored in pits or in large, crude baskets. People encouraged the bounty of their staple at Acorn sings held both in January and May.

Every three to four years, the Creator was believed to send Yuki a sudden abundance of army worms. In gratitude, these were joyfully gathered and consumed at a return food feast directed by a Sky shaman. Here, and every other time that food was consumed, the inedible parts and bones were carefully respected and returned to the habitat of the creature so that its soul would be reborn for use by future generations.

During winter, rituals and cult initiations were held. People also worked at their specializations. For men, these were the making of bows, mortars, pestles, nets, and beads. For women, it was basketry.

A Life

A woman knew she was pregnant when she stopped menstruating. Her gestation was watched for signs and portents. A large abdomen indicated a son, a smaller one a daughter. If a woman stayed on her back after intercourse, she produced twins. If she did not want a baby at that time, however, she used a herb or technique to abort.

For delivery, a woman sat or reclined in her home or that of her mother, assisted by midwives, who were regarded as adepts because their own deliveries had been easy. Men were not allowed at any birth. The umbilical cord was cut with a flint knife that was a family heirloom. When the navel stump fell off, it was salted and stored away to prevent the child from becoming dim-witted. The afterbirth was taken out and buried deeply to safeguard the child from its use for sorcery.

The baby was washed in warm water and placed in a basket lined with moss, fur, and soft deerskin. For the next ten days, the mother was steamed over a fire, washed in water, and scented with wormwood and pepperwood. She remained secluded in the back of the house for three months, eating only plant foods, using a scratching stick, and drinking through a hollow quill. If a wife of a leader, a feast was held to mark the end of her seclusion.

For the same three months, the father observed a mild couvade. He did not smoke, travel, gamble, or engage in heavy work so as not to adversely affect the child. If the paternity were in doubt, the husband claimed the baby by publicly steaming himself with fir needles and tarwood leaves.

A child nursed until it was two to four years old. If the parents died, there was no formal procedure for the adoption of orphans. Generally, they were simply taken in by a close relative, although they were thereafter stigmatized. The term meaning both orphaned and illegitimate was a grave insult. Orphans and illegitimate children, both called "brush rabbits," had to resort to informal sexual arrangements if they came from poor families.

Girls were given small pack baskets to use when helping their mothers. Fathers made tiny bows and arrows for their sons to use in play. A child was known by a vulgar nickname or kin term until someone offered to provide a name. Children of better families were named at a younger age than those of the poor. Female names were distinctively marked by a prefix (masak-).

At puberty, a girl was secluded in a menstrual hut. Over four days, she danced to acorn songs, three or four times daily, with other women to show that she had the vigor and stamina needed for life as an adult woman. She used a scratcher and a drinking tube, covered her head with a basket, and did not eat meat or grease. At her second menstruation, another four days were devoted to dancing to acorn songs, culminating in a feast of foods made from acorns. Thereafter, at every menstruation, the woman retired to the back of her house, used a fresh rush mat every day during seclusion, and did not look at the Moon.

When approaching maturity, children were tattooed. Girls were decorated on the chin; boys on the chest, arms, and wrists to mark standardized lengths for strings of beads of particular value and consistency. A woman applied the marks by rubbing soot into punctures made with a needle, flint, or pointed deer bone. Male puberty was marked by cult initiation. After puberty, brothers and sisters were more reserved with each other, avoiding any vulgarity or joking, because puberty was a prelude to marriage.

Yuki acknowledged occasional berdaches, both males and females, who were more rare, calling the former "man-girl" and the latter "women man-girl." Male berdaches acted as stretcher bearers during battles.

There were at least three types of marriage: sister exchanges, sororate or levirate, and informal (common-law) arrangements. A groom might be 18 and a bride as young as 13, but most couples married in their 20s. Families arranged marriages, exchanging gifts for a period that lasted from three months to a year. At a marriage ceremony, everyone feasted and the couple exchanged necklaces of beads. They lived with inlaws until their first child was born. Then they set up their own household.

Proper etiquette required that a husband be quiet and deferential to his mother-in-law, and a wife to her father-in-law. A husband could make obscene jokes around his -sters-in-law because, by the sororate, they were potentially his wives. When a spouse died, the levirate or sororate was invoked for the sake of any children. Thus, a brother-in-law replaced a husband or a sister-in-law a wife. Leaders and other wealthy men could support more than one wife and often practiced polygyny. The Yuki language has no word for divorce because it was never permitted on any formal basis.

A husband owned his own bows, arrows, fishing gear, dance regalia, and inherited beads or obsidian; a wife had her baskets, pestles, mortar, clothes, skins, and any inherited beads.

Yuki were not a unified group, lacking even a name for themselves as distinct from other humans. Their homeland consisted of the most rugged mountains in the Coast Range, varying in altitude from less than 1000 feet to over 7500 feet above sea level. About six regional or dialect bands, each made up of several towns, hamlets, and rancherias, had distinguishing names for every settlement and band.

Bands were oriented along a drainage system, but the overall population was most dense in the wet eastern areas with the widest valleys. Every Yuki had a vital sense of place; most intended to die and be buried at the spot where they were born.

A tysic of any Yuki community was its leader, also known as the capitan through contacts with Spanish. They were graded or ranked according to the size of the settlement for which each had responsibility. The Spanish and Americans wanted a single spokesman for all the Yuki, so a tribal chief was invented, but his role remained incidental.

Aboriginally, the most important figure was called a Big Leader because he directed a community large enough to have a Poison house rotunda near its center. Every time a new leader took office, a new rotunda had to be built at a site selected by a Sky shaman. Then a suitable oak tree was located to serve as a center post. It was carefully cut down while the new leader stood in its lower branches. He remained in the tree while it was carried to the site and set up in the earth. It appears from this that the new leader was equated with Taikomol as the builder of the first rotunda. After being built, it was managed by a man who was called "Mole" after the old Woman who supports the earth on her front paws.

Duties of a leader, whether man or woman, were conducting public rituals, hospitality to visitors, and repeated lecturing of the community to lead moral and worthwhile lives. He spoke this advice while standing on the roof of the rotunda. When the leader was a man, his wife supervised the activities of the townswomen.

If there were no mature male heir, a mother might act as regent for a young son. If there were no male heirs at all, the office passed to a close female relative. In all cases, a successor had to be a member of a chiefly family, rigorously trained and initiated into both degrees of the Creator Cult. A woman leader, however, could not go onto the rotunda roof, so she had to appoint a speaker to harangue for her.

Since the rotunda symbolized the cosmos, it is significant that a woman was excluded from the roof, which represented the sky vault – indicating that the sky was indeed a male realm.

The final selection of a chief had to be ratified by a community meeting held inside the rotunda. Men and women met there to deliberate while sweat bathing and smoking. Once they approved the choice, the new leader was called Big Guide and addressed as "my father, you." A similar assembly, conducted by a leader, selected the siger for a war expedition.

A leader wore a bearskin robe, beads, long hair, feathered headband, and other finery. He or she was wealthy, maintaining reserves by spending time in the manufacture of valuable beads out of clamshells traded from Bodega Bay. Items of wealth (according to 1940 prices) included thin clamshell beads ($1 per 100), thick clamshell beads ($2 per 100), baked magnesite cylinders ($5-$20 apiece) traded from the Southeastern Pomo, scarce dentalia through the Sherwood Pomo, and pieces of high quality obsidian. All of this wealth had to be personally acquired because it was destroyed at the death of the owner.

Family pedigree and visible items of wealth were the basis for social distinctions. A leader was the wealthiest person in his or her area. In high families, the men owned any of the items just listed, together with choice pelts of beaver, otter, mink, cougar, and elk. Some owned elkhide armor or fine bows made in the north but too valuable to use. Utilitarian baskets and tools constituted wealth only if they were in sufficient quantity. Yuki traded dried venison, fish, hides, and rope, receiving salt from Northeastern Pomo and seafood from Coast Yuki, often collected at Mussel Rock.

Despite lost wealth, social ranks remained stable, families staying rich, average, and poor through generations. The few exceptions of upward mobility depended on concerted effort, industry, trading, and advantageous (hypergamous, upward) marriage.

Shamanism among the Yuki involved many practitioners named for Sky, Earth, Sun, and Bear. Powerful shamans could either cure or cause a disease; they were ranked on the basis of the source and abilities of their powha. Sky shamans were most important, deriving their powha from the Creator. Sun and Earth Shamans were intermediate, while Bears were most limited.

A novice Sky shaman received a vision of Pal, acting as a representative of Taikomol. At that moment, the novice became unconscious from the overwhelming enormity of his experience. Other shamans found him and conducted a dance around the prostrate body to induct him into their fellowship. A Sky shaman could control all the lesser immortals and cure all diseases except those caused by fright or strong sorcery.

To become an Earth shaman, a man received a vision from dwarfs about two feet tall, and a woman received one from Deer bosses, who were female, enabling them to remove "pains" shot into a patient by such beings, thereby restoring hunting luck.

A Sun shaman was visited by Sun, the spouse of Moon, and given the ability to cure the bites of rattlesnakes and black widow spiders.

A Bear shaman behaved ursine − irritable, unpredictable, and sometimes violent. While physically strong, Bears had more limited powha than those immortals.

All of the shamans were said to hold periodic meetings where they "talked shop" and held contests to test each other's powhas, setting up a series of relative rankings.

Initiations into the Creator Cult also taught shamanistic and sorcery techniques. During induction into the first degree, boys were taught to embody ghosts. They were thrown into the rotunda through the smokehole and arranged on the floor, like the sticks that were used to create humans. For the next four days, they listened carefully to a recitation of the origin saga. They were also told enough about curing and poisoning (sorcery) to enable them to aid shamans. In this guise, they were known as Singing Doctors. For the rest of that winter, these boys remained in seclusion.

The second degree was an expression of the Kuksu cult found throughout central California. The Big Leader took charge of this initiation, supplying the novices with esoteric details of the epic and its songs, with more demanding requirements. Initiates had to remain motionless, silent, and fasting for four days. During the rest of that winter, boys worked diligently to perfect their skills at various crafts.

Accounts conflict about the initiation of girls. Those destined to become leaders must have gone through some kind of cult induction, probably receiving esoteric instruction in a separate house, away from boys. A more formal initiation may have involved both boys and girls, derived from the Obsidian school of the neighboring Wailaki, where all children fasted, sweatbathed, and engaged in many endurance tests.

Crimes included wife beating, theft, and murder, usually by sorcery. A leader adjudicated all disputes, setting the amount of valuables or treasures to be given to the victim or next of kin in compensation to settle the matter. If this violence happened repeatedly, that person was judged a persistent troublemaker and the leader had him killed.

Native Californians were remarkably peaceful, so Yuki were unusual in being proud of their war exploits. They would mount an expedition in response to charges of murder, sorcery, poaching, insult, or abuse of a kinswoman. Warfare involved both surprise attacks and formal battles, where each side wore distinguishing feathers. Weaponry included bows, slings, clubs, and knives. Wounded were carried off the field by berdaches. The first side to retreat lost the battle. If any of its wounded and onlookers were caught, they were massacred by the victors.

A victory dance of men and women was held, led by leading warriors. After the dance, the trophy heads, skins, and scalps were discarded. Winners were duty bound to offer compensation to losers. Beads and other valuables were collected and paid to the other tribe, in some cases to bribe them not to retaliate. Regardless of hidden motives, the desired outcome was the restoration of peace.

Yuki men and women sometimes tested each other. They would take sides in a sweatlodge and try to outlast each other in the intense heat. It is said that the women usually won. A tug-of-war might be held between two teams of men or of mixed men and women. They were never held men against women, presumably because the men were regarded as stronger, but it was unwise to put this to a test.

In the event of sickness, home remedies were tried first, or a tattoo was applied at a spot to end pain there. If an illness became serious, a shaman was summoned to diagnose and, hopefully, cure it. Agents of disease were called "pains", something like an animated splinter filled with blood, shot into the patient by an immortal or the Creator because of a breach of taboo or a mocking of tribal custom. Other disease causes were fright (soul loss), sorcery (poisoning), and such practical causes as drinking polluted water or the bites of rattlesnakes and spiders.

If requested to perform a cure, a shaman could never refuse or his powha would decline or leave him entirely since it had come to him to offer help. If denied the chance to do this, it went elsewhere. Should a shaman be reluctant to undertake a cure, however, he could delay his arrival by insisting that the payment was too small. In the most cronic cases, cures involved a full initiate of the second cult degree working in the rotunda, with the head of the patient near the center post. Lesser healings were aided by first degree singing doctors. All shamans could use massage, but each of them also had a specialty. If a victim ran a high temperature, that disease was diagnosed as poisoning, caused by individuals trained in sorcery, who spent nights mixing together menstrual blood, snakes, lizards, bugs, and salamanders to make a concoction magically shot into the victim. Motivation to do so was either the result of a "poison giver's" personal grudge or because someone had hired the poisoner to do this. Some of these givers where known, and routinely hired to get revenge. A whole community might also ask a skilled one to send poison into an enemy group.

At a death, men and women began to wail. Messengers were sent to nearby communities with the news. Close relations of the same gender washed and prepared the body for burial the next day. During the hot days of summer, the body was buried almost immediately. Otherwise, there was some delay to allow relatives to arrive. The house of the deceased was either abandoned, burned, or dismantled and moved. His or her name became taboo. Mentioning it was a grave insult, so a circumlocution had to be substituted.

For every Yuki, the life principal had a primary locus in the breath and a secondary one in the heart. At the moment of death, the breath-soul began to revisit all of its former homes and haunts. After a month of this, it went to Taikomol in the sky. The heart-soul seems to have stayed near its body. Souls of people whose blood spilled on the ground remained tormented on the earth forever, along with the souls of criminals.

Before burial, a body was covered with deer or bear skins, furnished with food, tools, and treasured wealth. Family graves were located in close proximity, but they never had a fixed order because available spaces would be obvious and thus encourage more deaths to fill them.

Those who prepared the body were considered polluted, having to wash and switch off with branches of wormwood and pepperwood. Mourners took the precaution of chewing angelica root. Women in mourning singed off their hair and covered the head and face with pitch. A widow would do this for a year, but an older person might endure it for five years.

Periodically, while memory survived, gifts were burned for the dead, if their family could afford this. Again, the poor were at a disadvantage. The dead lived contented lives in the sky, although some of them would visit the earth without doing harm.

History

The native population of California was decimated both by epidemics during Spanish control and by a deliberate policy of extermination carried out after the American takeover. At the time of the 1849 Gold Rush, settlers arrived in California already brutalized from the experiences of trekking across the continent.[56] In this state, surviving natives were considered more of an encumbrance to settlement than they were in other regions. Also, they were generally pacifists, so many offered little resistance when attacked and killed.

Yuki were also brutalized, but they were given a reservation in Round Valley, a portion of their aboriginal territory. This gave them the comfort of a sense of familiar place, despite the fact that they had to share it with remnants from other tribes. Among the survivors moved to the reservation were Wailaki, who spoke an Athapaskan language; Nomlaki Wintun and Concow Maidu Penutians; Achomawi, Shasta, and Pomo from Clear and Little Lakes, all of whom were classified as members of the Hokan stock.[57]

This kind of linguistic diversity among neighbors was typical of aboriginal California. The policy of relocating many different groups, sometimes former enemies, on the same reservation was also standard American practice since it provided more land for white homesteading and encouraged native factionalism, disruption and disorganization. Instead of divide and conquer, a motto of the Indian Bureau was jumble together and confuse.

56. Theodora Kroeber 1965: 53, 98.
57. Amelia Susman 1976.

Ritual

The major rites were the acorn sings of January and May, which dramatized the process of harvesting and preparing the acorn supply to insure a bountiful harvest. In addition to victory dances, return food feasts were held for potato-like roots, clover, and army worms. Elaborate dances were held in the rotunda during winter and in brush arbors in summer.

Summary

All of these data indicate that, for Yuki, Woman was exclusive, associated with women, woman man-girls, Mole, Deer bosses, plants, acorns, and the earth. Man was inclusive, bound up with settlements, man-girl berdaches, Coyote, dwarfs, animals, trees, and the sky.

The most obvious mediator is Taikomol himself, symbolized by the oak center post, rotunda, and big leaders. He is all-knowing and all-wise, the first being to think and to take mindful initiative to create everything else. He can aptly be described as the Mind of the Yuki universe.

Sources

Yuki culture was carefully summarized by Foster (1944). Related work was done by Edward Gifford (1937, 1939) and Alfred Kroeber (1932). Ethnohistorical research includes the work of Amelia Susman Schultz (1974, but done in 1939) and Virginia Miller (1979) documenting genocide and bureaucratic corruption.

KERES of the Southwest

Creation

Before everything else, Tsityostiinako existed as diffuse intelligence, although her later personifications include appearing to humans as a Man, Woman, or Spider.

The world itself originated from a blood clot, which grew into a Woman with head to the east, feet to the west, and arms to the north and south. For some purposes, this world also is a cube divided into four levels, arranged from top to bottom as Yellow, Turquoise, Red, and White Worlds. At the center of the Yellow World, connected to their primordial White womb, was Shipop^u, a passage into the underworld where life emerged and the dead return.

In the White World womb of Shipop^u, in total darkness, two Women appeared. As these sisters developed they became increasingly aware of Tsityostiinako (Consciousness), who directed their thoughts and intentions by telepathy. When mature, these sisters were given baskets containing seeds, figurines of male and female animals, and songs to animate these to populate the world.

Seeking light, they enlivened the images of burrowing animals like Mole or insects like Locust, and asked them to dig upward into the next world and to plaster the sides of the hole to make it safe. Evergreen seeds were planted to grow quickly into very tall tress for everyone to climb into the higher level.

These sisters settled in each of these upper worlds for four years, then moved to the next higher one. Finally, they came into the Yellow World, but the surface was too soft, so members of the Insect Priesthood were asked to cook and harden it. It would have then been perfect, but some witches (Two-Hearts) had joined the settlers without the women knowing it. For this reason, bad things still happen in the world, caused by selfish and harmful people who are witches.

The sisters continued to bring order, placing sacred mountains and patron immortals in the four directions, making the Sun and setting it on its present course, and providing people with personal names and matriclans. Yet all did not go smoothly; these sisters began to quarrel about their own relative powha. They fought a series of duels until one of them decided to remain with the Keres as their Mother and the other went off to become the Mother of either another tribe like the Navaho or of Europeans, to whom she supplied cows, pigs, sheep, horses, metals, money, and writing.

Keres began to move away from where they emerged or were created anew and began to seek the center of their world. They built several towns along the way, every time they had reached a likely center. The most important of these was White House, where the major esoteric priesthoods were instituted, devoted to Managing, Curing, or Protecting.

Managing Priesthoods were founded by sacred clowns to supervise the public rituals of the religious calendar. The Curing ones were divided into those which treated diseases caused either by witchcraft or by angry animals. The former were internal illness treated by a sucking cure, while the latter were external and doctored by brushing with eagle wings. The Protecting Priesthoods consisted of Warriors and Hunters, initiating men who had either taken scalps or killed an eagle, bear, or cougar.

At White House, men and women quarreled over who contributed more. To settle the argument, men and women lived apart. Men thrived on meat, but women wasted away eating crops. Four years later, these women were destitute and begged the men to take them back, which they did.

While living alone, some women gave birth to monsters, cannibal giants, who began to rampage the earth and kill everyone. Sun saw this destruction and took pity on Keres. He came to earth and gave two pinyon nuts to a virgin girl. From these, she conceived and gave birth to twin sons, who grew up very quickly and started to kill off the monsters.

White House was peaceful again until men started to gamble. At this time, the Katsina, immortals bringing rain from the West, visited the community in person. Once, during a tense game, someone mocked the Katsinas, who became very angry and mounted an attack on White House. They were winning the battle until the twins rushed to join the humans, turning the tide.

After the battle, slain Katsina were revived, but, even so, they withheld the rain, causing a prolonged drought, until a chaste and humble man danced long enough to convince them of his sincerity. They sent rain, but never returned themselves, instead giving humans permission thereafter to embody Katsinas with masks and costumes.

Whenever these masks were donned, Katsinas sent their spirits with needed rain to produce abundant crops which so increased their population size that the Mother of the Keres introduced death to keep the world from becoming overpopulated.

In time these twin men lost their sense of proportion and began to kill enemies indiscriminately, so the immortals held a council to decide their punishment. They brought a girl killed by the twins back to life to pursue them relentlessly. The Twins were finally driven to ask for help from the immortals, who instructed them in the proper way of protecting people and of harnessing the powha released by killing in the interests of public good. All of these teachings have since been passed down through the Warrior Priesthood.

With this new access to powha, Keres left White House and broke up into smaller communities which went on to found the modern towns of Cochiti, San Felipe, Santo Domingo, Santa Ana (Tamaya), Sia, Acoma, and Laguna (Kawaika'a). With the arrival of the Spanish in the 1540s, this native religion was persecuted and forced into increasing secrecy. In the process, many Keres converted to public Catholicism, hence many towns are named for the patron saint assigned to their church by early Franciscans.

World

This universe is populated by a vast array of immortals, led by Consciousness at the center or heart, with the sisters, twins, and Corn Mother. In keeping with the communalism of Pueblo society, each direction is associated with a class of beings, such as Katsina and Gomayowish in the west, Kopishtaiya in the east, Shiwana in the sky, and Maiyanyi in the ground. Each priesthood had patrons located at specific locales in the Yellow World whose boundaries are set by four sacred mountains, each linked with a color, weather deity, warrior, holy woman, animal, bird, snake, tree, etc., figuring in some ritual act.

Housing

Keres have lived in "pueblos" like apartment buildings for over a thousand years. Before that, their ancestors lived in pithouse villages. Slowly, over a few generations, rows of storage rooms behind the pithouses developed into massive house blocks and the pithouse changed into the kiva, a sacred chamber and men's club.

Often, a pueblo was built around an open plaza, which served as a work area and meeting place. Dug into the plaza were public community kivas that served as churches. Within the house blocks were smaller chamber kivas used by special priesthoods devoted to curing, managing rituals, and general wellbeing. In very large communities, each neighborhood had its own plaza, in addition to the main square, which was the focus for activities involving everyone. Each family occupied an apartment, opening off a plaza, and consisting of several rooms arranged from front to back on several stories. A family mostly lived in the front room, or outside on the stepped roofs in summer, and used the other rooms for storage of maize and other crops. Lower level rooms stored clan emblems and religious paraphernalia, hidden from the eyes of the unrelated or uninitiated.

Men and women shared the work of building a town. After the masonry foundations and the heavy timbers of the framework were set by men, women did most of the building. A work party of women, often close relatives, finished the walls with a coat of plaster and polished the adobe floors with smooth stones to make them more durable. Once completed, houses belonged to the women and their matriclan.

Men hunted and worked the fields to provide food for their families. More importantly, they devoted considerable time to religious duties as members of priesthoods or of the Kachina sect. Their prayers and dances were intended to bring rain, health, long life, and general goodwill for their entire community.

A Day

Every morning, a woman swept out her rooms before undertaking the arduous task of grinding maize flour for the day. Women often worked together for companionship, while boys playing flutes might serenade unmarried girls. Milling bins – consisting of a smooth, dished stone block (now called a metate) angled downward, slab walls, and a grinding block (called a mano, Spanish for "hand") – were set in the floor in groups of three so that the kernels could be ground into coarse, medium, and fine grades of meal.

Now, Keres eat three meals a day, mostly of maize stews, tortillas, chili, and meat. Anciently, meat was said to be more of a seasoning than a staple. Although some hunters did take bear and deer, most meat was supplied by communal drives for rabbit and antelope.

By occupation, men were farmers, hunters, weavers, metal workers, warriors, and ritualists; women were housewives, cooks, potters, basket makers, and auxiliary ceremonialists. The most vital task was the irrigated farming of maize, beans, and squash, supplemented by cotton and amaranth. Women tended small kitchen gardens that might include tobacco. Other activities included gathering pinyon pine nuts, fire wood, building materials, medicine plants, and raw materials for trade goods.

While some Keres continue these activities, most of them now work for wages in nearby Anglo communities.

A Life

During a birth, the right hand was used for ritual gestures because of associations with the category of Woman. In the event of a difficult birth, a member of the Giant Priesthood was called to render assistance. Every new mother and child was secluded four days, then ceremonial godparents named the baby outside as the sun rose on the fifth morning.

During childhood, youngsters played at adult tasks and roles. At puberty, children of the appropriate age and gender were initiated into the Katsina cult and pledged to secrecy.

Young adults arranged their own marriages subject to the approval of parents and matriclan councils. Newlyweds usually lived with her family until they had a child and built a home of their own nearby.

The organizational unit of the Keres was the town (called <u>pueblo</u> in Spanish), governed by priesthoods, arranged into matriclans, and integrated by two kivas (semi-subterranean churches) variously called East/West, Turquoise/Pumpkin, and Inside/Outside. Men were urged to join a priesthood if other members of the family belonged to it, or a parent had promised him to it as a child, or he made a personal vow to do so during a time of distress, or he had been successfully cured by it, or he was entrapped near its chamber while members were inside for a retreat of fasting, praying, and making offerings.

The present towns represent two patterns of organization, one is exclusive of Man and the other inclusive of Woman. The manly towns of Cochiti, San Felipe, and Santo Domingo initiated only boys into the secret of the Katsina, were governed by their priesthoods, and recruited to the kivas through the father. The womanly towns of Santa Ana, Sia, Acoma, and Laguna initiated both boys and girls, embodied both the Katsina and the Gomaiyowish, were governed by both priesthood and matriclan leaders, and recruited to the kivas through the mother.

While the matriclans shared authority in four of the towns, all of them recognized the vital role of the priesthoods, which were actually guilds (sodalities) with a tendency for memberships to run in particular families.

The head of the most powerful priesthood, usually called Flint Knife, was the Town Priest (cacique), a position with strong associations with Woman. Though a husband and father, "she" was installed wearing the garments of a bride and thereafter addressed as "mother" since "her" primary duty was to fast, pray, and meditate for the good of that town.

Complementing the cacique was the Country Priest, now replaced by two war captains named for the miraculous twin boys. They are selected from each of the kivas in alternate years. These captains served as the executive officers of the town and were particularly responsible for guarding its perimeters.

Both the Town and Country leaders had a staff of aides and messengers. For dealing with outsiders, each town also had a roster of officers added in response to a 1620 royal decree from the King of Spain to systematize Spanish colonial administration. These are under the supervision of a gobernador (governor), who handles matters pertaining to foreigners, crimes, and the Catholic church.

All of these officials were advised by a town council composed of male heads of households, retired officials, and native priests. The basis of all positions was legitimate access to esoteric (sacred and secret) knowledge affecting the welfare of the community and the world, derived from full details of the origin saga and to the rules for approaching various immortals.

The lowest category consisted of children and uninitiated women. Above them were members of the Katsina sect. Highest of all were the members of priesthoods, divided into novices, initiates, and adepts. Priests are considered "cooked" and everyone else "raw", while among the different degrees of a priesthood the process of cooking was equated with the level of instruction. Thus, a novice was cooking, an initiate was cooked and "knew something", and an adept was well done and "knew".

This communal way of life was all important for Keres and other Pueblos. Hence, crimes consisted of acting independent or selfish (against community needs), such as not helping with the cleaning of the irrigation ditches every spring, revealing esoteric "secrets" to women and outsiders, and disrupting the town by committing murder, rape, theft, or insult. The most serious offense of all was witchcraft, acting in an antisocial or inhumane manner. Punishment for this was confession rather than death, except in the most severe cases. The killing of witches was an African and European peculiarity; natives were content as long as they knew who they were, in keeping with their maxim "live and let live."

Crimes were generally divided into those of the inside or of the outside. Those of the inside related to the town, judged by the cacique and "her" staff, and, if necessary, punished by the captains. Outside crimes were judged by the so-called Spanish officials, with the advice of the theocracy. Most offenses were settled by compensation of goods or labor, but more serious cases could involve flogging, being confined in a tiny space until forgiven, or banishment. If a criminal or witch did not reform after several such punishments, they were killed in secret by a captain.

The four primary causes of disease were witchcraft, angry animals, psychological distress, and natural upsets. Witchcraft was treated by members of the Curing Priesthoods entitled to perform sucking treatments, while those able to conduct brushing cures treated disease caused by angry animals, especially Insects, who mystically caused skin eruptions and disfigurement. Psychological illness was handled by adoption into another matriclan to provide support and care from more relatives. Natural causes included eating unripe or contaminated food and were treated in a matter of fact way.

Cures were graded in terms of the priesthoods involved, number of curers, length of time, type of paraphernalia used, and, especially, the songs chanted.

When someone died, a relative of the same gender washed and dressed the body, and men dug the grave. A member of a priesthood conducted the funeral in ancient times; now, a Catholic service is held before a native one. Four days later, the same native priest returned to the home where the person died and exorcised the house and yard. During all these events, the left hand is used because death is associated with Man. A soul returns to ShipopU, from which it will later be reborn to another set of parents.

History

The modern towns have been in their locations for several centuries, and some populations, as at Acoma and Sia, have been in these areas for thousands of years.

Archaeologically, the Keres have been identified with the Oshara component of the Anasazi Tradition, going back 7,000 years in west central New Mexico. Between AD 800-1100, the center of the Keres, equivalent to mythic White House, was Chaco Canyon, containing over sixteen large towns and hundreds of smaller ones. After Chaco and environs, new towns were established along the Rio Grande, with the ruin now called Tyuonyi probably serving as a ceremonial center.

There also seems to have been a Keres concentration to the west, in the area now occupied by the Hopi villages. Until 1700, its most important community was Awatobi on Antelope Mesa. After the Pueblo Revolt of 1680-92, Awatobi again accepted Catholicism and in consequence was sacked in 1700 by Hopis, who adopted some women to perpetuate its clans and rituals.

Ritual

All of the Pueblos are justly famous for the complexity of their rituals and dramas based on their farming calendar. They include a bewildering series of feasts, public dances, private displays, masked incarnations, and return foods thanksgivings. The current repertoire has added fiestas, feast days, patron saints, and Masses derived from the Spanish Catholic Church.

Of these, the Matachinas Dance depicting troops of Spanish or Moorish (sometimes Native) dancers, and the gallo (rooster pull) are particularly dramatic. For the latter, horsemen compete to grab a rooster buried up to the neck, ripping it apart because the spattering of its blood on the ground is believed to bring rain, the ultimate desire of all Pueblos.

During June and July, each native priesthood takes a turn going into their chamber for an eight day retreat to fast, pray, and perform elaborate ritual feats, usually called kiva magic, while avoiding females.

In February and November, all of the priesthoods met simultaneously, each in its own chamber, for four days to mark the crucial solar rites renewing the world as the Sun changed direction along the horizon. During the winter, the sun rose more and more to the south; then, for summer, it moved toward the north. On the last night, each priesthood set up paraphernalia in its chamber that included painted altars made of wooden slats, colored sand paintings, insignia of degrees, and other proofs of their access to powha.

During summer, Katsina dances were held to bring rain for growing crops. Spanish persecution made the use of masks secret in the Rio Grande towns, so now the public versions of these dances do not use them.

Summary

Keres culture was intensely anthropomorphic, pervaded by a Man/Woman opposition mediated by Mind—as Consciousness—that was fully expressed. Man included a sacred language, white ceremonial costume, turquoise color, kivas, the boy twins and war captains, priesthoods, left, Sun, animals, death, and the directions of north, east, and above. For Woman, these were the ordinary language, black costume, yellow paint, houses, sisters and the cacique, matriclans, right, Earth, plants, birth, and the directions south, west, and below.

Sources

The Keresan Pueblos were the lifelong concern of Leslie White, who published ethnographies for five of the seven towns: Acoma, Sia, Santa Ana, Santo Domingo, and San Felipe. The town of Laguna were treated by Elsie Clews Parsons, Franz Boas, and, most thoroughly, Florence Hawley Ellis. Cochiti has been described in several monographs, summarized and augmented by extensive research by Charles Lange (1959), the best single account of a Keresan Pueblo. A dissertation by Jay Miller serves as the basis for the version given here. It intends to make sense of the Keres as a unified cultural entity, contrary to the prevailing opinion in the Southwest which regards them as a mosaic bridge influenced by neighboring Pueblos.

YUCHI of the Southeast

Creation

Old Woman Who Was The Sun met with Birds to decide how to get earth. After considerable discussion, they agreed to send a messenger, an earth diver, to the bottom of the sea. Beaver, then Otter, dove and drowned. People despaired until Crayfish (Crawdad) asked to try, saying the water would turn bloody if he failed, but muddy yellow if he reached bottom.

He dove and was down a long time. People waited. Then the water turned yellowish, and they were glad as Crayfish emerged with earth between his claw-fingers. Though only a speck, Old Woman made it expand to form a vast if soft land. Everyone made a pact to stay off the ground by gliding, running very fast, floating, or hovering.

Buzzard became the inspector. Once, when he was gliding over it, he noticed that had Bullfrog settled on the land. Very angry, he struck Bullfrog hard enough to make his eyes bulge out. Later, he discovered Raccoon ensconced and, in the ensuing argument, blackened his eyes. Exhausted, Buzzard tried to fly away but instead plummeted to earth, raising rugged mountains on impact.

Other animals were created and met with Old Sun Woman to decide how to light the world. After much discussion, they asked Glowworm, Moon, and Star Spider try out but each was too dim. Finally, this council selected Sun herself. She went into the sky but the world was in constant sunlight until Chipmunk suggested that night be created to alternate with day so people would have privacy to create babies. Everyone thought this was a good idea, and Moon and Star Spiders took dim positions in the night sky.

Chipmunk was so delighted with his fame that he kept boasting of his own brilliance. Everyone began to shun him, but still he raved. Wildcat became increasingly angry, but when he tried to deliver a fatal blow, Chipmunk jumped aside, though sharp claws raked down his back, leaving stripes.

Once the land had topography and denizens, it hardened so that everything else could live on its surface.[58] Later, a woman went to the creek to fetch water as she always did, but this time noticed that drops of menstrual blood from the Sun had spattered on the ground. Carefully gathered these up, she hid them at home until a crying baby boy was heard. She raised him as her son, never letting him touch the earth until he was initiated into manhood by being scratched on his arms and legs. Since then, all boys have similarly be initiated at the annual Busk.

Growing strong quickly, he was ready for marriage so his mother took out one of his ribs and created his wife. Their children were the first Yuchi, calling themselves the Tsoyaha, "offspring of the Sun." Among them were special individuals with dark skin so closely identified with the Sun that their death caused a solar eclipse. Indeed, a prophecy says that if all Yuchi ever disappear, or if the Busk (Green Corn) is not held, then the Sun will never rise again and the world will die.

Other useful items were added to the Yuchi world from time to time. Among these was

---

58. Gunter Wagner 1931.

tobacco, which grew from a drop of semen left at the spot where a couple conceived a son.[59]

As humans settled in, Ironman carefully watched the behavior of each being in order to provide a name for its species and derivative matriclan, such as Raccoon, Bear, etc. Ironman also instituted the moiety halves of Chiefs and Warriors inherited from fathers to sons.

World

The Yuchi drew much of their symbolism from nature, especially for creating distinctive beaded neckbands with emblems of sky, clouds, earth, sun, moon, and more. They shared a common belief in an antagonism between sky Thunder and something like a sea serpent.

With Great Lakes tribes, they believed in a powerful composite being, living in lakes or other bodies of water, called the Underwater Panther. Some say it has the body of a large cat, the tail of a snake, and the antlers of a deer. During one Busk, an effigy of it, made of stuffed deerskin with body painted blue and horns yellow, rested in front of the north arbor while a Turtle Dance was held in its honor.[60]

At the limits of this world were the four directions, each equated with certain qualities: North = green-blue (grue) = sky, East = white = propitious = sunrise = life, South = red = war = turbulence = fire, and West = black = misfortune = sunset = death.

Housing

In 1791, on the Chattahoochie River in Georgia, William ? Bartram was impressed by the compactness of a Yuchi town set in a vast plain along a bluff. Houses were large and well built, with walls of lathe and reddish plaster and roofs shingled with slabs of cypress bark. Bunks were set along the inside walls for sitting and sleeping.

Summer dwellings were square arbors with open sides and brush piled atop a frame supported by four corner poles. Smaller houses consisted of quonset huts made of bent over saplings, ten feet high and sixteen feet square, covered over with bark shingles or mats.

Households and compounds were built around a central plaza, called the square, which was the focus for community activities. Because the mother of the Sun took him to the first Busk, traveling along a Rainbow, to be scratched and thus initiated, the square ground was also called "rainbow" and the annual rite "on the rainbow."

In the center was the town fire, symbolizing the Sun, made of four logs set along the cardinal directions to form a cross (+). This fire represented the Sun. At every Busk a new fire was kindled and the old ashes sprinkled to mark paths to the north and south arbors, which were painted red and occupied by Warriors, and to the west one, painted white and used by Chiefs because it faced the rising sun.

All Yuchi belonged to the town where they were born, but new members, such as foreign spouses, were adopted at a Busk. One of the reasons that ancestral Yuchi can be identified is that their towns were so compact and orderly around a plaza and council house.

After they were moved to Oklahoma, Yuchi lived on rural, dispersed farmsteads. Yet, a

---

59. By contrast, in Tibet, tobacco was produced from the menstrual blood of a demoness (Epstein 1975: 44). These ethnographic examples and counter-examples establish the range of variation possible in human thought, action, and experience.
60. Frank Speck 1909: 111.

sense of three former towns was perpetuated by three square grounds used for rituals, most especially the Busk. In other words, while the town households broke up and scattered, the public plaza was retained as a focus for community and communal activities. Many of the functions of the council house, moreover, were transferred to the Protestant churches that became another focus for Yuchi community sentiment and decision making.

As the name implies, the square had an inside surface of bare earth and four outside edges. At Kellyville, where a new chief was installed during the 1975 Busk, there are open-sided, brush-roofed arbors on the north and south, where Warriors sit, and on the west side, occupied by Chiefs. On the east is a mound about four feet tall composed of dirt swept up from every cleaning of the square. At the center is a hearth where a fire is kindled during rituals and fed by a cross of four logs, pushed inward to be consumed.

Year

A staple of the diet was maize, as food and as a drink called <u>sofkee</u>, a sweet, viscous mixture of ground cornmeal and water. Annual activities concentrated on field crops, augmented by hunting and fishing. Rituals paid particular attention to these natural cycles, reminding the Yuchi of their obligations to the land.

Genders were codependent. Women tended maize, beans, squash, and pumpkins in fields defined by upright stones decorated with personal marks. Women also kept house, raised children, and worked in soft materials, such as hide, clay, basketry splints, and textiles. Some families also tended a plot of tobacco near their home.

Men engaged in politics, waged war and contests, worked in hard materials (stone, wood, later metal), and hunted in forests outside the towns, alone or in groups, with bow and arrow or blowgun, before they acquired rifles. After contact, Yuchi added potatoes to their other crops, and men became the farmers.

Each animal and species had its own protecting immortal so a hunter needed special songs to convince an animal to allow itself to be killed. If the hunter had good intentions, respected life, shared his success with others, and was otherwise worthy to receive that meat, the animal died, regardless of any personal hunting skill or ability. The crux of all this sincerity, therefore, was the songs because they most closely mirrored the rhythms basic to life.

The full series of these songs was learned and used by shamans, but individuals could pay to learn particular tunes. Since the entrails of large animals were considered a delicacy, they provided appropriate payment for such knowledge. Once songs were acquired, however, they could only be used effectively if the husband and wife were chaste during the hunt.

Like other peoples in the Southeast, Yuchi used a fish poison. After it was mashed and placed upstream, stunned fish rose to the surface to be gathered up. Some were roasted to eat immediately, and the rest were prepared for storage by men and women working together to clean and salt them.

A Life

Yuchi had a belief in reincarnation. Anciently, a birth hut was built with a door to the east, associated with sunrise and life, and the pregnant woman delivered lying on her back, assisted by old women acting as midwives, later burying the afterbirth to protect the newborn from premature death from sorcery. Something as closely linked with life as this placenta could be used to kill someone in revenge for a grudge against the family, envy of a healthy baby, or jealousy of the parents.

A father desired a son and a mother preferred a daughter, but all children were welcome. For a son, the father made a tiny bow and arrow, wrapped them with the umbilical cord, and threw them into a dense thicket to encourage the boy symbolically to become a good woodsman. The cord of a baby girl was buried under the family wooden mortar, and the father carved a tiny mortar, pestle, and two pot stirrers to be kept in the home. These acts encouraged the girl to become a good homemaker.

A baby was washed immediately after birth, but not clothed until named on the fourth morning. Preference was given to reviving the name of a deceased maternal uncle or aunt, according to the sex of the child. Names were carefully selected because they influenced the lifelong temperament of that child. Some made reference to the matriclan, but this was not an important consideration. If a name turned out to be inappropriate or the child became seriously ill, the name was changed to gain another temperament. Twins and deformed infants were believed to be sent among humans as moral guides and examples, reminding everyone that life was a gift and no one was perfect.

For a month after the birth, the father was expected to remain idle, a mild couvade indicating concern for his baby. As children grew older, they became increasingly proficient at adult roles and careers. A father had responsibility to train his sons properly, and a mother taught her daughters.

At puberty, a girl was secluded four days in a menstrual hut with the door facing east. Her mother brought her food in dishes made of unbaked clay, used only once. After this seclusion, a girl was sought by suitors because she was now eligible for marriage. Until menopause, the girl returned to a menstrual hut every month to protect her male relations from any dangers emanating from this periodic expression of vital cosmic rhythms.

Male puberty was indicated by a cracking voice and celebrated by initiation at the Busk when every townsman was scratched on the calves, arms, and chest. This Scratcher used the jaw of a garfish in the past, now a comb imbedded with pins or a sterile needle, to produce an outflow of blood symbolic of purification and acts of valor. All men were scratched at every Busk, together with any boys who had come of age.

Of these, four boys particularly admired by the community were selected to serve as guards, each carrying a seven foot sapling. These bare poles with leafy tops served as insignia and threatening weapons.

Yuchi marriages usually did not involve gift exchanges. A couple established their own residence as full adults. Important men were expected to have several wives so they could better fulfill their obligations of hospitality and generosity. If there was a divorce, children lived with their mother.

The focus of Yuchi was the town, each occupied by over 20 matriclans and two patrimoieties. Yuchi use a term for matriclan that translates as "on the house" together with a particular species name. Thus, the Bear clan is called "bear on the house," making species, clan, and household synonymous. Further, Yuchi tradition records that each clan once occupied a separate town.

This link between clan, town, and animal forbid individuals from insulting or eating their namesake, but they could handle or use pieces of it. Thus clans were mutually interdependent because those pieces needed for tools, clothing, or decoration had to be acquired from members of other clans. Particular clans also provided special services.

Thus, the Bear Clan supplied the Town Chief, while other leaders came from the Panther, Wolf, Turtle, and Deer, similarly numerous and therefore influential.

Ironman also gave two groups for Yuchi men to inherit through the father, Chiefs and Warriors, expressive of the basic dichotomy between Peace/War = White/Red so important among Southeastern cultures. The head of the Warriors usually came from the Panther Clan, as that of the Chiefs came from the Bear. Chiefs were supposed to be thinkers, orators, and distinguished role models; while Warriors were expected to be aggressive, spontaneous, and outgoing. Formerly, Warriors used black face paint, adding some highlights in red; while Chiefs decorated their faces in red, blue, and yellow paint.

The leadership of each town reflected the Civil/War dichotomy. The Town Chief was aided by three men and an heir, of proper Bear clan and Chiefs memberships, who acted as subchief. The War Chief, also called Police Chief, belonged to both the Panthers and Warriors. He also had a staff of three, one of whom acted as Scratcher at the Busk. Two heralds announced decisions and also served as butchers and cooks at ceremonies.

The town council consisted of all initiated men, called into session periodically by the Town Chief. Seating was by patrimoiety and deliberations usually ranged from sharing advice among the leaders to ratifying a succession. Offices were held for life unless conduct led to public displeasure, censure, and removal. To elect or ratify a successor, men formed a single line until they were asked to step out in a certain direction to form a separate row. The line with the most men determined the vote.

While the Town Chief was respected as a font of knowledge and sage advice, regard for him was tinged with fear because he was also a shaman of considerable powha and ability. He supervised the collection and mixture of the medicine plants at the Busk to create the Black Drink or, more pleasantly, the Herb Water, a medicine with awesome symbolism, consumed to purify participants. Meanwhile, the War Leader had charge of the sacred fire, Scratcher, various games, and numerous dances.

According to Yuchi, the Chiefs had higher status than the Warriors. The basis of this distinction was the rightful possession and beneficial use of esoteric knowledge and mystic powha, as typified by the shamanic attributes of the Town Chief. The most vital representation of this powha was the Herb Water, a mixture of plants and other ingredients representing all of creation. As the Town Chief was the apex of this system, so foreigners were beyond its serious concern. In the Yuchi language, this was indicated by a special form of pronoun (wey instead of hey) that was applied to anyone not fortunate enough to have been born a Yuchi.[61]

As men became older, they wore longer ceremonial jackets, supposedly inspired by European hunting styles, called Red Stick coats in honor of the conservative Upper Creek faction, which also provided the nucleus for the Seminoles, defeated in 1813. They took their name from the war post, known in French as Baton Rouge, set up when a war party was recruited. Warriors joined by striking it and reciting their past deeds of valor.

Traditional crimes were murder and adultery, together with some minor offenses. Clansmen were expected to avenge the murder or maiming of a fellow member, ideally using the very same weapon. Yet punishment was never unmixed with compassion. If a murderer could hide out until the next Busk and manage to enter the square during that

---

61. Hans Wolff, Yuchi Phonemes and Morphemes, with Special Reference to Person Markers, International Journal of American Linguistics, 14 (4): 240-243.

celebration, he had to be absolved by the offended clan.

Among the Yuchi, a persistent womanizer was mobbed and injured by either all the townspeople or just the women. For flagrant adultery, both the man and the woman had their ears nicked or cut off, a change from the usual double standard that only punished the woman.

Anyone who ate their clan animal or refused to attend the Busk was either fined or whipped, depending on his or her attitude and any extenuating circumstances, for such disregard of the communal ethic so important in Native America. More than just anti-social, they acted anti-human. Hence, the only valid excuse for avoiding punishment was a greater social need, such as treating the starved or sick.

In general, Yuchi, and other Southeastern tribes like Creek and Cherokee, held that many diseases were caused by specific animals and cured by associated plants. Sickness, called "trouble" by Yuchi, responded to a variety of remedies, which escalated with the severity of the case. The most simple were home cures like emetics and sweat baths; the most serious involved calling a shaman, who looked into a pot of water until an image of the animal causing the disease was revealed and the appropriate plant medicine could be prescribed.

When a Yuchi died, relatives washed the body. A man had his face painted in a manner appropriate to his patrimoiety. Men dug the grave, formerly into the floor of the house and now in a cemetery, and the prone body was lowered in and covered by planks. The head was to the west, with food, tobacco, and valuables placed nearby. After the grave was filled in, a fire was built at the head end and kept burning four nights to light the way of one of the four ghosts to the afterworld.

Two other souls hovered near the kin, and the fourth remained at the place where the death occurred. If the traveling soul safely passed under a cloud that rose and fell like a bludgeon, it took a rainbow trail to the place called Far-Overhead, arriving on the fourth morning. Simultaneously, on earth, a shaman conducted a feast for the dead.

Bad people suffered another fate. Their souls became dwarfs who lived deep in the woods and killed everyone who intruded on them.

History

The ancestors of the Yuchi seem to have dwelt within the modern state of Tennessee, initially to the west in the Kentucky Basin of the Tennessee River and then in the southeastern corner as the Mouse Creek Focus on the middle and lower Hiwassee River just prior to face-to-face contact with Europeans, a period usually called the proto-historical. Nearby was the Dalles Focus, which has been traced to the Koasati. Modern Yuchi claim a homeland in South Carolina and eastern Georgia.

By 1729, they had joined the Creek Confederacy, where they were recognized as a single town, and, in 1836, they were forced with other allies to move to Indian Territory (now Oklahoma). After Removal, they settled as three communities in the area called Cross Timbers near Tulsa. Yuchi sent a chief to the House of Kings and four men to the House of Warriors within the Creek Assembly at their capitol in Okmulgee until 1906, when tribal governments of the "Five Civilized Tribes" were disbanded to make way for Oklahoma statehood.

Ritual

The major ceremony of the Southeast, probably derived from Yuchi, is the Busk, a regional version of the Green Corn or Maize Rite practiced by most farmers of the East as a thanksgiving harvest rite. The term Busk derives from the Muskogean Creek term poskita, "to fast," but the Yuchi called their ceremony "In The Rainbow Big House."

This rite was scheduled by the Town Chief to coincide with the full moon when the maize was ripe, usually in July. When the date was set, a tally stick was discarded daily as a countdown. On the first day, people arrived at the square, the women setting up their camps in accustomed places around the periphery.

At dawn on the second day, a new fire was kindled by the Town Chief. People feasted until dusk, while the men sang, danced, and tried to jump over the earth mound. Males drank Herb Water, according to age and rank, at set intervals. After being thus cleansed and purified, the men were scratched using a comb of needles repeatedly dipped into the Herb Water. Anciently, at noon on the second day, a captive was burned at the stake in honor of the Sun.

During breaks in the proceedings, men smoked tobacco as an offering. All morning, any women, children, foreigners, or dogs entering the square were beaten by the aides and stripped naked as punishment for violating that sacred precinct. In the afternoon, lacrosse or double racquet ball, called the "brother of war" because of its violence, was played around a tall post at the edge of the square. Features of the ancient military complex such as the war cry have been continued by ballplayers.

At the end of the afternoon, women went into the square, many silky streamers hanging down their backs, to perform the Ribbon Dance, or to join the men in the Buffalo Dance. Other women were busy cooking the first maize of the season for the evening meal. Social dances lasted all night.

These events might be repeated for the next few days if people had time available and money enough to provision the camps. Singing, dancing, jumping the mound, and scratching involved only the men, as did the games. All of the campers participated in the feasting and the social dances that filled the night. Visiting among Yuchi and friends was prolonged for as long as possible.

Summary

This Yuchi world was organized into concentric realms associated with Man as exclusive at the extremes of the inner square and the outer forest, or Woman as inclusive in the town and fields. Within each town, matriclans, households, and Chiefs were concerned with the sustenance and cooperation of everyone; the Warriors with their protection and defense. Men were expected to function away from the community as an exclusive grouping, engaged in trade, sports, and warfare.

In sum, for the Yuchi, Woman has existed from the very beginning, as has Old Sun Woman. Indications are that Woman is inclusive because menstrual blood, an epitome of the Womanly, created both the boy who fathered the Yuchi and the rib that became their mother. Semen, as an epitome of Man, produced both a son and tobacco, a plant important among men for social and ritual use. While the rib to wife episode may have been borrowed from the Bible, it has been given a distinctly Yuchi meaning.

Mediators for this dichotomy of genders included the Herb Water and the Underwater Panther, combining many animals and habitats in its grue body linked it with men and the forest and yellow antlers evoking women and maize.

Sources

The classic ethnography of the Yuchi is Frank Speck (1909), referring to earlier work by William Bartram, Albert Samuel Gatschet, and John Swanton. Bauxar (1957) looked at Yuchi archaeology and ethnohistory. The language has been studied by Guntar Wagner (1931), Hans Wolff (1951), James Crawford, and W. L. Ballard, who also looked at the cosmological symbolism of their Busk (1978). During the past decade, Yuchi have been actively recording their own traditions.

IV.
INVASIONS and EVASIONS

European invasions of the Americas were largely successful not because of superior technology or pretensions to God-given "civilization," but because of microbes turning America from a virgin into a widowed land. Advancing with colonial devastation was denial and distortion, a failure to understand or respect the native traditions already ancient in this "New (only to them) World." Indeed, a saving grace throughout this takeover has been the creativity and humor shown by natives as they devised "end runs" around official policy.

Invasions and displacements of natives rooted in the land were, of course, long familiar everywhere else, so-called handmaidens of war and empire since long before the Romans. What remains less well known were the various evasions used by the natives to counteract European presumption, arrogance, and self-righteousness.

In any situation, either among native peoples themselves or between natives and invaders, a limited repertoire of outcomes was possible, escalating into armed conflict. Demands of hospitality required that anyone who arrived on marked trails or open beaches be treated as a guest, able to make many demands on the hosts. In the process, of course, hosts watched guests to assess relative strengths and weaknesses. If the visitors were merely passing through, nothing further happened.

If the guests had come to stay, however, several strategies were invoked. An alliance might be proposed, each side agreeing for its own purposes. Alternatively, an alliance might be feigned to wait for a weak moment to attack. Sometimes, a better location might be suggested, to provide space between the communities or to misdirect the others and, hopefully, lead them astray, perhaps to perish on their own. If the visitors were many, the local town might be abandoned, either left intact or burned down, like Moscow in anticipation of Napoleon.

Once settlement occurred, however, other kinds of accommodations and evasions were called for. Specialized go-betweens (brokers) appeared, interpreting and misinterpreting for each side. Laws and taxes to be imposed and enforced got confused, misunderstood, and shunted aside. People intensified the differences between their living styles and approach procedures, preventing easy contact. Veiled threats and intimidations kept people further apart. Hardships, while debilitating, served a purpose in terms of strengthened cultural identity and survival. Distortions on both sides held out hope for uniqueness.

Following a roughly chronological order, this chapter concentrates of the most dramatic examples of the encounter, regardless of their actual location since they clearly had direct impact on the Americas.

TACITUS: Germans, Indiens, and Others

When Cornelius Tacitus wrote Germania in AD 98, he incorporated attitudes and opinions long part of Roman (and European) ethnocentrism about scattered tribes without the unity of a state, as was eventually forged for Germany by Otto von Bismarck in 1871. To turn the tables and to spare native American people further haughty abuse, yet to serve as a reminder − to set a warning tone about much of what has been written by outsiders, particularly biased and narrow-minded ones − what Tacitus said of the Germans will be summarized under A, then compared with (Rome) under (B), and with [Native America] under [C]. In this manner, a reader's reactions to such biased written worda can be assessed.

Because Tacitus was a Roman writing for other Latins, his perspective colored the record.[62] Native customs and gods lost their distinctive identities and instead were equated with better-known Roman or Classical equivalents. We are spared how the Roman learned about the Germans, thus avoiding all the presumption about explorers (better known as tracers, exploiters, and expanders) trekking through the wilderness (long someone else's familiar home.) Instead, Tacitus began with geography.

A.   Located between Gaul (modern France) and Rhaetia (imperial provence of East Switzerland), bordered by the Rhine and Danube Rivers, Germania's population seemed long settled, largely because, Tacitus thought, no one else wanted to go to a place with a bitter climate and dull, ugly landscape clogged with forests or swamps.

The original Germans, later called Tungri, were the first Teutonics to cross the Rhine and drive Gauls off the land. Ultimately, these settlers (or invaders, depending on your perspective) traced their mythic origins to three brothers, who gave their names to three German groupings: Ingaevones in the north, Herminones in the center, and Istaevones in the south.

B.   (Romans had a similar heroic saga about their founding by Romulus and Remus, twin boys suckled by a she-wolf. Nothing was said about German naming customs, though they are universally important for defining personal and social identity. A Roman usually had three: a praenomen = personal name like Lucius or Sextus, a nomen = clan name like Julius or Flavius, and a cognomen = family name like Caesar. Sometimes added was an agnomen = nickname like Cicero "warty" referring to his family's tendancy to have a nose shaped like a round and dented chickpea. Other cultures had other naming practices. Among the Parthians, most kings had the name of Arsaces, their BC 248 founder.)

C.   [Spanish explorers in the Southeast noted a tendency for the same name, more like a title, to be applied simultaneously to a chief, village, and locale. Otherwise, names signaled both personal and social identity. In many areas, personal names were secret, too intimately linked with the self, to protect the wellbeing of that individual, although other members of this family shared in the secret. Instead, nicknames and kin terms were used to identify people. Where clans existed, self designations also made reference to the namesake or founder of the grouping. Thus, a member of the Corn clan might be named Tassel, or someone of the Killerwhale clan might be Shining Fin. More generally, men were named for animals and other images of strength, while women were named for flowers and images of beauty.

A.   Without the sinister motives of Nazis two thousand years later, Germans were described as "untainted by foreign intermarriage," pure, unique, and peculiarly uniform in terms of their "wild, blue eyes, red hair, and a huge frame fit only for violence." A boy came of age when he was given a spear and shield.

B.   (For Romans, a boy reached manhood when he put on a toga. Indeed, in Rome, the word togati (toga wearers) meant citizens. Among Irish Celts, strict laws fixed the type and color of clothing by social class. A king could wear seven colors, a poet six, a chief five, and so on, down to ordinary people who could wear only a single drab color.)

C.   [Native America lacked such restrictions on dress, although exotic trade items like copper, turquoise, and seashells were owned only by members of leading families. Children passed into adulthood when a boy killed his first game and a girl harvested fresh food. Sometimes, a tribal initiation was involved, particularly for girl's puberty.]

---

62. H Mattingly, Tacitus on Britain and Germany 1948, published at the end of World War II with a sense of having survived ancient forces of history.

A.   While their environment prepared Germans to endure cold and hunger, Tacitus wrote, they could not cope with hard work, thirst, or hot weather. They took no "normal pleasure" in wealth and treasure, had not the wit and skill to train horses to perform intricate maneuvers, and lacked the patience to plow, plant, and wait for a harvest.

B.   (Tactitus here was drawing an invidious comparison with the covetousness of his fellow Romans, who craved gold and silver. Indeed, their society was based on slave owning and conspicuous wealth.)

C.   [Baron Lahontan,[63] Roger Williams, and other colonial writers also used their own version of "free and open" Native America as a foil for showing up European failings. When Spain set up its colonial empire in the New World, their model was Imperial Rome, granting both land and native residents to enrich the new owner and overlord.]

A.   Germans lived apart, avoiding crowds except in battle. Their houses were rudely made of timber, lacking the security of stone and tile. They dug caves for warmth and storage, like root cellars. Clothing consisted of a short cloak, sewn animal skins, and women also wore linen undergarments. People washed after arising from sleep, and were much given to banquets (feasts) which included drinking bouts. Food was plain – game meat, wild crops, and curdled milk.

B.   (Freeborn Romans dressed and ate well, sometimes too well at an orgy.)

C.   [While there were no dairy foods in the Americas, people ate what nature provided, and they could grow or trade. All public and family events were celebrated by feasts.]

A.   German marriages were "austere" and monogamous, a husband bringing dowry to his wife's family. Adultery was very rare, and punished by shaving the wife's head before she was stripped and beaten. (Note the double standard that absolved the other man.) By instilling good morality, Germans benefitted without having to try to pass good laws. Families were close, uncles and aunts as concerned as parents in the care of children. Men in particular had a sacred bond with the sons of their sisters. Women had a strong voice in all matters, goading men to victory, serving as political hostages, and providing holy prophecy. After death, famous men were cremated using special woods in the pyre.

B.   (Romans, like other Mediterraneans, assumed a strong father figure as head of the family, whose honor resided in its women, who "needed" to be sheltered and protected. The singular contribution of the Romans, later adopted by the British, was a system of universal law for all citizens. The catch, of course, was a very narrow definition of who constituted a citizen.)

C.   [While kinship throughout the Americas was largely bilateral, traced equally through both parents, farming groups were usually matrilineal, emphasizing the female line. In these matriclans, the mother's brother served as the father figure (better, as male mother) for his sister's sons. Marriage was a moral contract, but both partners had full personal autonomy in all their actions. Polygyny was typical of leaders, and rare polyandry occurred in the Basin. Cremation was a frequent practice throughout western portions of the Americas.]

A.   For Germans, important matters were discussed by the whole community, minor ones only by the chiefs. Councils were regularly scheduled at the full or crescent moons. Fines were paid both to the leader and to an offended family. In severe cases, a criminal paid with his or her life.

63. Louis-Armand de Lom d'Arce, Baron de Lahotan (1666-1715) gave voice to such comparisons through dialogues with his native guide, La Grangula, modeled on the Onondaga Chief Otreouti, in his <u>New Voyages to North America</u> 1703.

B.   (Rome was governed by its citizens – strictly freeborn males, but leadership was vested in the hereditary nobility.)

C.   [Native America was filled with consensus societies. Hereditary leading families had a special relationship with a place and its spirit patron owner(s), who enabled them to look after the wellbeing of a greater than human community.]

A.   German families of noble name and pedigree were given special distinction. They owned slaves, and their sons joined the ranks of a leader's companions, learning how to govern. Kings succeeded by right of birth, while leaders emerged through valor and commanded by example because only the gods could demand obedience.

B.   (Roman society was based on life and death control of others, with a strict hierarchy of ranks and classes.)

C.   [While Native America had its "high" families, they led more by moral example than by force. Invoking deities, however, did have the ability to coerce. While a chief could not compel, the spirits did. Throughout the Americas, war captives were slaves, forming an underclass among Northwest Coast tribes.]

A.   Tacitus arrogantly equated Mercury with the chief god of the Germans, distorting him in terms of the Roman pantheon, but, today, we know him as Wotan (Odin), who was also the chief Norse god. Since these gods of Nature could not be contained, their sanctuaries were springs and groves rather than temples. The will of the gods and impending fate was revealed by casting lots or by auguries, ranging from avian flight patterns and bird calls to twitches by sacred horses.

Other legendary figures were equated with Hercules and Ulysses. At Asciburgium (Asberg), Ulysses supposedly left an altar, inscribed with his father's name of Laertes. In other words, in addition to the sacred natural settings, some places were consecrated as holy by the deeds of an immortal hero.

B.   (Roman religion was devoted to sustaining the state. Over time, its pantheon incorporated gods from throughout the Empire, including a special altar for an Unknown god, just in case. Priests and priestesses, as aspects of this institution, served temples and conducted sacrifices, each specifically directed toward certain outcomes. For example, when large animals, such as oxen, were ritually killed, the head was held up for a sky deity or down for an earthly one.)

C.   [Worship in Native America was directed to Nature, as populated by the spirits and powha transmitting at particular locales and features. The most common religious practitioners were shamans with special ties to powerful spirits, but among farming and other tribes with food surpluses, priests and priestesses coordinated scheduled rites observing plant growth cycles and sacred objects, often inside a temple or community hall. This association of priest, temple, and bundle included sacred places and tribal fetishes. Native American deities have suffered a similar distortion because of incorrect comparisons. Thus, Hurricane, a Caribbean high god, now only survives as the name of a tropical storm.]

A.   The last half of Germania was devoted to the many German tribes, particularly in terms of their military strengths or weaknesses. Tacitus, the year before, had similarly considered the tribes of Britain in his biography of his father-in-law Agricola ("Farmer"), military governor there in AD 77-84, but he downplayed two great women leaders of the Britains, Boudicca of the Iceni (East Anglia, who led an AD 61 revolt) and Cartismandua of the Brigantes.

In Germany, the Cimbri, once a mighty nation, were reduced to a handful after 210 years of war against Roman legions. Borders and identities shifted. For example, the Marcomanni took Bohemia from the Boii in BC 8. After present-day Cologne was founded by Claudius in

AD 50, the Ubii local people renamed themselves the Agrippinenses in honor of his wife, Agrippina.

Tacitus dwelt, also, on distinctive tribal customs, such as the practice of Chatti men to let their hair and beards grow until each had slain an enemy to "repay the price of birth." After thus proving worthy of parental respect, they remained clean shaven. Some men became professional warriors who led the life of nomads "without home, land, or business," attaching themselves to various leaders. The Suebi, a collection of tribes over half of Germany, wore their hair in a knot at the side of the head. The Semnones, foremost of the Suebi, held a national ritual in the grove where they were created by their god. Other groups worshipped Nerthus, Earth Mother. Among the Naharvali, the priest of their sacred grove wore female garments and supervised rituals for the Alci, twin brothers Tacitus equated with Castor and Pollux. The Gothones were distinguished by round shields, shorts swords, and kings. The Suiones used ships pointed at both ends, and stored their weapons together under the custody of a slave. The Sitones were ruled by women.

Overall, because of their fixed abodes, weapons and shields, and great fondness for travel, Germans stood apart from neighboring Sarmatians, who traveled in wagons or on horseback. For the benefit of Roman rule, Tacitus hoped that if the Germans would not love the empire, then they continue hating each other.

B.   (Tribus, the Latin origin of the term tribe, referred to native groupings throughout Europe and, in particular, to the local kinship groups involved in the founding Rome.)

C.   [While Native Americans once identified themselves primarily in terms of their town and river drainage, recognizing larger tribal commonalities based on geography, language, and ritual (like the Naharvali); wholesale destruction from diseases, dislocations, and despair, encouraged peoples to coalesce into larger political groupings based on tribes, districts, regions, areas, and, finally, reservations.

While often accused of being "nomads" who never "improved" their land, Native Americans, for generations, followed seasonal movements among a series of set camps and resorts near various resources. Neither nomads nor opportunists, native changes to the landscape by controlled burnings, irrigation, or mound building were ecologically sound.]

HANS STADEN, Captive in Brazil

One of the strongest literary traditions in the Americas is the "captivity narrative" in which someone, usually Protestant, shows the hand of God helping through awful trials and tribulations.

Among the oldest and best of these is the account by Hans Staden, a German Lutheran born in Homburg who went to see America.[64] His father was a teacher so he had some education. Prior to sailing, he trained as a gunner, a valued talent in this violent age.

He made two voyages. The first (June 1547 - January 1548) lasted sixteen months and took him to the eastern tip of Brazil. The second (April 1549 - February 1555) lasted six years and included almost a year (1554) in Tupinamba captivity along the southeastern coast near modern Rio de Janeiro. All tolled, he was gone eight and a half years.

Written in a direct style, his book, published in 1557, is a fascinating, sometimes chilling, eye-witness account of life in these early colonies. The Marburg edition had 56 woodcuts to illustrate the text, 33 in Part I and 23 in Part II. The first part describes both of his voyages. The

64.   Hans Staden, The True History of His Captivity 1557 printed in Marburg, Germany, republished 1929 with block picture plates.

second part reports ethnographic details about the Tupinamba and Brazilian natural peculiarities from his own perspective.

Introductory material includes a testimonial from Professor Dryander, citing clergy and the local noble, to prove Staden's authenticity. Since travelers of that time were often fond of fantastic and embellished reports for the incredulous, Staden was careful to name his ship mates and companions along the way. These men, many of them Germans, could verify his adventures.

The Brazil trade was bitterly contested between the Portuguese and French. Yet the men involved came from all over Europe. Each nation also had its local native allies, supplying the trade and battling enemies. Staden, along with other Germans, got caught up in these disagreements.

To reach Brazil, Staden went to the German neighborhood in Lisbon, where his host found him passage as a gunner on a Portuguese ship delivering convicts, seizing booty from foreign ships, and returning with brazilwood, monkeys, sugar, and parrots. After 84 days at sea, sighting huge runs of tuna and St Elmo's Fire, they landed at Pernambuco. There, Staden was hired to defend a nearby fort, surviving a month of siege without losses.

The ship then continued along the coast, before returning to Portugal after 108 days at sea. After a rest, Staden left Lisbon on an English vessel that landed in Spain. The Conquest of Peru had goaded other adventurers and Staden joined an expedition bound for Rio de Plata (plata = silver) with high hopes. Four days after 1549 Easter, three vessels set sail, but, while crossing the Atlantic, they got separated. After six months, Staden's vessel made landfall at an unsure rendezvous and the shore crew bluffed them into thinking the worst. After a tense time, the cruel joke was revealed and everyone rejoiced, though local conditions never improved near Santos, where they were stranded for two years.

For part of the year, natives lived nearby and supplied them with food in exchange for fish hooks and knives. During these encounters, Staden learned to speak some Tupi, the native language. The rest of the time, they ate whatever they could find. Finally, the captain divided the crew into land and sea parties. Staden went with the ship and survived its wreck.

A nearby Portuguese colony, running a sugar mill, saved them. The local Tupinikins were their allies, while the Tupinamba, confederated as the Tamoio, were enemies loyal to the French. Early Portuguese ships had killed and enslaved many of their relatives.

Over a hundred years before, all these Tupi speakers moved from the interior in response to a prophetic call to find Paradise. Fierce warriors, they displaced ancient inhabitants along the coast. Expanding and populous, Tupi fragmented into disparate groupings. Feuding was constant, but raiding largely occurred when supplies were bountiful after August harvests of fruit and manioc or November fish runs taken with nets and arrows.

Staden was employed as the gunner at a fort for four months, and agreed to continue for another two years. By then he had several native slaves, including his own hunter. Once, when Staden went to the jungle camp to collect his meat, he was captured by Tupinamba warriors from a town called Utatuba, a log palisade around seven houses located half way between Santos and Rio de Janeiro. Though mauled and stripped naked, he suffered only a leg wound, which he attributed to God's mercy. An attempt to rescue him failed, and he was bundled into a canoe. To test his courage, he was constantly reminded what a fine meal he would make. At night, he slept in a "net." Both canoe and hammock were novelties to him.

At the town, warriors – to purify, sing, and pray – secluded themselves in one of the houses, while Staden was left in a house filled with women.

The two brothers who had captured him gave him to their father's brother so he could earn a new name by killing Staden for a feast. Everyone tormented him, while he thought of the sufferings of Christ. Taken to a fresh mound of earth near the house of the town leader, Great White Bird, a woman shaved off his eyebrows and tried for his red beard, but he resisted. Led to the center of the plaza, he danced with the women, using a stamping step accompanied by strings of cocoon leg rattles and a waving feather headband.

A few days later, they removed his beard using scissors traded from the French. Since Staden was captured from a Portuguese settlement, these warriors assumed he was Portuguese and their enemy. He insisted that he was a German, someone else allied with the French. When a young French trader was asked to confirm this, he spoke French to Staden, who did not understand. The Frenchman said to eat him. Captive slaves from other tribes were not as sure. His red hair and foreign speech made him seem different from the Portuguese.

As preparations began for the death feast, Staden developed a severe toothache and stopped eating. He lost weight and the host became concerned. Taken to the town where the skulls of slain enemies decorated the entrance posts of that stockade, that higher chief, who wore a lip plug labret of greenstone and six necklaces of shells, insisted he was not Portuguese.

He was taken back to Utatuba, where preparations continued until Tupinikin warriors attacked in 25 canoes. Staden joined the defenders hoping to escape. He could not, but the doubts of his captors increased, since he had seemed willingly to fight their enemies.

That night they deliberated in the plaza. Staden spent the time pondering the moon. When men noticed this, Staden claimed that the moon was angry with them for daring to eat Christians.

The next morning, the warriors went to the rescue of another town attacked by the Tupinikins, delaying the feast. While they were gone a Portuguese ship came to trade. Staden pretended that a brother Frenchmen was among them, but the ruse did not work.

Soon word came from the absent Tupinamba that an illness had struck the family of Staden's owner. That leader asked Staden to reverse the sickness and make them well by praying to his God. With some uncertainty, the captive did so. While eight relatives died, including mother, brother, and children, the chief did not. In return, he spared Staden from death.

Relying on the courage of his convictions, Staden now, to threaten his hosts, called upon his God often. Everything he did was filled with portents. Once, after reading a book, a fierce wind blew up that disrupted life for some time. Another slave who continually mocked him took ill and was eaten.

He met the French trader again and shamed him into recanting. Still, his owner was angry that Staden did not ask the trader for a knife that he could leave behind. Staden promised that his own French family would ransom him with a load of axes, mirrors, knives, hooks, combs, and scissors.

Staden still sought escape, particularly when others were executed and served at feasts. He went into great detail about what these rituals involved. The wooden club used was treated with elaborate care and attention. The man who used the club underwent strict purifications before assuming a new name, usually that of his victim.

After five months of captivity, another Portuguese ship came. On board was a Frenchman he knew well. Though unable to escape, Staden was given many trade goods that pleased his hosts into suspecting he really was French.

Later a French ship arrived and Staden tried to escape, but it left without him. To save himself, he explained that he had swum out to remind the sailors to have his family send back many trade goods for his hosts. Once again, Staden eventually saw the hand of God in this since that ship was lost at sea.

When the Tupinamba launched an attack in 38 canoes, Staden was taken along. Throughout the expedition, warriors told their dreams so as to predict the outcome. The raid was successful and prisoners, including five Christians, were taken. Staden stayed with them, when he might have escaped, to pray and console, but he could not save them from roasting.

Later, he twice got everyone's attention. He had erected a cross of reeds near his home. While the warriors were away, a women had removed it and given the rushes to her husband to use as sandpaper. When he returned, he called upon his God and it rained heavily for several days. In response, men put up another cross for him and the rain stopped. Later, while fishing, a thunder storm arose and threatened the party. Staden prayed, and the storm passed them by.

Increasingly wary of Staden, his hosts gave him to the chief of another town, with a warning to treat him carefully. Luckily, fourteen days later, a French ship arrived and carried Staden away. So as not to offend his hosts, the captain had ten sailors pretend to be Staden's brothers sent to fetch him home.

He had no sooner been rescued, however, than he was shot in a skirmish with a Portuguese ship, but, in time, with the help of his God, recovered.

His ship left Rio at the end of October 1554 and arrived in Normandy on 20 February 1555. From there he went to Holland and England before returning home to Germany, where he wrote his account.

The second part described the route to Brazil; the diversity of tribes, climate, rivers, and terrain; and native customs and manners. He began with the dwellings, located near wood, water, game, and fish. Houses were up to 150 feet long, with a rounded roof over one room. A stockade of palm trees surrounded each town. Fire was made by rubbing sticks. Natives slept in hammocks. Men used bows and arrows to hunt and fish. The people were handsome, though without modesty since they went naked. Their tools were made of stone, sometimes with wooden handles.

They ate meat and fruit. Women planted manioc (tapioca), digging up the root and replacing a branch so the bush would regenerate. Food was boiled with green peppers. Many did not have salt, but some tribes made it from palm ashes.

Every house had a leader and all chiefs belonged to the same family. While "the young defer to their elders," everyone could act according to their own free will. Furnishings included containers made of baked clay. Women chewed boiled manioc roots to make a fermented drink consumed socially. Men shaved the top of their heads, to show off their wounds. While they wore no clothes, they painted and decorated themselves with care. Many wore stone plugs in the lower lip and cheeks. Important people wore valuable shell necklaces, but most wealth consisted of feathers. Men were named for fierce animals, taking a new name every time they killed an enemy or prisoner. Women wore earrings and paint, and were named for birds, fish, or fruit. They cracked and ate lice in revenge for being bit.

Kings (major chiefs) had several wives, but each one had her own fire. Her sons hunted for her until they married. Children were betrothed early, but they did not marry until the girl became a woman. Couples were discrete. A chief went to each house some mornings to scratch the legs of all the children with a sharp-toothed fish jaw. This strengthened them, but also served as a threat in case of bad behavior. Then the scratches were deep. Their idols were gourd rattles, blessed every year by holy men called Paygi (shamans). Some women went into ecstatic trance and predicted the future when they revived.

Canoes were made from large sheets of bark. War campaigns were motivated by hatred of the enemy. Expeditions were planned by chiefs, who urged all warriors to report their dreams so as to foretell success. They attacked yelling, stamping, and blowing trumpets. Weapons were bows, arrows, shields, and the fumes of hot peppers. Fire arrows with wax tips were used to ignite the enemy town. Warriors carried special cords to bind up captives.

When men returned with a captive, women and children beat him. He was bound, decorated with feathers, shaved, and made to dance. They gave him a wife, but any children were likely to be eaten when grown. He was well fed.

When the feast was ready, the club to be used was decorated with tassels, paint, and etchings. The prisoner was painted, decorated, and bound with a special tether around his neck. All night, hosts and guest sang and danced around the club.

At dawn, the captive was led into the open, his former home destroyed, and the tether was wrapped around his waist. While people held the ends of the cord to keep him in the center, he threw stones at them while making made two fires before waited for the club to arrive.

When shown the club, he prepared himself. After ritual phrases about revenge were exchanged, the prisoner was clubbed. Sometimes, he had enough mobility to dodge for a bit, displaying his bravery. Afterward, the clubber went into seclusion to purify himself, later assuming a new name. The body was taken to the fires and cut up. Everyone received a piece to cook and consume.

In ending chapters, Staden described unfamiliar wild life of Brazil. These included monkeys, armadillos, opossums, jungle cats, vampire bats, bees, flamingos, pawpaws, cotton, sweet potatoes, and peppers.

The final chapter summarized his journey and named important companions to witness his deeds because "the world is closed to none whom God assists."

GERM WARFARE in Mexico

At the risk of summoning up "the dark legend" of Spanish brutality, events leading to the conquest of the Valley of Mexico present a chilling sequence of what happened throughout the Americas. Even more deadly than the bloody weapons, wolfhounds, and horses that terrorized native peoples were the germs that devastated populations which had no immunities because the cold screen of the Arctic, where Old and New Worlds were closest, prohibited the transmission of bacteria, viruses, germs, and microbes that caused epidemic diseases, such as the Black Death of the 1300s, which periodicly depopulated Asia, Africa, and Europe.

Early Franciscan missionaries taught writing to the surviving sons of Aztec nobles, ostensibly to prepare catechisms and other liturgical documents to strengthen their Catholicism. Once they had learned to write, however, this alphabet was also used to preserve their ancient traditions and comment on their present conditions. Father Bernardino de Sahagun and his workshop of native writers assembled texts and drawings to produce a dozen volumes called The History of the Things of New Spain. After providing a full ethnography of the Aztec State, the final volume chronicles the Spanish invasion.[65]

Elsewhere in Latin America, literacy preserved other traditions threatened by Christianity and European chauvinism. In Guatemala, a 1557 alphabetic copy saved the Popul Vuh, the Quiche Mayan account of their creations (see below). In Peru, Don Felipe Guaman Poma de Ayala provided block prints, along with a Quechua and Spanish text, to describe the glories of the Inka Empire and later Spanish colonial abuses in A First New Chronicle On Good

---

65. Miguel Leon-Portilla, The Broken Spears 1992, updated.

<u>Government</u>, preserved for centuries at the Royal Danish Library in Copenhagen.

Unlike college notions of history, native views blend the personal, cosmic, and practical with a regard for time that is not linear but mystically both simultaneous and cyclical.

During the decade before Hernando Cortez landed, omens foretold of coming Aztec disaster. A flaming ear of corn filled the night sky, an important temple was struck by lightning and burned, a lake boiled over, abnormal animals were seen, and monstrous humans stalked the land. Then word came from the coast that floating mountains had appeared carrying man-like beings.

Moctecuhzoma consulted his seers (also called wizards), but they could not explain the source of the danger or propose a remedy. Angry, Moctecuhzoma had them killed, along with their families, and their houses leveled to the ground. At a loss, spies were sent to watch these beings, who seemed human. Eventually, their pale skins and strange ways suggested the prophesy of Quetzalcoatl, a divine king of the Toltecs who promised to return. While this was a possibility, caution was advised. After spies watched what seemed to be a fishing expedition, messengers were sent with gifts, emerald quetzal feathers, turquoise inlaid plaques, and finely made gold ornaments.

At the sight of the gold, the eyes of the strangers glowed and they acted covetous. They smiled broadly, fingering the gold like monkeys and snorting like pigs. Those messengers became fearful because these actions seemed dangerous and threatening. Indeed, the messengers were grabbed and bound while preparations went on around a bulky object. Suddenly, this cannon was fired and the messengers quaked, but they could not run away. Impressed by the ability of these strangers to summon thunder, they returned to Moctecuhzoma to report that the strangers were gods. Before they gave their report, however, Moctecuhzoma had two captives sacrificed and this blood sprinkled over the envoys to remove any lingering danger that came from their contact with, sight of, and verbal exchange with these deities.

Spies reported that the strangers had left their ships and were moving inland. Along the way, as during every other trek across America, various delegations met them, each with their own agenda. Some wanted to lead them astray, others wanted to fight them, and still others wanted allies for their own wars against enemies. To test the foreigner's abilities, Moctecuhzoma sent an envoy in which someone impersonated him, but the Spaniards saw through this ruse, probably on the advice of a native ally like Marina, a native woman polyglot who became mistress to Cortez.

Thus, when the invaders met men from Tlaxcala, bitter enemies of the Aztecs, they helped slaughter people from Cholula, a valley east of modern Mexico City containing the largest earthen mound in the Americas.

Tlaxcala princes became converts to seal the alliance, but when one of them asked his own mother, Yacotzin, to be baptized, she rebuked him for abandoning their ancestors. Her son insisted that she had not choice, but she asked for time to decide what to do. As the son left, he ordered that his mother's rooms in the palace be set ablaze. Not surprisingly, she emerged and asked to become a Christian, receiving the name Doña Maria.

Gathering Tlaxcalan and other allies, Cortez swelled his ranks by the time he reached Tenochtitlan, the Aztec capitol city. They were made welcome by a wary Moctechuzoma, who sent food and gifts. Cortez and part of his army soon left to deal with the forces of Panfilo de Narvaez (see next section) who were sent from Cuba against him. Within a month, both armies had joined under the banner of Cortez and his promise of gold.

Meanwhile, in the city, occupying Spaniards waited for an opportunity to seize control.

During an important ceremony, they surrounded that temple plaza and hacked to death most of the dancers. These men had been fasting, most for twenty days and some for a year, so they were defenseless.

Shocked and grieving, Aztecs rose against Spaniards and drove them from the city. Some invaders were so laden with gold and other heavy objects that they drowned fleeing over causeways. Moctecuhzoma was killed, and Cuitlahuac, a hard liner, was elected by the lords of the four quarters to succeed his brother.

Aztecs were now in a advantageous position, well led and united. Spaniards rallied outside the city, strengthened by the return of Cortez and his increased army, who laid siege to the city.

All previous carnage paled in comparison to what happened next. For seventy days, smallpox and other epidemics ravaged the native population. The new emperor and tens of thousands more died, either of the disease itself or of starvation because not enough people survived to nurse or feed the others.

Cuauhtemoc was selected to succeed his uncle, assuming the onerous responsibility of surrendering to the conquistadors. He tried to rally his forces and attempted supernatural retaliation, but both these failed. Finally, the end was signaled by an omen. Huge flaming spirals filled the sky, and, the next day, Aztecs gave up.

Natives fleeing the city were searched by soldiers looking for gold and loot. Anyone who opposed them was killed. Some were branded as trouble makers, had limbs amputated, or were otherwise mutilated.

During the 80 days between the massacre at the temple and the surrender, an estimated half a million natives, both Aztecs and Spanish allies, died, most from disease. Especially decimated were the ranks of the Aztec nobility, who traced their descent from the marriage of an Aztec woman to Acamapichtli, a royal Toltec from Culhuacan who became their first <u>tlatoani</u> or "emperor."

Surviving daughters married or mated with conquistadors to continue noble lines, but, by and large, the elite of Mexico derived from Spain. Cortez pressed the conquest, ending with the title of Marques del Valle with a grant to the Valley of Oaxaca from the Spanish monarchy.

Alvar Nunez **CABEZA DE VACA**

Of the 300 men with Pamfilo de Narvaez in Florida only four survived, wandering eight years across what became the southern United States, over about two-thirds of the continent. They sustained themselves, alone and together, by living with austere native groups and gathering their own food, in addition to occasional efforts as traders and curers.

The most famous survivor was Cabeza de Vaca (1490-1557), descended from illustrious families. His paternal grandfather was Pedro de Vera, one of the most sadistic of the conquerors of the Guanche peoples of the Canary Islands. His mother's family had been honored with the title "Head of a Cow" for their part in a victory over the Moors in 1212.

After a military career in Italy, Spain, and France, Cabeza de Vaca was appointed second in command and treasurer of the Narvaez expedition in 1527. The commander was an inept bungler, who divided his forces and perished with them at sea. Of the dozens who survived initially, only four remained after a short time. They set out for Mexico by land and were rescued by a Spanish slaving expedition in Sinaloa in 1536. While the other two survivors fade from history, the fourth man was a Moorish slave named Estevanico, who went north in 1539 with Father Marcos, a Frenchman from Nice in Spanish service, and was killed outside the walls of a

Zuni pueblo in modern New Mexico.

Sailing from Mexico, de Vaca returned to Spain just as de Soto was preparing to leave, yet his tales of hardship and poverty did not deter this soldier made wealthy by the looting of the Inca. De Soto even tried to enlist de Vaca as his second in command, but, after the experience of Narvaez, the weary survivor wanted his own expedition. De Vaca expected great wealth from Florida, but he also wanted to establish a humane order that recognized the full humanity of native peoples, a hard-earned lesson from his years of wandering.

The king agreed to this ideal and appointed Cabeza de Vaca as governor of the South American provinces called Rio de la Plata. He arrived in 1540 and within a few years had prohibited all slaving, raping, and looting of native peoples. The result was that he was deposed and sent back to Spain in chains in 1543. There he awaited trial until 1551, when the Council of the Indies sentenced him to eight years in Africa. De Vaca's wife spend all of her fortune on appeals before the king intervened, annulled the sentence, awarded a pension, and placed de Vaca on the royal council. Unlike other of his contemporaries, he died in honor both in life and in history.

Bartolome de **LAS CASAS** and Spanish Humanism

For all the maimed and disfigured natives left by conquistadors in their wake, a legacy of hope survived both in terms of a new generation of mixed racial descendants, the mestizos, and of principals of international law applied to everyone.

Spain was a great center of scholarship before Columbus sailed across the Atlantic, with keen minds devoted to the study of legal theory and justice in accord with ancient Roman and ecclesiastical law. Learned men began protesting the treatment of native peoples almost from the beginning of the encounter. To justify their right to conquest, the Spanish monarchy sponsored a curious document called the Requerimiento (requirement) explaining the Biblical history that founded the Papacy, which in turn gave Spain the right to occupy the New World. This treatise was to be read to native people just before they submitted or were attacked. Since it was read only in Spanish, the ludicrous consequence was that no native ever understood it. Indeed, it was mostly read − upholding the letter but not the spirit of the law − to trees, empty huts, and fields.

Other actions, tentative at first, had greater impact. For example, just before Christmas in 1511, Father Antonio de Montesinos preached a fiery sermon in a thatched church on the island of Hispaniola, the first Spanish colony in the New World, condemning the cruelty and tyranny committed against native peoples.

Among the settlers hearing these words was a man who would take up this message and proclaim it throughout a long life. He was Bartolome de las Casas (1474-1566), whose father had sailed with Columbus on the second voyage and who preserved in his own writings the only surviving account of Columbus's journal.

Born in Seville, he attended the University of Salamanca, served by a native slave brought back by his father. In 1502, he went to Hispaniola as a colonist, acquiring native slaves to work his mines and build his estate. He added more slaves and land during the conquest of Cuba. Though he was refused the sacraments at least once because he held slaves, he continued to enjoy his privileges.

Yet, after stirrings of conscience, in 1512, he took holy orders, probably the first to do so in the Americas. Then, in 1514, while preparing a sermon, he read in Ecclesiasticus (chapter 34), "He that sacrificeth of a thing wrongfully gotten, his offering is ridiculous, and the gifts of unjust men are not accepted." His life was forever changed. In delivering this sermon on 15 August 1514, he gave all of his native slaves to the Governor. He was then forty years old and would

118

live for another fifty-two years.

Twice, with royal approval, he tried to establish utopian Christian native communities in Venezuela and Guatemala, but was thwarted by constant slave raids and hostility.

Still, las Casas persisted and finally convinced Carlos V to seriously reconsider Spanish efforts in the Americas. On 16 April 1550, Carlos suspended the conquest until his theologians could decide on a just way of proceeding. During August and September, a tribunal in Valladolid heard a momentous debate between las Casas, arguing for the basic humanity of native peoples, and Juan Gines de Sepulveda, a theologian well versed in Aristotle, arguing for the natural inferiority of natives. While the issues were mighty, after the debate, those judges scattered, never to proclaim a decision. In hindsight, however, it appears that de las Casas won the debate because he continued to publish, while the works of Sepulveda were suppressed during his lifetime, although his memory was long revered by various opportunists.

Publication often assured preservation. For example, of the two first-hand accounts of the de Soto expedition, that by his private secretary, Rodrigo Ranjel, is known only from a summary by Gonzalo Fernandez de Oveido y Vales in the first comprehensive history of the Americas. More than a pasteup, Oviedo broke into the commentary to criticize the ruthlessness of de Soto and his men, both in Peru and La Florida.

Not surprisingly, the English were quick to translate and publish these self-criticisms of Spanish colonization, giving rise to the so-called "black legend" of Spanish cruelty, whose pictorial representations were provided by the Protestant engraver, Theodor de Bry, in a thirteen part series called Great Voyages (1590-1634).

Yet, among the educated elite of Europe, if not its officials, the humanity of American natives had wide popularity, and was strongly confirmed in Papal Bulls by Paul III in 1537 and by Urban VIII in 1639. The sad corollary of this attitude, however, was that Africans were imported into the Americas to replace natives as slaves.

Measured in term of numbers, rather than wealth or comfort, the Spanish enterprise was hugely successful. Throughout Latin America, people trace ancestry to both European and indigenous soils and have created remarkably blended cultures. Mixtures of economies, societies, and religions abound, with life style more important than color or finances for determining who is native, mestizo, casta, creole, or hispanic elite throughout modern Spanish America.

Hernando **DE SOTO** according to an Inka

Only during the early years of the Spanish colonies could a son of mixed ancestry join the governing elite. Foremost among these was Garcilasco de la Vega. In addition to writing a distinguished account of the Inka empire before and after the Spanish conquest of Peru, de la Vega also interviewed survivors of the six year meander by Hernando de Soto through the modern Southeastern United States to produce a literary masterpiece. It is especially ironic that a skilled native writer had to interview illiterate conquistadors to provide the fullest account of the havoc they left among chiefdoms along the Gulf states, both in terms of mangled bodies and wholesale epidemics.

El Inca Garcilaso de la Vega was born, a month before de Soto left Havana in May of 1539, to a Spanish officer and an Inka princess, who were never legally married. He was baptized as Gomez Suarez de Figueroa, but, after leaving Peru and settling in Spain, he created an identity befitting his own literary aspirations, taking the name of a distinguished poet related to his father and preceeding it with the self-designation "El Inca." His life as a soldier, writer, and minor cleric took him from the Peru of his foremothers to Spain, where he was buried in a crypt in his own chapel in the converted mosque that is the cathedral of Cordova.

After centuries when European scholars published reports based on oral interviews with native authorities, Garcilaso's 1605 Lisbon publication relied on such an interrogation of a de Soto veteran who was his neighbor in Spain, along with insights and understandings gained as a child among his Inka relations together with erudition from a classical education and his own concern for literary style.

His writings about de Soto overlapped with his work on a history of Peru before and after the Spanish conquest. Each is filled with digressions and observations held together by a strict adherence to chronology. La Florida is divided into six books, one for each year of the expedition.

In addition to evoking the reckless enormity of a thousand invaders marching through the swamps and plains of the Southeast, Garcilaso had a personal reason for honoring de Soto, who, as a young soldier in Peru, closed the career of Lord Inka Atahualpa just after he took the throne from his half-brother Huascar, who had ruled the heartland from the capitol at Cuzco.

Their father had divided his domain between this rightful heir by his sister-wife and Atahualpa, his son by a foreign noblewomen from Quito, who received this northern province.

Because his ethnic background precluded claims to the racial purity required of the Lord Inka, Atahualpa was ruthless about securing his own position. When his army occupied Cuzco, on the pretense of a victory celebration, he demanded that all royal women and children assemble at a park outside the city. Over many months, his soldiers tortured and butchered them all.

Only a few children escaped. Among these were the mother and the uncle (Francisco Hualla Tupac Inka Yupanqui) of Garcilaso. By extolling the exploits of de Soto, who was the first Spaniard to denounce Atahualpa and to take part in his subsequent capture, torture, ransom, and murder; El Inca thus revenged the murder of his Inkan relatives.

The riches gained by de Soto in Peru financed his expedition through La Florida. He requested this region as a personal possession from the King of Spain, and received it only for the duration of his life. If riches were found, then the terms would be renegotiated.

Others had previously tried to colonize the region, but they had failed. Juan Ponce de Leon had come to the Florida peninsula with 80 men in 1521, Judge Lucas Vazquez de Ayllon tried with 220 in 1526, and Pamphilo de Narvaez bungled a force of 400 in 1528 (see Cabeza de Vaca above). Less famous but much more important for the success of de Soto was another Narvaez survivor, Juan Ortiz.

Each of these invasions spread havoc because, long before they arrived in a place, European germs pushed ahead wiping out many local people. Diseases, once introduced by Europeans, advanced everywhere as a vanguard to actual confrontations. Such diseases spreading from the Caribbean into South America may have begun the destabilization of the Inka empire and opened the way for dynastic struggles that eased the Spanish conquest of Peru. In addition to the diseases unintentionally unleashed by these intrusions, an obsession with gold, jewels, and quick riches impelled Spaniards ruthlessness.

With great sympathy, Garcilaso wrote of Hirrihigua, a local Florida leader much abused by Narvaez and ever after hostile to Spanish. Garcilaso remarked that the chief converted to Catholicism, but "the Devil" make him renounce his vows. While this was an age when the Devil was a palpable presence in human affairs, the hostility of native peoples had nothing to do with any concept of evil so very foreign to their own philosophies.

Juan Ortiz had the initial misfortune of being a slave in the home of Hirrihigua, who tried to kill him whenever he went into rages, but women kept him safe until, a year and a half later, he escaped to a neighboring chief. There he lived for the rest of the ten years between the arrivals of Narvaez and de Soto

Why did Hirrihigua go into rages? Garcilaso explains by taking pains to show all of the emotional dimensions of native peoples, ensuring that his readers realized that Indiens were fully human. This chief became enraged when he recalled that his mother had been devoured by war hounds, which accompanied every Spanish expedition to terrorize native communities.

Moreover, Hirrihigua himself had been disfigured by orders of Narvaez to punish him for some misdeed. His nose, if not also his ears, had been cut off. His anger at the Spanish returned "each time that he attempted to blow his nose and failed to find it." Such cruelties were regarded as necessary to locate gold and gems or to cower locals.

De Soto did the same during the four years of wandering. Natives slow to answer were tortured, and hostile villages were burned. Dogs and horses were used to threaten, maim, or kill.

Beginning at Tampa Bay, his forces went north and west through the Florida panhandle, northeast through Georgia and South Carolina, west into Tennessee, southwest through Alabama, northwest through Mississippi, north then west through Arkansas, and, after the death of de Soto, meandered southwest through Arkansas, a tip of Louisiana, and western Texas before retracing their route back to the Mississippi River, building transport, and fighting their way downriver and along the coast to reach New Spain (Mexico). By the end, almost three-quarters of the thousand member expedition were dead, along with several hundred pigs that had been bred from the dozen swine brought along as a source of meat. A few escaped into the wild to become feral razorback hogs.

Native communities were in their last glory. Powerful hereditary leaders of distinguished families, carried around on litters, had coordinated the lives of thousands. Intricate rituals accompanied all events, whether civil, military, or religious. This orderly world had been damaged by earlier coastal contacts with the Spanish, but these chiefdoms remained largely in control of their own fates. Away from the mangrove swamps of the coasts, forests were park-like because every year thickets were burned over and tended by human caretakers under chiefly direction so that all animal and plant life would thrive.

As de Soto left one town and moved on to the next, natives were taken prisoner to act as guides and translators. Those who led Spaniards astray were mercilessly slain or thrown to Irish wolfhounds. Still, the terrain was so alien and confusing that de Soto was never entirely sure of misdirection unless a confession under torture justified his suspicions.

The great diversity of languages throughout the Southeast, as with the rest of the Americas, made multilingualism a requirement for effective leadership. After Juan Ortiz was able to remember his lapsed Spanish, he stood at the end of a chain of languages that started with the one most recently met. Unoccupied buffer zones separated political and linguistic communities. Given this diversity, de Soto received from Ortiz a decidedly garbled message in less than fluent Spanish so misunderstandings were rife.

Garcilaso glosses over these difficulties, except to comment that his own fluency in Inkan Quechua had similarly faded during his residence in Spain. To add luster to their harangues, his natives speak like Roman senators. Not only was this fitting for his literary aspirations, it also reflected the strong appeals to Rome that Spain made in setting up its empire in the New World. Classical forms of administration and tribute were used as prototypes for the Spanish endeavor.

At Acuera in central Florida, that leader, also called Acuera, announced that he knew the Spanish only too well from previous expeditions. Professional vagabonds, he called them, who lived by robbing, sacking, and murdering inoffensive people for their own profit. Mortal and perpetual enmity was his only solution for dealing with such inhuman intruders. He demanded that his followers bring him two Christian heads for every week that the Spanish remained in his territory. During the three weeks of their stay, fourteen heads were taken to Acuera. Such was the hatred of the intruders. Even after the headless bodies were given Christian burial, natives dug up these graves, dismembered the bodies, and hung the pieces from trees. De Soto ignored this grisly message to go home.

For comparison, similar sentiments were expressed by Shakespeare in <u>Henry VI, Part 3</u> (Act I, Scene 3, lines 27-31) where Lord Clifford says, just before he kills Edmund, Earl of Rutland, the young son of the Duke of York

> No, if I digg'd up thy forefathers' graves
> And hung their rotten coffins up in chains,
> I could not slake mine ire, nor ease my heart.
> The sight of any of the house of York
> Is as a fury to torment my soul.

In north Florida, where three brothers shared the leadership of Vitachuco, the younger two were more conciliatory but the eldest was hostile, expecting the very earth to help destroy these Spanish interlopers. He called for fissures to swallow them, hills to crush them, winds to hurl trees on them, and birds to drop poison on them. Barring all these, he would capture all of them so he could bake half and boil the rest. Still, the Spanish coaxed through diplomatic channels until Vitachuco seemed friendly, but this was only to make his ruse all the more effective.

Like many of the native prophets who came in later centuries, Vitachuco rallied his people with promises that the cosmos itself would join their cause. When they turned on the Spanish, they lost the battle and many drowned in flight. Taken prisoner, Vitachuco was accorded the respect of his rank and "quality" but used this lack of restraints to try to kill de Soto with his fist. He almost succeeded.

At Cofitachiqui in present South Carolina, that ruler was a woman and Garcilaso cast his narrative to evoke the meeting of Marc Anthony with Cleopatra, again to underscore a Roman ideal. The expedition first heard of this province from a boy who had been raised by professional traders and so had a wide range of knowledge about places, people, and goods. He thought that yellow metal could be found there. The expedition assumed this was gold, but he probably meant copper, which was more valuable in native terms of prestige.

A younger woman served as the representative of this "queen," explaining that food was scarce because a great pestilence had killed many people during the past year. In all likelihood, this was the disease vanguard of de Soto and his men. Unable to feed the troops, the woman nevertheless earned their goodwill by allowing them to loot thousands of freshwater pearls from her local temple.

In other towns, native allies of the Spanish used their protected status to desecrate the temples of their enemies if they got the chance. Though mostly innocent of this destruction, the Spanish received blame in many towns for facilitating traditional enmities on a greater scale since they defended their allies regardless of their actual guilt. These temples, sometimes built atop huge earthen mounds laboriously raised with basketfuls of dirt by the faithful, were the very heart of each community. By tacitly allowing their looting and destruction, Spanish aggravated existing hostilities. At Cofitachiqui, however, permission to take the pearls kept local women in positions of leadership.

Though Garcilaso heightened the description with comparisons to Roman and Greek parallels, this native temple was impressive. As in previous towns, such temples were repositories of tribute and offerings, cult centers for the worship of ancestors, armories for stockpiled weapons, and the sepulchers for the bodies and bones of deceased members of elite families.

The temple of Cofitachiqui was rectangular, a hundred feet by forty, with benches set along interior walls. Wooden chests holding the bodies of leaders rested on these benches, each below a carved portrait statue of the man, woman, or child placed inside. Smaller boxes and baskets nearby were filled with pearls or skins. After looting these, De Soto had over fifty pounds of pearls sent to Havana as hopeful news of his expected gains.

Six pairs of standing interior posts were carved to look like giant warriors, each pair holding a different type of weapon. Along the upper walls were two rows of carved women and men holding weapons decorated with inlay, pearls, and tinted fringes.

The roof of canes and reeds was decorated, both inside and out, with many shells and long strands of pearls. Interior walls were also made of woven canes. Behind these walls were eight side rooms, each storing a different type of weapon.

As impressive as such a temple was, Spanish visitors were incapable of viewing it as holy. While great skill was shown in its design and construction, it only indicated to the Spanish and their priests what conversion to Catholicism could do to improve native lives. Ironically, the alternative term used for these native edifices was "mosque," which carried the hostile burden of Spain's fight to expel the Moors.

Native resentment continued to build and new local alliances were forged in the face of Spanish threat. A huge war leader named Tuscalusa lured the Spanish into a trap at Mobila, near modern Mobile, where a pitched battle resulted in many casualties. De Soto was wounded and most supplies, horses, and pigs were lost.

To hold his weakened force together, de Soto decided to move north, away from the coast and rescue ships, into the interior. Already at least one Spaniard had deserted to live with the Indiens. Others might do the same.

The five priests with the expedition had lost all of their vestments, along with wine and wheat flour to make wafers for holy communion. Since nothing locally grown or made could substitute for these, thereafter only the "dry mass" was celebrated without the Eucharist. Difficulties such as this absence of familiar European products fostered theological debate, eventually opening up many more possibilities for God's divine plan than Europeans had ever thought likely.

Lessons could be learned from all novel situations. While there was much deliberate and some accidental miscommunication between natives and Spaniards, every encounter brought bits of new understanding. The first winter at Tallahassee, de Soto's men were shown the strength of native bows and arrows, which easily pierced chain mail armor. For their own safety, soldiers adopted quilted tunics impervious to arrows and spears.

During their retreat inland, survivors suffered terribly from a lack of vitamins and salt. After a low fever, living bodies began to turn green, to rot, and to slowly die. Natives had shown them an herb whose ashes cured the disease, but Spaniards continued to die because they felt it was "beneath their quality" to do anything so base as to imitate an Indien, even if it meant saving their own lives. Garcilaso called this outcome a just punishment for those sixty soldiers who let pride get in the way of good sense.

After the death and double burial of de Soto, Luis de Moscoso de Alvarado led the survivors into Texas and back to the Mississippi River. There they entered a land they presumed was inhabited by herdsmen because there was so much meat available. Yet they never saw a live buffalo or learned about the enormous herds. For part of the way, they were deliberately misguided by a boy for eight days until Moscoso became suspicious and fed this valiant saboteur to the dogs.

As they prepared to settle into a native town along the Mississippi from which the inhabitants had fled, an old woman who had stayed behind warned Moscoso that the river was due to overflow as it did every fourteen years. Sure enough, when the brigantines were nearly built, a huge flood hampered final construction but made launching them much easier.

A local confederacy of ten tribes attacked the Spanish. As survivors floated down the Mississippi, they battled large canoes, each fleet of a different color, filled with warriors. Eventually, some of the Moscoso party reached Mexico, where they fought among themselves about their degree of success.

Garcilaso noted that these men thought only of precious, portable wealth, not of rich farmland or abundant fruits. Long term benefits of the Southeast went unrecognized by Spain for another century. By then disease had taken such a terrible toll that later visitors doubted the reliability of Garcilaso and other more accurate eyewitness chronicles.

POPUL VUH: Sacred Text of the Quiche Maya

The Popol Vuh describes the creation and history of their world from the standpoint of the Quiche Maya of Guatemala, and, in particular, the Kavek patrilineage. As such, it is the oldest and longest example of precolumbian literature in the early colonial record, a great epics of world literature that appears widely in multicultural anthologies because the text has long been translated into Spanish, French, and German.[66] In Mayan it represents a uniquely American epic which resonates throughout the New World where successive creations, underworld journeys, tests of fortitude, and hero twins occur in the traditions of many tribes and regions. Its themes are as old as the interactions of deities and humans in the Americas.

Scholars suspect that the story of the Popol Vuh was formulated about two thousand years ago during the Late Preclassic since many of its incidents are depicted on painted pottery of the Classic period (AD 300 to 900). Recently, these images have been used to create an hour-long video depicting the early portion dealing with Mayan creation.

The epic was also the subject of one or more hieroglyphic codices or accordian-fold books for which the Mayans are justly famous. All but five of these books were destroyed by early Spanish missionaries.

About 1557, Mayans literate in Spanish wrote down a Quiche version of the Popul Vuh coopting the alphabet they had learned from missionaries. It was a version of this text, now at the Newberry Library in Chicago, that copied by Father Francisco Ximinez (1666-1730), a Dominican parish priest, in 1700 to illustrate the workings of that language at the end of a comparative triple grammar intended for missionaries. Brief versions also exist in libraries in Guatemala and Europe.

66. Dennis Tedlock, Popul Vuh 1985.

Because numbers counted (and more) for Mayans, spelling conventions are put aside to make Arabic numbers all the more obvious.

When finally made on the fourth attempt, the first 4 humans could see across time and space, but the gods, wanting no equals, limited their vision to the nearby and obvious. In partial compensation, they provided an ilbal called the Council Book (Popul Vuh) for the Quiche nation of highland Guatemala. Among Yucatec Maya, the same function was provided by local Jaguar Priest (*Chilam Balam*) books, setting out systematic cycles, often astronomical, with predictive value for earthly events. Indeed, ever person and event in this epic has astronomical, calendrical, and divinatory aspects.

Beginning with an empty sky and calm sea, Hurricane (Sky Heart) comes down to discuss with Quetzalsnake ideas of an earth and growth, setting these in motion by "bestowing," which is simultaneously a sowing, dawning, sprouting, and bursting forth. They intend beings to walk, work, talk in fluent measures, visit shrines, give offerings, and worship them in accord with calendrical rhythms.

Their first attempt lacked arms and speech, becoming animals of today. The second was formed of mud, amorphous before dissolving utterly. Before the third attempt, the gods consulted their grandparents, Matchmaker and Midwife, prior to all marriages and births, who, as diviners and daykeepers of the 13 numbers and 20 names making a 260 day cycle, approved the use of wooden figures, able to look, talk, and multiply, but unable to regulate their work nor prayer. Hurricane sent a tempest, beasts, and angry artifacts to eradicate them, except for a few who become monkeys.

Building suspense, instead of taking up the fourth successful attempt, the account turns to double twin sons (1 and 7 Hunahpu) and grandsons (Hunahpu and Shbalankey, spelled Xbalanque) of the first grandparents. Both sets of twins are expert rubberball players, while the sons also gamble with dice and the grandsons hunt with blowguns.

These episodes, quite typically for the Americas, are arranged by place rather than chronological time, the first on the earth and the second in the underworld (Shibalba).

A father and his two sons (7 Macaw, Zipacna, Earthquake) pretended to great powers so Hurricane sent the grandsons against them. Claiming to be sun and moon for the wooden people, 7 Macaw is shot by the twins while eating high in a fruit tree, breaking his jaw and crashing to earth to unleashed the flood ending this era. Posing as shamans, the twins pretend a cure that instead extracted all his teeth and shiny metal eye disks to form the prototype for scarlet macaws, though he becomes the Big Dipper and his wife the Little Dipper.

Crocodilian Zapacna revenges an attempt to kill him by changing the gods of alcoholic beverages, Four Hundred Boys, into the Pleiades. Twins then lure him with a pseudo-crab into an impossible situation that turns him to stone.

Earthquake is lured by the aroma of a claybaked bird into becoming clay encased himself, fixed in the east to balance his elder brother in the west.

Now the account reverts to the twin sons, particularly 1 Hunahpu, who fathered 1 Monkey and 1 Artisan. These four play at a ballcourt in the east, sometimes watched by falcon, messenger of Hurricane. So enthusiastic is their noisy sport that they offend the lords of the underworld, led by 1 Death and 7 Death, along with lords of lesions, jaundice, emaciation, edema, sharp pains, and death by vomiting blood.

Lords 1 and 7 Death challenged 1 and 7 Hunahpu to play in the underworld court at the western edge of the world. Bypassing traps set along the way, these twins choose the Black Road at the crossroads where color-coded directions intersect, taking them east to west through the dark cleft in the Milky Way. Subjected to various tests, they failed to keep a torch and two cigars intact after a night in the Dark House and so were sacrificed the next day. Their bodies are buried in the ball court, but the head of 1 Hunahpu is placed in forked branches that soon bear fruit as the first calabash tree to disguise his skull.

Fascinated, Blood Woman, daughter of the Lord Blood Gatherer, is reaching toward the tree when the skull spits into her palm, making her pregnant with the twin grandsons, and decrees that the face of a father will continue in his sons.[67] After six months, when her pregnancy is obvious, she denied to her father, quite literally, that she knew any man with a face. Unyielding, he ordered Owls to sacrifice her with a White Dagger and bring back her heart in a bowl, but they relent and lead her up to earth, producing a substitute heart of aromatic croton tree sap that thereafter becomes the preferred underworld incense. Not surprisingly, Blood Woman is equated with moon phases, and, after tests of her success in the garden, is given refuge by Grandmother Midwife.

Once born, these twins (Hunahpu and Shbalankey) are mistreated by their half-brothers 1 Monkey and 1 Artisan, but they never complain, happily blowgun hunting until they maroon their siblings atop a tree to become monkeys. Outraged, their grandmother makes four tries to redeem them but she keeps laughing because they are so ridiculous. Finally, they swing away into the trees forever as a sign of Mars, whose retrograde motion corresponds to their attempted reprieves.

The grandsons plant a cleared garden, but every morning it is overgrown by forest. Hidden, they discover chanting animals, and rush them, breaking tails off rabbit and deer, entirely missing jaguar and puma, but capturing rat, who promises them ball gear left by their father and uncle in house rafters in return for future pilfering of stored grain. The next day, while their grandmother and mother go for water to soothe their throats after eating hot chili stew, rat crawls under the roof and chews through bindings so the gear falls down to the waiting twins.

of course, their noisy enthusiasm again provokes the underworld lords, who send a summons to be below in 7 days to the grandmother, who sends a louse to relay it. Soon, in an all-consuming chain, the louse is swallowed by a toad, snake, and falcon, who is shot in the eye by the twins and cured with ball pitch so it now has a black eyepatch. Then these creatures are spit out in reverse order until louse delivers the demand. First going to their grandmother to leave a eternal token of maize while punning on the day name AH, they go below on the day named Hunahpu. At the crossroads, they send ahead a mosquito to sort out manikins from lords, who shout their own 12 names when stung. Overcoming all traps and passing off a macaw feather and fireflies as all night torch and cigars, these twins finally play ball, rebounding a pseudo-skull with hip yoke to reveal the White Dagger inside, which pursues them to no avail. During the second round, the twins allow themselves to lose and be confined for the night in the Razor House filled with voracious flint knives, who are calmed with the promise of slicing through animal flesh. In the morning, the twins pay their forfeit of four bowls of flowers, cut by ants from the lord's own gardens. Angered, lords gash through the beaks of the nightjar (poorwills and whippoorwills) guards. Succeeding nights, the grandsons survive Cold, Jaguar, Fire, and Bat House, where Hunahpu is decapitated by a wing. While his brother carved him a squash head, old man opposum made four dark streaks along the sky as a harbinger of the coming sun. Thereafter, opposum brought in each new 360 day year begun by only four day

---

67. Such a remark is distinctive of matrilineality where substance comes from mother and distinctive appearance from father (Miller 1997: 102).

names (Deer, Tooth, Thought, Wind).

Using Hunahpu's real head as the ball, Shbalankey hit it out of the court. While rabbit pretended to bounce away as that head, the real one was returned to its own shoulders, and the squash retrieved from an oak grove to be put into play to shatter and show up the lords as fools. Celestially, these events correspond with appearances of Venus in the west and east.

Summoned to a pit where the lords are brewing alcohol, the twins thwart any tests by jumping inside. Unknowingly following secret plans by the grandsons, the lords grind up these bones and pour them into a river. In five days, the twins become catfish, then human the day after.

Disguised as entertainers famous for burning houses and sacrificing people without lasting harm, the twins are summoned to the underworld, where they murder 1 and 7 Death. Thereafter, other lords can only prey on those weak or guilty.

Throughout these ordeals, grandmother has faithfully prayed, planted, and made offerings. The twins tried to revive their uncle, insisting that he name all the parts of his body, but he could only say mouth, nose, and eyes, which remain major characteristics to this day.

These difficulties overcome, the narrative now returns in flashback to the fourth and final creation of humans able to walk, work, talk, and pray before the real sun. Fox, Coyote, Parrot, and Crow discover a mountain filled with yellow and white corn, which, like the twin's bones, is ground up by Midwife and mixed with the water used to wash her hands to model Jaguar Quitze, Jaguar Night, Mahucutah, and True Jaguar to head the first 4 Quiche patrilineages as androgynous father-mothers with perfect prayer, vision, and knowledge. Greatly alarmed, the gods fog their eyes. Next they give them wives, named domestically, Celebrated Seahouse to Jaguar Quitze for founding Cauec lineage, Prawn House to Jaguar Night for Greathouse, Macaw House to Mahucutah for the Lord Quiche line, and Macaw House for True Jaguar, who have no sons.

All these events are in the dark east, where the first four visit great cities, particularly Seven Caves at Teotihuacan and ultimately Tulan to entice patron deities. Cauecs benefit from Tohil, Greathouses from Auilix, and Lord Quiches from Hacauitz. In time, Tohil (Tahil, Obsidian Mirror) becomes patron of five patrilineages, while the other patrons foster separate dialects. After a hailstorm extinguished all fires, Tohil pivots inside his sandal to show humans the use of a firedrill. Other Mayans plead for fire and receive it if they promise to be embraced and suckled by Tohil, later discovering that this means their hearts can be cut out in sacrifice.

Singing while passing cords through their ears and elbows to draw blood, Quiches leave Tulan backpacking their new gods until they reach the highlands, accompanied by Rabinals, Cakchiquels, and Tsutuhils. There, after a great fast, these three gods are hidden away in arbors. At the namesake of Hacauitz, Quiches, standing by ranks on ridges, greet the first true dawn appearing only that once as a whole person, and turning all the patron gods to stone except for White Sparkle Striker who becomes keeper of the game animals and stone fetishes, dressing entirely in dawn red. Though far flung, all Mesoamerican nations recognized this instant of the first dawn as a hallmark of their unity.

Disguised as backcountry rustics, Quiches still spoke with their stone gods and decided to plunder travelers as blood sacrifices. Though deflected by rain, mist, and mud, these other tribes found the cause of their losses and sent two maidens as the first prostitutes, "barkers of shins," to tempt these other gods at a bathing pool. Rebuffed, they come back with cloaks painted inside with either jaguars, eagles, or yellowjackets, who enliven to sting these enemy leaders.

Hostile warriors on a massive night assault are put into a deep sleep by Quiches, who remove all the metal on their weapons and clothing, along with their eyebrows and beards. The next morning, advancing, they see the Quiche palisade surmounted by defenders (really wooden puppets) wearing that stolen metal. When all 24,000 attack, Quiches release four large gourds filled with yellowjackets and wasps, routing the enemy under their serenely view. Thereafter, survivors pay tribute.

Victory assured, the first 4 approach death before another 52 year cycle begins on Deer day. Jaguar Quitze left a sacred bundle of flames as they all vanish. Later, the sons of these 4 pilgrimage eastward, visiting Nacxit (Plumed Serpent) who gives them emblems of highest rank to become "keeper of the mat" for the head of state and "keeper of the reception house mat" for the collector of tribute. The Greathouse lineage leader was given the title of "lord minister," and Lord Quiches became "crier of the people."

Returning in fiery splendor with these titles manifested in canopies, thrones, musical instruments, cosmetics, jewelry, animal tokens, and books; rulers marry carefully and establish important cities, expanding into 23 palaces and 4 pyramids. Each succeeding high lord is described in terms of shamanic or military abilities, within a symbolic national fortress. In five generations, Quiches were powerful enough to ennoble their own authority at their namesake city, whose greatness came from its prior gifts as well as from religious austerity through fasting, praying, and blood sacrifices during 180, 240, and 340 day retreats. Eventually, Quiche lords were like gods, receiving tribute of turquoise, jade, and quetzal feathers, the ultimate iridescent fruits of earth and sky.

After 12 generations, Pedro de Alvardo destroyed their capitol, confiscated all tribute, hanged their lords, and gave them Spanish names. The surviving alphabetic account was probably transcribed about the start of another 52 year cycle on 2 June 1558 (Julian calendar), perhaps in time for Juan Cortes to take it with him to Spain in 1557 to plead in vain for restoration of tribute rights.

The text ends with a list of titles of successors that may hint at those with the valor and skill to preserve this ancient record of their nation for the future global community.

ENGLISH EFFORTS

With the defeat of the Spanish Armada in 1588, the British intensified their plans to establish colonies along the Atlantic seaboard. Following martyred 1570 Jesuits and the 1585 aborted Roanoke colony of Sir Walter Raleigh, settlement was made at Jamestown in 1607 by John Smith, a well traveled soldier of fortune. This bog was unhealthy and many colonists died. Later, outlying communities called "hundreds" were founded and health improved, particularly when Englishmen followed the native practice of moving with the seasons.

Native communities were led by Powhatan, who had recently formed a powerful chiefdom over the region. Circumstantial evidence suggests a connection between his family and Don Luis de Valasco, the native who was captured on the Virginia coast in the 1560s and tutored by the Spanish in Mexico, Madrid, and Havana. When he came back with a 1570 Jesuits mission but resumed his chiefly office, including taking several wives, the priests were outraged. In response to their public criticism of him, Don Luis led the attack that martyred them. Similarly, when tribes like the Chesapeakes resisted Powhatan, he exterminated them and settled allies in their former territory.

The starving and bullying English made constant demands on Powhatan food reserves and land. After Powhatan turned the leadership over to his brothers, they executed well planned massacres in 1622 and 1644 to drive the English back into Jamestown and out of the satellite hundreds. These attacks were moral statements rather than military defeats because of the finesse with which they were accomplished.

While starving colonists demanding native food were sometimes found dead with bread stuffed in their mouths, a clear statement that they "choke to death" on their unreasonable appetites, during the 1622 attack, about a third of the colony were killed using their own tools, a message that they were "working everything to death."

As the Virginia colony expanded, Powhatans were crowded off their lands. Small reservations were set aside for their exclusive residence and use, and, while these were reduced in size over the centuries, such shelters still serve survivors.

Instruction in the doctrine of the Church of England remained informal, although there were some converts, the most notable of whom was Pocahantas, the favorite daughter of Powhatan. She married the widower John Rolfe, who started the English tobacco industry despite objections from the royal court of James I. Their union sealed an alliance between English and Powhatans that eased tensions and gave natives remarkable protection over the centuries because so many prominent Virginians claimed decent from Thomas Rolfe, the son of this marriage.

Of the colonists, only George Thorpe actively sought conversions from natives, intending to found a college for native children. His attempts to remove native children from their homes were so offensive that Thorpe was killed and mutilated in 1622, when distinguished officers of the colony rapaciously divided up his estate.

The confident strength of Powhatans is indicated by their dispersed residences. Families lived on farmstead scattered along rivers, rather than in fortified villages like their Siouian and Iroquoian neighbors to the south and west. Community cohesion instead depended on isolated temples, where treasures, idols, and the dried bodies of elite ancestors were kept near their sacred fire. While each community had a temple, that for the entire nation was located in Uttamussak at the mouth of the Pamunkey River.

Late in the 1600s, while local natives were away, Robert Beverly and some friends violated one of these temples and wrote a description. Since Powhatans were then politically weak, it is significant that their religious institutions remained strong.

Around the perimeter of the enclosure were standing posts, each carved and painted with a threatening face to warn off the curious. In the dark inside, Beverly and his friends found shelves holding three bundles, which they ripped open. Inside the first were the bones of former leaders, in the second were carved and painted weapons, and in the third were the wooden segments of an articulated human figure which served as an idol and an oracle.

Later, when Beverly boasted of this sacralege to a native friend, the man was visibly shaken both for the desacration of the temple and for the lack of spiritual retribution on Beverly and his friends.

In 1620, England allowed the settlement of Puritan dissenters or Pilgrims at Massachusetts Bay. A buffer zone along the Atlantic was intended to separate this colony from that of royalist Virginia. As an avowedly religious community, conversion was an important goal of these English Calvinists.

Their colony was founded just after a 1616-18 decimating epidemic. Demoralized and depopulated, local natives could not resist this Puritan intrusion.

Because Roman Catholic missions were viewed as irresponsible, allowing conversions that were superficial and insincere, Puritans established extremely high standards that had to be met before baptism and full "churching" (admission) were permitted. This regime blended praying, preaching, and instruction with careful scrutiny of meticulous behavior showing that natives had made a radical change and were leading rigidly Christian lives.

Since reverends saw this severe depopulation as the hand of God clearing the way for English settlement, little was done to relieve local suffering until the 1640s. Colonists were unable to comprehend the vast chasm that separated their perceptions of native life from its own cultural basis. With classic wrongheaded distortion, most assumed that there was nothing of substance in native life so any and all outside offers to "improve" it would, of course, be gratefully received.

What the English viewed as disorganized, chaotic, and wandering was actually a meticulously planned series of seasonal movements to take advantage of regional bounty. A mixed economy of hunting, farming, fishing, and gathering had taken centuries to perfect. Yet the colonists wanted all of this ecological resourcefulness to be replaced, overnight, by yeoman male farmers living with their families in cramped houses.

Traditionally, women were the mainstays of the native economy, contributing three-quarters of the food supply by farming maize, beans, and squash, along with their gathering of nuts, roots, and berries.

In 1637, Puritans incinerated hundreds of Connecticut Pequots who had taken refuge in their palisaded fort. Learning of this horrible carnage, native peoples opted for a low profile and hit and run tactics. The English then took over the Pequot monopoly of the lucrative trade in wampum, cylindrical beads much prized throughout the region.

During this war, a native visiting from Long Island was taken prisoner and became the servant of an English family. Since this youth spoke both English and his own Algonkian language, he was sought out by John Eliot, Puritan minister of Roxbury, to provide instruction in a native language close to that of local Massachusetts tribes.

Thus began a briefly successful "Red Puritan" mission, whose legacy included a strong tradition of native literacy in their own languages and the first Anglo-American publication of a book, the 1663 Eliot Bible in the Massachusetts language.

While firm in his convictions, Eliot had the wisdom to bend when natives insisted on certain requirements. In 1650 he settled converts at Natick, a model Red Puritan community. A fishing weir, long attracting natives there, remained in the aboriginal ownership of the Speene family, who willingly shared the fish as they did the town site. Granted legal title to these 6,000 acres seventeen miles southwest of Boston, converts quickly built, with the help of English carpenters, a foot bridge, a meeting house, and three streets lined with houses. The foot bridge spanned the 80 foot wide Charles River, had a central arch of nine feet, and rested on stone abutments on either bank.

Once settled, Naticks assumed the burden of spreading the Puritan message, as tempered by Eliot. Since they did so in the native language from a native perspective, they were largely successful. Of the five points basic to Calvinism (total depravity, limited atonement, predestination, irresistibility of grace, and perseverance of the saints), Eliot taught only the first two and rephrased them to suggest that repentance opened the way to forgiveness and that atonement was without limits. The three more difficult tenets he postponed until the converts could understand and accept their severity. Even so, his sermons on the utter depravity of humans and the pains of Hell terrified many natives.

Regarding local conditions as hopeless, converts were drawn to Christianity as a panacea for their despair. A frequent hope was to survive as individuals and families within a community living in ancestral territory. Their special status as Christians also gave them advantages before

Puritan law, and provided better access to manufactured goods.

Because he (wrongly) saw native life as unfixed, confused, and ungoverned, Eliot designed Natick to be a model community. Leaders drawn from hereditary families were replaced by elected representatives. Tribute that had formerly been given to the chief became tithing to the town. New legal codes punished idleness, moving about, long or unruly hair, polygamy, fornication, wife beating, powwowing [shamanic curing], using bear grease to protect the skin, killing lice between teeth, and holding elaborate mourning ceremonies.

For all their piety, no one in the Natick community was "churched" until they underwent thorough examinations toward acceptable testimonials in 1652, 1654, and, finally, 1659.

At first, Eliot assumed new converts would move to Natick, but most refused to leave their homelands. Thus, instead, new Praying Towns were founded, each in a separate ethnic region. Over time, fourteen Praying Towns grew up around the bay and another seven in the Nipmuck country of central Massachusetts before war broke out in 1675, led by Metacom. Known to the colony as King Philip, he was retaliating for the loss of his people and lands. Incidents leading to the war included the murder of John Sassamon, Natick secretary to Philip. Suspicious of his loyalty, three native men were convicted of his murder. As they were hanged, one rope broke and that man confessed to the crime before he was hanged again. Alerted, Philip moved up the timing of his attack.

A brutal Puritan counterattack threated Praying Towns so often that converts were moved to safety on a island in Boston Harbour. There, they languished, starved, and died until desperate survivors paid their own way back home.

The few resettled Praying Towns then suffered from constant Mohawk raids. In 1678, Mohawks carried off 22 Natick captives and burned them to death. In retaliation, Natick supplied scouts and soldiers for English offensives. In time, the last Praying Towns broke up and people drifted back to the areas where their ancestors had lived. Only in places like Mashpee and Gay Head, where the land was set aside as a reservation, did people maintain a tribal community.

Before Eliot preached in the language, Roger Williams had mastered enough of Algonkian grammar to give sermons at Plymouth, before he fled a charge of heresy to found Providence, Rhode Island. While aboard ship bound for England, he wrote a phrase book of Narragansett that ingeniously questioned the moral superiority of English Christians by invidious comparisons between native generosity and Boston hypocrisy.

On Martha's Vinyard and other islands off the coast, the Mayhew family continued a less publicized native mission over 163 years and five generations. While Eliot worked through a community organization and enjoyed publicity as the "Apostle to the Indiens," the Mayhews acted through individual natives, and left a less cohesive legacy.

Literacy was an important component of both missionizing programs. The bible and text translations were intended to allow converts to read divine word in their own languages. Unlike Mexico, however, where native scribes also used the alphabet to preserve their own ancestral traditions, Massachusetts, sensitive to British legalisms, used writing as a mnemonic to recall details of legal transactions such as sales, leases, wills, oral agreements, bills, letters, daybooks, ledgers, and petitions, along with church records of births, banns, marriages, or deaths.

HBC (Hudson's Bay Company)

For over 300 years, the dominant presence throughout the north has been the Hudson's Bay Company, chartered in England in 1670. Building upon overland native trade routes learned by French adventurers, this huge joint-stock company expanded to the west over several centuries. From Hudson's Bay, it moved into the Great Lakes (1670-1763), north central Canada (1764-1821, during intense trade rivalries), the Yukon (1822-1885), and, most recently, the High Arctic of the Northwest Territories and Quebec.[68] Today, as The Bay, its stores cross Canada.

For two centuries Rupert's Land (most of the interior) belonged to this company, before relinquishing it to the government of Canada in 1869. Throughout this vast region, the Hudson's Bay Company was, by royal charter, "the law of the land."

The incentive to begin the company was the golden opportunity to resupply the northern tribes with trade goods after the destruction of the Huron Nation in 1649. Scattered Huron survivors forever lost their key role as middlemen in the Northeast trade.

While the English had the resources and willingness to pursue this trade, they knew little about dealing with native peoples and wisely relied on French Canadians for advice and labor. Therefore, instead of the rigidity with which English always dealt with colonial peoples, the more relaxed and tolerate French attitudes kept interrelations cordial.

Seeking a standard of exchange, the Hudson's Bay Company adopted a monetary unit called "made beaver," which was the value of an adult beaver pelt of prime quality. All goods, furs, and provisions were priced accordingly. For example, a marten pelt was officially valued as one-third of a made beaver.

Over time, traders developed special relationships, often by claiming kinship with local leaders, who thereafter served as trading captains. Such men, and a few women, spoke effectively, knew the regional trade networks, and bargained with the best.

Despite strictures forbidding relations with native women, many laborers and some officers took native wives "without benefit of clergy, according to the country." Given the strong obligations of brothers-in-law to exchange gifts, native men abetted these liaisons by encouraging their daughters and sisters to accept employees as mates.

In 1821, HBC became the giant of the North by merging with its largest rival, the Northwest Company, whose members included famous explorers like Simon Fraser and Alexander Mackenzie.

The array of this trade was indicated by Arent De Peyster,[69] British commander at Detroit, on 4 July 1779 during a council at L'Arbor Croche, Michigan:

> Which, for good reasons, I think meet,
> In this grand council to repeat!
> Smoked red-deer skins, for warriors' shoes, −
> Item − large birch-bark northern canoes,
> Masts, halliards, sails, flags, oars and paddles,
> Broaches, medals, bridles, saddles,
> Large rolls of bark, awls, watap*, gum,
> Lines, punges, pipes, tobacco, rum,
> Guns, powder, shot, fire-steel and flint,
> Salt pork and biscuit, without stint;

68. Arthur J. Ray, The Hudson's Bay Company and Native People 1988; HBC Archives at Winnipeg, A Brief History of the Hudson's Bay Company, 1968.

69. Collections of the State Historical Society of Wisconsin 18: 387-388, 1908. Helpful definitions: watap = pine root for sewing canoes, Pani = a generic term for native slaves because so many were taken from the Pawnees, milk = alcohol (in this context).

Rich arm bands, gorgets and nose bobs,
Made of French Crowns and Spanish cobs;
Lac'd coats, chintz shirts, plum'd hats for chiefs,
And for your beau, silk handkerchiefs;
Paint, mirrors, blankets, moultins, strouds,
To clothe the living and make shrouds
For those who might in battle fall,
Or die by rum, at Montreal.
You made me likewise, close the graves
Of War-chiefs, slain with Panis slaves;
Clothe each child, old men and women,
Give nets, hooks, lines, grease and mandamin [maize];
Knives, scizzars, combs, hoes, hatchets, spears,
And kegs of <u>milk</u> to dry your tears,

In time, a distinct population grew up around these posts. Known as <u>metis</u> (French for "mixed"), these people formed a distinctive and wide-spread community, which survives today, blending traditions from Old France, Celts, Canada, and Native America. Legally, along with natives and Inuits, <u>metis</u> form the First Nations of Canada. Unlike natives, however, they have had to struggle to gain a land base. Twice, in 1870 and 1885, under the leadership of Louis Riel (1844-85), Red River Uprisings fought for, but lost, <u>metis</u> independence from Canada. Continuing communities along the Red River near Winnipeg and throughout the north owe their modern location to the roles their ancestors played in fur exploration, trade, and settlement.

MORAVIAN MISSIONS

The Unity of Brethren (<u>Unitas Fratrum</u>), known as the Moravians for the section of Eastern Europe where their teachings took hold, were Pietist Protestants who traced their beliefs to John Hus's 1415 martyrdom and thus represented a renewed church sixty years before Luther's Reformation.

Their watchwords are "In essentials unity, in non-essentials liberty, in all things charity." Further, congregations were arranged by gender, status, and age into "choirs," very much like the separate but equal division between men and women that characterized Native America. Thus, their regard for consensus and choirs appealed to native converts. For example, a Labrador Inuit woman wore a colored ribbon on her parka to indicate her choir: pink for unmarried, blue for married, and white for widowed.

The Moravian Eskimo mission began in Greenland, then spread to Labrador. A first attempt in 1852 ended quickly when Inuits massacred the Moravians in retaliation for abuses by whalers. Eventually, Jens Haven, who spoke Greenland Inuit, established the Nain mission in 1770 – with help from Merkok, an Inuit woman who, with her son Tutauk, had been captured during a naval skirmish and taken to England in 1767. After seeing English might, she hoped this mission would save her people.

Moravians had total control. To meet expenses, they set up a trading post in each community to collect furs and sell guns, ammunition, clothing, tea, twine, nails, tools, and some tobacco. Alcohol was strictly forbidden. Also, tourist arts like baskets and ivory carving were encouraged.

Because of their emphasis on fine music and Bible reading, by 1884, most Moravian Inuit were literate in their own language, with a locally-printed newspaper and books. Most churches also had singing groups, using German, Danish, English, and Inuit music, and some had brass bands.

Nonetheless Moravians taught a divine plan, espousing the domination of nature, that was destructive to the local ecology. With guns, Inuit overhunted caribou merely to collect sinews. To feed many sled dogs, they overfished local waters. To fill wood-burning stoves instead of more efficient oil lamps, they destroyed nearby forests.

After almost a century, the relative isolation of these Moravian Inuits ended in the 1860s when cod fishermen moved north, following warming ocean currents. Meeting Inuit in summer camps, away from missions, these men did great harm by introducing diseases, alcohol, damaging foods, and social conflict. They fathered mixed children, known as "settlers," who were educated by the Moravians in English rather than in Inuit.

After years of declining fur prices and a growing Canadian presence, in 1926, Moravians leased their posts to the Hudson's Bay Company and left Labrador.[70]

Based on the model of these Greenland and Labrador missions, in 1885, the Moravian church sent missionaries to the Yup'ik Eskimo along the Kuskokwim drainage of western Alaska. Among them was Rev. John Killbuck, a Delaware Indien. While Killbuck and the Yup'ik recognized common affinities, there were also many difficulties.

While traditional Delaware had beliefs about the importance of an all-encompassing "awareness" and a definition of "people" that included all life, not just humans, like that of the Yup'ik, Killbuck was a dedicated Christian missionary who believed that only humans could be "people" and that the endless feasting and celebrations of the winter were not worship, but instead a waste of time and effort.

Surprisingly, when the Killbucks spoke of "waking up" or "opening the eyes" of the Yup'ik and of "spreading light," their message rang true to Yup'ik beliefs in self-enlightenment. In time, despite some distortions, this Moravian mission succeeded, and, today, a Yup'ik man presides as the local Moravian bishop.

RUSSIAN ALASKA

With the defeat of the Mongol Tartars by Ivan the Terrible in 1552, the Russian state, relying on cossack adventurers, moved relentlessly eastward toward Siberia. Its proven strategy for holding conquered territory was to establish forts, called <u>ostrogs</u>, along each important waterway. In this manner, Russians advanced river by river, backed by prior forts, each a collecting point for native tribute in furs.

In tandem with the forts, priests converted natives to Russian Orthodoxy, but tolerated many native customs. More personal bonds were forged when Russians served as godparents for baptized natives. In some cases, however, conversion was forced upon native hostages held to assure the good conduct of their communities.

By 1641, this policy of forts, tribute, and domination reached the Pacific coast. From Siberian ports, cossacks went east, beginning with the 1647 voyage of Semen Dezhnev, a merchant-navigator, using the <u>koch</u>, a vessel adapted to the polar seas from the Viking ships that had earlier colonized Russia.

70. Crowe 1991: 138-140, 96-99; Arctic 1984: 511-513.

On his death bed, Peter the Great signed orders that sent off the first expedition of Vitus Bering, a Dane, in 1728. In 1741, Bering reached the American shore to claim Alaska and the Pacific coast for Russia, challenging Spain and England.

Using native Siberian traders and maps, Russians reached the Aleutian islands, brutally subjugating resident Aleuts (properly Unangans) in the 1760s. Rival trading companies, forced labor, diseases, and disrupted family life took a heavy toll. In 1788, aware of the demoralized conditions in Alaska, the fur tribute was abolished, although it remained in effect in Siberia until 1917.

From a 1783 foothold on Kodiak Island and grandiose plans for empire, in 1799, the Russian-America Company was given a 20-year monopoly by royal decree of Tsar Paul I, with full control of the lives of all native Alaskans.

With this mandate, Aleksandr (Alexander) Baranov, the chief manager or governor of the company, embarked on a ruthless program of forced labor in which native men were taken away from their families to hunt sea otters for three years. Since officials insisted that kayaking was best learned in childhood, only native men had such necessary skill. A few Aleut men were sent as far as Fort Ross in California, where they were rented out to American skippers in return for a percentage of their sea otter pelts.

Since Russian nationals remained a small but powerful minority in Alaska, many of these acts of oppression were committed by native allies. For example, to move the Russian capitol further down the coast to Sitka in 1799, Baranov intimidated local Tlingits by arriving with three ships and a fleet of Aleutians in 550 baidarka watercraft. Backed by this force, Baranov soon reached an agreement with Tlingit leaders to allow the fort to be built in exchange for trade privileges and protection. To provide fish and game for his table, Baranov detained the crews (120 men) of 60 Aleut vessels at Sitka, but sent the others home. Intertribal tensions caused by this Aleut and Tlingit face-off found an outlet when, on the way back to Kodiak, over a hundred of these men died from eating contaminated shellfish. Kodiak was plunged into even greater despair, and Tlingits were accused of using witchcraft to poison the mollusks.[71]

To avert hostilities, the company refused to trade guns or ammunition. Instead, Tlingits got these weapons from American or English vessels and used them well, destroying the Russian fort at Sitka in 1802. In 1804, aided by a navy vessel, Baranov punished the Tlingit and rebuilt Sitka. In 1805, Tlingit leveled the fort at Yakutat forever.

Orthodox clergy and navy officers, continually shocked by the abuse of native rights, had Baranov removed in 1818. Thereafter, the governor was always a ranking naval officer. Further, when the company charter was renewed in 1821 and 1844, greater (but not better) concern was given to the treatment of natives. In 1828, conservation measures for fur bearing animals were instituted, but the 1867 sale of Alaska to the United States (to keep it away from Spain or England) thwarted these efforts. Moreover, American racial attitudes only made life harder for native peoples in Alaska. The sea otter, hunted without regulation almost to extinction, suffered most of all.

While Orthodox clergy were expected to convert by example rather than coercion, they were backed by the Russian state.[72] Thus, the spread of conversion coincided with the expansion of the empire as Siberia was colonized. Sometimes, however, the church spread faster than

---

71. Lydia Black, The Story of Russian America, Crossroads of Continents, 1988: 70-82; Richard Pierce, "Russian and Soviet Eskimo and Indian Policies," Arctic Handbook 4: 119-127.
72. Sergei Kan, The Russian Orthodox Church in Alaska, Arctic Handbook 4: 506-521.

officialdom.

Conversion of Aleuts and other coastal Alaskans was the last stage of the Russian movement eastward. Initially, military defeat and severe depopulation so demoralized native populations that the new religion came as a relief in troubled times. Sometimes, conversion was the result of force. For example, the first Koniag Eskimo converts were children sent as hostages to live with Russian officers.

Petitions by Alaska fur traders asking for Orthodox clergy were answered in 1793 when the Holy Synod and Catherine II sent a group of eight monks and two novices with Archimandrite Iosaf Bolotov to Kodiak, where the first church was consecrated in 1796 and Bolotov appointed bishop. He and most of this mission drowned returning from his 1799 investiture in Siberia, the same year the Russian-America Company was given the Alaskan monopoly, both as a business venture and outpost of the Russian state. Unchecked, Baranov fully imposed his ruthless and oppressive policies.

Remaining clergy were feeble and relations were strained between the church and company because of the "immoral" behavior of the promyshlinniki (trading roust-abouts), who both coerced native men into hunting for the trade and exploited native women, fathering a mixed population of "creoles." In time, some creole sons became members of the married clergy. The first, in 1810, was Prokopii Lavrov, but he moved to Siberia because he was unable to force the company to improve the lot of his people.

By 1823, Monk Herman, declared a saint in 1971, was the only missionary left. He lived as a hermit for 14 years on Spruce Island, providing a haven for natives fleeing the worst offenses of the traders and helping natives to identify with Orthodoxy as a means for both their spiritual and physical salvation. Russian Orthodoxy truly became a "grass roots" movement and still remains a strong aspect of modern Aleut and Tlingit identification.

Plans to end the failing mission were vetoed by Tsar Alexander I, who sent more clergy, including Ivan Veniaminov, a remarkable man canonized as Saint Innocent in 1977. Settled among the Aleut in 1824, Veniaminov and Ivan Pan'kov, an Aleut leader, designed an alphabet based on Cyrillic script to translate scriptures. Among his compatriots was Iakov Netsvietov, a Creole priest who also corrected faulty translations.

A decade later, Veniaminov was transferred to Sitka (then called Novo-Arkhangel'sk, "New Archangel"). There, he faced stiff opposition from local Tlingits until a smallpox epidemic in 1837 killed many of the elders and shamans. Survival rates soon improved when the company began inoculations. Those who submitted willingly learned to value Russian help, while those who refused usually died during the next plague.

Slowly, Veniaminov won over members of the Tlingit nobility, and others with them, through his willingness to fit church rules to local conditions, tolerate most native customs, use native languages, and provide a moral example. After the death of his wife, Veniaminov entered the celibate clergy as a monk. In 1840, he became Bishop Innocent and published a three volume study of the Aleut, the first professional volumes on a North American tribe. He ended his career as Metropolitan of Moscow, from 1868-79.

As bishop, Veniaminov toured Alaska and found that Orthodoxy had become the major focus of Aleut community integration, with local leaders serving as church wardens. Churches were added along the coast and, in 1845, a mission began in the Yukon.

With the sale of Alaska to the US in 1867, however, Orthodox came under attack by American missionaries, particularly Presbyterians, who demanded a less ornate and more aggressive version of Christianity forged by European capitalism. Many natives, suffering under

American racial attitudes, clung to Orthodoxy.

Aleuts were constantly challenged by American officials to learn English and go to school, even though they were already literate in their own language using Cyrillic letters. Such writing was clearly judged un-American. Tlingit towns at Kake and Wrangell, in 1869, and at Angoon, in 1882, were shelled by an American man-of-war in punishment for acts the navy itself had provoked. During the 1898 Klondike Gold Rush, the navy also broke the centuries-old monopolies of the Chilkat nobles to trade into the Yukon through these mountain passes.

Without the financial support that had been provided by the Russian-America company and the Russian state, in 1870, the Orthodox bishopric was moved to San Francisco, and later to New York. As a bulkward for their beliefs, local churches started brotherhoods dedicated to temperance and mutual aid.

After the Russian Revolution in 1917, American Orthodoxy became established with its own resources, although it only received self-government from the Russian church in 1970. New clergy, however, could not be found, and churches returned, by and large, to their grass roots from "lay readers" who led prayers and conducted necessary rituals at birth, marriage, and death.

Throughout its long and difficult history, Alaskan Orthodox has been sustained by its use of native languages, a married native clergy, and a general acceptance of native beliefs which blended well with its own mystical traditions of sanctifying the land.

THOMAS JEFFERSON

A keen intellectual, Thomas Jefferson set a strong course for the understanding of the native peoples of the United States and North America.

While he wrote voluminously, Jefferson's only published book is the modestly titled Notes on the State of Virginia. Written during the American Revolution in response to questions raised by French allies, nervous about future prospects and benefits, Jefferson was then 37 and Governor of Virginia.

Its 23 chapters took "notice" of boundaries, rivers, mountains, cascades and caverns, mines, vegetation, population, militia, navy, natives (Indiens), counties and townships, charters and constitution, law and justice, colleges and roads, Tory assets, religions, local customs, commerce, European imports, measures and currency, public income, histories, and memorials about the Virginia. Appendices illustrated a draft constitution, an act for establishing religious freedom, and, in later editions, an examination of the 1774 murder of the family of Logan, a Mingo (Ohio Iroquois) leader who, with great eloquence and pathos, lamented that he was left to mourn alone.

Jefferson quoted Logan's speech in his chapter called Query VI while refuting the claim of Count Buffon and other French scholars that "vapors" in the soil of America were defective and caused its inhabitants to degenerate. After commenting on the great size and diversity of American animals, he considered the aboriginal peoples, arguing against certain claims made by these Frenchmen about native stature and ardor. As evidence of insight and ability, he quoted Logan's speech and named the murderer, but subsequent evidence has left the murders unsolved.

Query XI looked at the natives of Virginia, briefly discussing political, cultural, and linguistic differences among the Powhatan, Mannahoacs, Manacans, and their neighbors. Rather than appreciating the farming skills of these tribes, he repeated the distortion that these people lived "on the spontaneous productions of nature," though he did note that native lands were acquired not by conquest but by proofs of purchase. Seeking evidence of large scale labor in "monuments," he hoped for something like a common ditch for draining farm lands, but instead looked to local "barrows" or earthen mounds.

Curious about these mounds throughout the landscape, Jefferson excavated one about two miles from his Monticello estate. While much legend and fantasy was associated with such mounds, including the existence of a pre-Indien civilization of Mound Builders, he correctly concluded that local natives had built and used them for burials. By this insight, he laid the foundation for future American archaeology.

To understand the origin and distribution of native tribes, however, Jefferson thought it was best to look at language, particularly the names for common objects, noun and verb inflections, and principles of regimen and concord (that is, grammar). This chapter ended with a chart of known American tribes and their estimated populations for 1759, 1764, and 1768.

As a culmination of these thoughts, he drafted the guidelines used by Lewis and Clark during their exploration of the newly acquired Louisiana Purchase, which began American expansion into the West.

Jefferson left the White House with a large collection of native vocabularies collected by himself and others, including Lewis and Clark, but the trunk holding them was stolen from the Potomac dock. Since a few pages later washed, the thieves, disappointed that the stout lock protected only papers, tossed them into the river.

Albert Gallatin, Jefferson's Swiss-born Secretary of the Treasury (the first to balance the national budget) followed up on this work and produced an early linguistic map of the eastern United States. John Wesley Powell made such linguistic mapping an early goal of the Bureau of American Ethnology. Franz Boas, Edward Sapir, Carl Voegelin, and Joseph Greenberg have continued these efforts.

WENATCHIPAM FISHERY

On 9 June 1855, the Yakama Treaty was signed at the Walla Walla Council, along with two others with Walla Wallas and with Nez Perce. Isaac Stevens, Washington Territorial Governor, head of the northern US railroad survery, and Indian Commissioner, hurried through this sixth of ten treaties, although a native uprising, growing public opposition, and the agitation leading to the Civil War postponed their congressional approval until 1859.

Instructions from DC insisted he was to gain legal (strictly according to Anglo-Saxon conventions) title to as much Washington Territory land as possible, since many its best sections had already been usurped by settlers. To accomplish this, he was to provide certificates to head chiefs as a means of consolidating as many tribal groups as possible under an appointed native treaty signer on the smallest bit of land, either a reservation kept back from the ceded territories, if a community were lucky, or away from their homelands, if they could be forced to move. Most did not budge. Languages, kinship, and food preferences were not adequately considered.

Both Salishans and Sahaptians were lumped together at Walla Walla, where one of the greatest travesties involved a fishery near modern Leavenworth in the homeland of the Psk^waws, who were Salishan speakers who are now better known as Wenatchi, the more euphonious name given them by neighboring Sahaptin bands who eventually joined the reservation of their Yakama kin.

Kamaiakin, the man Stevens wanted to be head chief of his fabricated Yakama Nation, was a distinguished member of a chiefly family, but he avoided as much as possible succumbing to American pressures. One of the few things he did on his own initiative was protect the fishery of the Psk^waws, friends and kin through intermarriage, in Article 10 of that treaty. According to notes, Kamaiakin "desired a small piece of land at the place called Wenatshapam – where the

Indians take many fish – for the Pisquouse and Methows." In the wording of the treaty, however, this article reserved, at most, six square miles at the forks of the river, the junction of Icicle Creek and the Wenatchee River for "the use and benefit of the aforesaid confederated tribes and bands," not specifically its traditional Salishan owners, the Psk^{w}aws, or its frequent reciprocal users, the Methows. Because the river flows out of Lake Wenatchee, it has (had) the only sockeye salmon run in the ceded Salish territory. Chelan Falls blocks any such run into that lake, while the run into Canadian Lake Okanagan eventually became the western border of the Colville reservation.

Psk^{w}aws, who did not join their closest kin on the Colville Reservation until forced in the early 1900s, lived along their river and shared their fishery with Salishans like the Methows and other welcome visitors. Yet, according to the federal government, that fishery belonged not the to Psk^{w}aws but to a "legal fiction" known as the Yakama Nation, composed of Sahaptians.

In 1892, after white settlement choked the Wenatchee valley, increasing pressure on the Psk^{w}aws and their fishery, Jay Lynch, the Yakima agent 100 miles away, asked if article 10 of the treaty had ever been acted upon. As far as DC and the Yakamas (erroneously) knew, it had not. Thus began a parade of absurdities, with the federal government repeatedly blaming the victim for their own ignorance.[73]

In 1892, the Yakama agent placed the fishery as a strip three miles wide from Lake Wenatchee for ten miles downriver. This was 20 miles above where the natives, treaty, and prior officials had located it at the Icicle fork. Rather than admit their error, agents compounded it by insisting on that general locale and holding meetings, not among the Psk^{w}aws, but over a hundred miles away at Yakima. One native was so amused by all these mistakes, since they did not involve his people, he asked,

> "Does the Great Father in Washington think a salmon is an eagle that lives on top of a mountain, or does he think a salmon is a deer that lives in the woods and hills, or does he think a salmon is a mountain goat that lives among the rocks of the snow-covered mountains."

Yakama's remarks remained vague and general about the fishery being far away, remotely known, and unused by them. All true, but very misleading. When money was discussed for these 23,000 acres, $.50/acre was suggested since the land had forest, water, and some farm land not yet taken by settlers. By comparison, land along the railroad right of way was sold for $5/acre. During the 6 January 1894 council, Psk^{w}aws snow bound so only Yakimas attended, and sold the land, using the money to build their own irrigation system in 1894.

The Psk^{w}aws took out homesteads to stay in their homeland, but suffered greatly. As one inspector lamented,

> "Are we a nation of thieves and unmitigated scoundrels? Are we devoid of all sense of honor? Does 70 millions of people because of their superior numbers and intelligent propose little by little to derive the sorely depleted tribes in the west of the small patrimony their more magnanimous conquerors, the early settlers in this country, gave them, or more properly speaking, allowed them to retain after wresting from them the heritage which had descended to them from generation to generation. Will the interest of private individuals or the greed of corporations be allowed to sully our nations honor?"

On 4 July 1937, still pleading injustice, Chief John Harmelt and his wife, both blind, burned to death in their cabin on their Wenatchee homestead.

73. John Bower assembled these records for use by the Colville legal office.

In all, the US government in its ignorance, despite paying for a knowledgeable survey, took away the vital Psk^{w}aws fishery and gave it to a collection of foreign-speaking tribes over a hundred miles away. It mis-surveyed that fishery on a whim, then demanded that it be sold as "surplus" during crucial meetings in bitter winter cold when Psk^{w}aws leaders could not travel, insisting all the time that it knew best despite all available evidence proving otherwise. After relying on it for centuries, the Psk^{w}aws lost their fishery and received, in 1965, some money in final recognition of their ownership. As they say, "You can't count on money to return each year to feed you, the way you can with salmon."

LUSHOOTSEED SHAMANISM ON TRIAL

Multiple inabilities of local settlers to grasp or understand native culture is sadly illustrated by a 1874 trial involving Puget Sound Lushootseed of Washington. On 14 December 1873, as his wife Susie lay dying, Harry Fisk shot Dr Jackson, a Squaxin shaman, once in the head with a rifle and then twice in the body with a pistol. That Jackson did not die immediately after the first shot must have been taken as an indication of his considerable powers.

Fisk, whose father was white and mother native, worked as a translator for the local superintendent of Indien affairs, using this authority to serve as an intercultural go-between around Olympia, the state capitol, so his relations with other Lushootseeds must have been sometimes strained by his employer's demands. During a potlatch in Seattle a week before, one his enemies hired Dr Jackson with nine blankets to project an evil power (masatchie tamanawas in Chinook jargon) into Susie, presumably because Harry's own strong allies protected him. Certainly, the speed with which Susie became mortally ill was another indication of the intensities of power involved.

When other remedies, though shamans or medicines, proved of no avail, Fisk went to Olympia, found Jackson, handcuffed him under the pretense of making an arrest, and took him to Mud Bay, an off-reservation native community five miles away, where Susie languished in the home of Indian Sandy. Confronted with his victim, Jackson was calously unmoved so Susie demanded that Harry kill him to lift her condition. Fisk aimed, but the shaman resisted, then took a while to die, pleading for a weapon to defend himself from men standing nearby, such as Lewis with a wood ax. Half a day later, as Susie herself died, her voice became that of Dr Jackson gloating of fatal triumph. As a result, native witnesses concluded that Fisk had taken the right course at the wrong time, waiting a week too long.

During white preparation for the trial, however, the judge and opposing lawyers developed legal strategies for this first case involving a native murdering another native. Their positions are instructive, if wrongheaded. Previously, such crimes had been left entirely to native justice, because as this judge explained to the jury "An Indian is a man if he kills a white man, but loses his identity if he kills an Indian."[74] Not until 1885 did the Major Crimes Act impose federal jurisdiction on reservations.

In this era of US Grant's peace policy to put Christian reformers in charge of reservations, the prosecutor sought to use this trial to force natives into the American mold, while the defender argued that believing in witchcraft was an insane delusion justifying self-defense without criminal intent.

In twenty-two pages of instruction, this judge insisted that law was an objective search for truth, rejecting any plea of insanity, yet suggesting, by taking into account the defendant's "level

74. Brad Asher 1995: 19.

of civilization," the legal doctrine of mistake, an eminently reasonable and justifiable action based on misunderstood facts, according to the law "which covers the soil on which he did what he has done."[75] After a trial that allowed several native witnesses, an all white, all male jury, deliberating eight minutes, tendered a verdict of acquittal on 31 March 1874.

Denying powha as first cause, according to Lushootseed belief, and misunderstanding the great and proven intensities displayed by Dr Jackson's heartlessness before the ill woman, his own protracted dying, and his revealing final confession from Susie's own mouth, Fisk was entirely justified. That he was tried and freed by Americans, however, gave some of Jackson's relatives a counterclaim for revenge that was never fulfilled. Rather, another possible outcome, suggested by present Jackson family claims to descent from an aunt of John Slocum, may have led to the founding of the Indian Shaker Church at Mud Bay, site of this murder, about a decade later in 1881.

LIVING TREASURES

Every year since 1982 (except 1988), at least one Native American has been named a National Heritage Fellow by the National Endowment for the Arts in recognition of their contributions to the artistic diversity of the United States. The equivalent of the Japanese designation of "living treasure," these awards recognize excellence in the traditional and folk arts with a grant of $10,000, which is more money than most of these people have ever seen in a lump sum.

In order, these native artists have been an Osage ribbonworker, Chitimacha basketmaker, Eskimo carver, Lakota quill artist, Cochiti potter, Comanche flutist, Tlingit Chilcat weaver, Anglo-Comanche storyteller, Kiowa regalia maker, Apache fiddle maker, Ojibwe painter, Lakota flutist, Hupa-Yurok artist, Nez Perce cornhusk weaver, Cherokee musician, Alaska Athabascan basketmaker, Menomini-Potawatomi regalia maker, married Yupik artists, Mesquakie singer, Passamaquoddy basketmaker, and Skagit storyteller. Each represents the epitome of a living tribal tradition.

In September of 1994, eleven National Heritage Fellows traveled to Washington (DC) to receive their recognition. Among them was Vi Taqʷšəblu Hilbert, a Skagit storyteller and linguist living in Seattle. There she met Liz Carroll, an Irish-American fiddler; Clarence Fountain and the Blind Boys, African American gospel singers; Mary Mitchell Gabriel, Passamaquoddy basketmaker; Johnny Gimble, Texas swing fiddler; Frances Varos Graves, New Mexican colcha embroiderer; Sosie Shizuyi Matsumoto, Master of the Japanese tea ceremony (chado); D.L. Menard, Cajun musician; Simon Shaheen, Palastinian oud player; Lily Vorperian, Armenian embroiderer; and Elder Roma Wilson, African American harmonica gospel musician.

Awardees arrived on Tuesday in time for a reception at the Women's National Democratic Club. On Wednesday morning, Hilary Clinton, the First Lady, presented the awards in Caucus Room 325 in the Russell Senate Office Building. Thursday night, a banquet was held at Dumbartan House, a restored mansion. Friday night, a concert was held in which all of the awardees displayed their talents, followed by a pizza party that went into the night. A last gathering was held Saturday Night in rural Maryland as, over the weekend, allowing for some sight seeing, these fellows left for home.

75. Brad Asher 1995: 19.

While the fellows were well tended during their stay, there was a certain irony that the native artists shared the limelight with so many other traditions with a strong presence elsewhere in the world. Only the African American gospel artists were also unique to the Americas. Moreover, in terms of the media, newspapers and broadcasters spent much more time with the popular, Anglo-oriented musicians familiar to their audiences. Though under-appreciated, the native artists displayed an integrity and vibrancy uniquely American.

Unlike those other artists, however, when Native American artists cease to pass on their techniques, they are extinct, gone from the earth forever.

III.
TIME FRAME
FOR THE AMERICANIST TRADITION

So much has happened in Native America that it is impossible to put all of it between the covers of a single textbook. As incentive to look elsewhere for the people, places, and events that have changed the Americas and the world, this time line presents entries that are starting points for expanding the story of increased understanding and of cultural masterworks in the human record. Each century is arranged separately to highlight particular dates, rather than present a continuous chronology, as others have done,[76] more attention is given to contemporaneous happenings. While not exhaustive, most of the high, and some of the low, points are included, particularly for the last five thundred years. As sustained examples, dates listed for 1540 De Soto, 1547 Hans Staden, or 1770 Moravians are fully treated in the next section.

1900s

1900 A federal investigation halted the amateur excavation of Pueblo Bonito in Chaco Canyon, New Mexico, leading to decisions about American archaeological treasures and the passage of the Federal Antiquities Act of 8 June 1906; Arthur Evans excavated Minoan Crete (to 1908)

1900-1975 Leslie White, prolific Puebloan researcher and evolutionist

1902-72 Julian Steward, classic Basin researcher and evolutionist

1903-1949 Archie Phinney, Nez Perce folklorist, linguist, reformer, BIA official

1904-1977 D'Arcy McNickle, Flathead Selish writer, reformer, administrator

1906-1991 Fred Eggan, Americanist famous for work on comparative kinship, especially in the Southwest

1906-1985 Homer Barnett, Northwesternist concerned with innovations

1912 Jim Thorpe (Sauk-Fox), Louis Tewanima (Hopi), Joseph Keeper (Cree) competed in Stockholm Olympics; Alaska Native Brotherhood founded and organized into camps on models of Protestant and Russian Orthodox men's groups.

1914-18 World War I

1920 Norman Wells discovered oil reserves in the Northwest Territories (Canada)

1922 James Teit died

1924 All Indiens made US citizens in recognition of native service during World War I

1926-28 Brookings Institute studied the economic and social conditions of tribes for the Meriam Report (1928) entitled <u>The Problem of Indian Administration</u>

---

76. Major references for this chronology included Barry (1972), Grun (1979), Jennings (1993), Franklin (1981), Schele and Freidel (1990), Snellgrove and Richardson (1968), and Washburn (1988: 617-699). Thanks also to Donna Steinburn, Robert Keyes-Back, Ann Schuh, Larry and Michiko Epstein, Judith Henchy, Olive Dickason, Andie Palmer, and Jere Bacharach.

1927 Native Administration Act (South Africa) made the British Crown supreme over tribal paramount chiefs

1929 22 June, third beam expedition of Emil Haury and Lyndon Hardgrave discovers in Whipple Ruin at Show Low a charred timber (HH-39) filling out the Southwest tree ring record

1931 Native Brotherhood of British Columbia formed on 1912 Alaska model, but with its own chapters called "branches."

1934 John Collier's Indian Reorganization (Wheeler-Howard) Act

1939-45 World War II

1940 Handbook of Federal Indian Law by Felix Cohen

1944 National Congress of American Indians formed in Denver

1946 Indian Claims Commission (to 1978) decided recompensation for undervalued land sales; Philippine independence from US

1947 Dead Sea Scrolls (BC 22 - AD 100) found

1951 Bureau of Indian Affairs relocation program to displace Indiens into cities; Canadian Indian Act dropped prohibition against potlatching and the pursuit of any native claims

1953 American Society for Ethnohistory founded; 13 tribes dropped from Federal control and thus "terminated"

1954 US schools desegregated

1964 BAE (Bureau of American Ethnology) disbanded

1966 Rough Rock Demonstration School founded and run by Navahos

1970 Blue Lake, a sacred emergence site, restored to Taos Pueblo (expropriated in 1906 for a national forest); American Indian Movement (AIM) started in Twin Cities

1971 Alaska Native Claims Settlement Act

1972-85 Alkali Lake, a Shuswap reserve in British Columbia went from total alcoholism to 95% sobriety

1973 Wounded Knee II, 1954 Menomini termination rescinded

1975 Dene Declaration asserts aboriginal rights in Northwest Canada and Alaska

1978 American Indian Religious Freedom Act; Indian Child Welfare Act (native children should be raised by native families); Oliphant v Suquamish Indian Tribe (tribes did not have jurisdiction over non-natives living on the reservation)

1980 Canadian Supreme Court recognized Inuit "aboriginal rights" but excluded mineral rights; Greenland home rule

1990 Native American Grave Protection and Repatriation Act (NAGPRA) returned burials and stolen artifacts to tribes; over half of all registered Indiens were urban; Elijah Harper, a Cree member of the Manitoba legislature, kept ratification of Canadian federal-provincial accord because full standing of First Nations not recognized

1800s

1800 Washington DC new US capital

1801-73 Pierre Jean de Smet, founded Northwest Jesuit missions (1840-46)

1802 Tlingits destroyed Sitka (New Archangel), rebuilt 1804

1803 Napoleon's France sold to US much of its usurped Spanish West as the Louisiana Purchase

1803-5 John Rogers Jewett (1784-1821) captivity at Nootka Sound

1803-6 Urey Lisianskii, Russian explorer

1804-06 Lewis and Clark expedition, planned by Thomas Jefferson

1805 Tlingit destroyed Russian post at Yakutat

1806 Simon Fraser explored the Stalo River renamed for him

1806-1872 Benito Juarez, Zapotec elected President of Mexico in 1861, 1867, 1871

1809-28 Description de l'Egypt, 23 huge tomes derived from Napoleon's invasion.

1809-93 Karl Bodmer, German painter of the Plains

1810-74 Alfred Jacob Miller, painter

1811 Battle of Tippecanoe routed Shawnee Prophet (Tenskwatawa) and made William Henry Harrison a popular hero

1812 War of 1812; Russians founded Fort Ross in California; Elgin Marbles taken from Athens to London; Philadelphia Academy of Natural Sciences begun

1814 Andrew Jackson defeated "Red Stick" Creek patriots at Battle of Horseshoe Bend, helped by native scouts and allies; Creeks forced to cede 20 million acres; Eight Canadians were hanged, drawn, and quartered from their US sympathies on 20 July; Oblates (Catholic Order of Mary Immaculate) founded at Marseilles, France

1815 Battle of New Orleans

1815-59 Robert S. Neighbors, murdered Texas Indian agent

1815-73 George Gibbs, Northwesternist and treaty agent

1817-96 Horatio Hale, lawyer, linguist, and Iroquoianist

1818 John Barrow's plan for British Navy to explore Arctic

1818-81 Lewis Henry Morgan, League of the Iroquois (1851), toured the West 1859, Systems of Consanguinity and Affinity of the Human Family (1871), cousin terminologies (Hawaiian, Eskimo, Iroquois, Sudanese, Crow, Omaha) Ancient Society (1877) where three stages, beginning with Lower Savagery, were defined by their inventions: Middle = fire, Upper = the bow, Lower Barbarism = pottery and farming, Middle = domesticated animals, Upper = iron tools, and Civilization = writing

1819-25 William Parry explored eastern Arctic three times

1820-1903 Herbert Spencer, English social evolutionist

1821 Hudson's Bay Company merged with Northwest Company; Mexico seceded from Spain

1822-1884 Gregor Mendel, laws of heredity (1865)

1822-1895 Louis Pasteur

1823 Many Oneida from central New York forced to Green Bay, Wisconsin

1824 Bureau of Indian Affairs set up

1825 Erie Canal built

1827 Fidelia Fielding (Djiits Budanaca, "Flying Bird," 15 September - 1908), Mohegan diarist; John James Audubon (1785-1851), Birds of North America (to 1838)

1828 American dictionary by Noah Webster (1758-1843); Russian America Company instituted conservation measures to protect the sea otter, ignored by American officials after 1867

1828-1895 Ely Parker, Seneca leader, Union Army general, advisor of Lewis Henry Morgan, first native Commissioner of Indian Affairs

1828-35 Cherokee Phoenix published in Sequoyah syllabary

1828-89 Joseph Lightfood, Bishop of Durham, refined the biblical creation date to 9:00am, 26 October, BC 4004.

1830s Shift from ship-based to land-based fur trade along Northwest Coast

1830 Andrew Jackson's Indian Removal Act

1831 Nat Turner (1800-1831) Rebellion

1831-1848 Lord Kingsborough, squandered family fortune on lush facsimile editions of native Mexican classics

1831-36 Voyage of the HMS Beagle, Charles Darwin (1809-1882) on board as naturalist

1831-1885 Helen Hunt Jackson, reformer, A Century of Dishonor (1881), Ramona (1884)

1832 Japanese color block prints of Ukiyo ("floating world")

1832-1918 Hubert Howe Bancroft, American historian

1832-1907 Albert Samuel Gatschet, linguist at Bureau of American Ethnology (BAE)

1832-34 Maximillian Alexander Philip, Prinz von Wied-Neuweid toured tribes along the Upper Missouri River, while Karl Bodmer sketched and painted for their book (1839) and plates (1841)

1834 Hunchback of Notre Dame by Victor Hugo

1834-1902 Major John Wesley Powell, Basin Numic research (1868-80), founded BAE (1879-1964), advocate of science in federal policy

1834-1909 Sheldon Jackson, Presbyterian missionary and education commissioner in Alaska

1834-36 California missions secularized by bishops into parishes

1835 Pablo Tac, a Luiseño, wrote an account (published a century later) of his people at mission San Luis Rey while living in Rome

1836 Cherokee trail of tears; Battle of the Alamo; Hudson Bay Company's Beaver first steamship along the Northwest coast

1836-41 George Wilkes, US exploring expedition around the world

1837 Mandan smallpox kills over 90%; Tlingit smallpox; Queen Victoria (1819-1901) assumed the English throne; Mount Holyoke College founded

1837-39 George Winter (1809-1876) watercolors of Great Lakes natives

1837-99 Daniel Garrison Brinton, MD, first anthropologist at a university (Pennsylvania, 1886), classification of languages of North and South America (1891), American literatures

1837-1913 J Pierpont Morgan, patron of research

1838-1923 Alice Fletcher, Plains anthropologist and reformer

1838-1908 Otis Tufton Mason, 12-18 American ethnic environments (early form of culture areas), Women's Share in Primitive Culture (1894)

1839 John Stevens and Frederick Catherwood toured Maya ruins

1839-1914 Charles S Peirce, American logician

1839-1915 Frederick Ward Putnam, set up museums and research at Harvard, Chicago 1893 Columbian Exposition, American Museum of Natural History, and Berkeley

1840s Beaver exterminated, fur trade shifted to bison hides

1840 Ivan Veniaminov (1797-1879), Russian Orthodox priest (canonized 1977), published on Aleut and Tlingit, became a monk (1840) and Metropolitan of Moscow (1868); With Ivan Pan'kov, an Aleut leader, devised a Cyrillic script about 1824 that made Aleuts literate

1840-1924 Major Richard Henry Pratt, founded Carlisle Indian School (1879) after being warden at Ft Marion, Florida

1841 Oregon Trail; James Evans (1801-46), Methodist missionary at the HBC post at Norway House in Manitoba soldered together a tin canoe, and devised Cree syllabics for translations printed using a press for compacting furs, type melted from tea chest lead, ink combined from soot and sturgeon oil, and deerskin covers; Edmund Albius, a former slave, perfected a pollination technique for vanilla, a Mexican Totonac domesticate

1841-45 14 Ioways tour Europe

1842-1912 Karl May, German writer about Winnetou, a very fictional Mescalero Apache

1843 British Archaeological Institute founded; Sioux recaptured some of the Cheyenne sacred arrows from the Pawnee

1843-1925 John Hillars, photographer of the Great Basin

1845-48 Ill-fated arctic expedition of Sir John Franklin kills 129 members of the British Navy in 2 crews northwest of Hudson's Bay; 40 later expeditions trying to learn their fate complete the exploration of the Canadian arctic

1846 US colonized New Mexico and California; Mormon exodus from Navoo, Illinois to five locations, including Utah

1846-48 Paul Kane (1810-1871) painted images of the Northwest

1846-52 Rudolph Friederich Kurz toured Mississippi and Missouri Rivers for erotic sketches and journal

1846-1933 William H Holmes, archaeologist, BAE director

1847 Whitman Prebyterian mission destroyed by Cayuse

1847 Caste War of the Speaking Cross, successful Maya revolt in Yucatan until 1900; rituals of Cruzob (Spanish word for "cross" + Mayan plural, Crosses) continue to this day

1848 Most Seneca Iroquois elect officers in place of hereditary chiefs; Russians sold Fort Ross to John Sutter, who found gold in the Sacramento River; Revolts in Germany, Italy, and France; Ancient Monuments of the Mississippi Valley by Ephraim George Squier and Edwin Hamilton Davis

1848-95 James Owen Dorsey, Episcopal missionary and Siouianist

1849-51 California Gold Rush

1849-1915 Matilde Coxe Stevenson, classic Puebloan ethnographer and women's rights advocate

1850s Laan, Southern Tutchone trade chief in the Yukon, rose and fell

1850-70 Bini ("mind"), Carrier prophet, known in boyhood as Sami from his MB before he assumed the Beaver moiety chiefly name of Kwiis; this prophetic powha passed from that MB to his own B Lex, who took the name of Sisteyel after visiting heaven, to Bini, to Louis, and Mrs Jim Michel, who was forbidden any role by the Catholic priest and became crazy before dying

1850-1930 Jesse Walter Fewkes, Hopi ethnographer and Southwestern archaeologist

1850-1914 Adolph Bandelier, Swiss-American Southwesternist

1852-1936 Clarence Moore, a wealthy Philadephian, spent winters in Southeast excavating major sites from his 100 foot steam launch The Gopher for Academy of Natural Sciences of Philadelphia who sold these superb artifacts to the Heye Foundation in 1929, now within National Museum of the American Indian

1852 Dogribs began bringing 8,000 caribou to Fort Rae for provisioning the York boat crews; 16 August James Savage, translator, polygamist, and trader at the Fresno Reservation, is killed in a disagreement over California Indian policy

1854 Japan opened to foreign trade

1855-1942 C Hart Merriam, zoologist and ethnologist of California

1856 Neanderthal skull found near Dusseldorf; William Duncan (1832-1918), Evangelical Anglican missionary, arrived at Port Simpson to begin lifelong work among the Tsimshian

1857-1932 Francis La Flesche, Omaha scholar

1857-1900 Frank Hamilton Cushing, BAE scholar at Zuni and Florida Keys

1857 Mountain Meadows Massacre (Utah); Bishop Paul Durieu, OMI, developed native leadership system at Oblate missions in Canada

1858-1942 Franz Boas, comparative Americanist, founder of academic anthropology in the US

1859 On the Origin of Species by Natural Selection by Charles Darwin

1859-69 Suez Canal

1859-1937 John NB Hewitt, Tuscarora anthropologist

1859-1938 Adrian Gabriel Morice, OMI, missionary in British Columbia after 1880

1860s Qillarsuaq (Kridlak), a shaman, led a migration of Canadian Inuit from Baffinland 1800 miles to the Polar Eskimos (Thule Inuit), reintroducing kayaks, snowhouses, bows, fish spears among survivors of a devastating epidemic fifty years before

1860s-70s Ipikvik and Tukkolerktuk (Joe and Hannah) trained, guided, and saved a generation of Arctic explorers, including Charles Francis Hall, sent by God to find survivors of the Franklin Expedition (1860-65)

1860-1943 Ales Hrdlicka, physical anthropologist opposed early dates for human occupation of the Americas

1860-1936 Charles Curtis, enrolled Kaw (Kansas), real estate shark, Vice President of US (1929-33) under Herbert Hoover

1861 Smallpox spread from Victoria, British Columbia, throughout the Northwest, killing over half of the native population

1861-65 War Between the States (Civil War)

1861-1921 James Mooney, Irish patriot, journalist, BAE ethnologist famous for his sympathetic comparative study of the 1890 Ghost Dance

1862 Red Cross began

1862-1921 James Murie, Skiri Pawnee ethnographer

1863 US National Academy of Sciences

1864 Sand Creek massacre of Cheyenne and Arapaho in Colorado; first US salmon cannery

1864-1956 Frederick Hodge, BAE Southwest archaeologist, adversary of Frank Cushing though they were married to sisters

1867 US "brought" Alaska from Russia, without consulting native inhabitants; British North America Act established the Dominion of Canada

1867-1957 Frances Densmore, prolific BAE ethnomusicologist

1868 Treaty of Fort Laramie with Sioux; Hampton Institute (VA) founded to educate ex-slaves, (after 1878) natives; Emancipation Proclamation denied natives the right to vote; Canadian Indian Act for the gradual civilization of native peoples

1868-1925 Edward Curtis, famous photographer of Native North America

1869 Red River Rebellion led by Louis Reil, metis seminarian; Rutgers-Princeton started intercollegiate football; American man-of-war shelled Tlingit towns of Kake and Wrangell; American Museum of Natural History founded in New York

1870 Wodziwob Ghost Dance; Canada assumed Rupert's Land from Hudson Bay Company

1870-1947 Clark Wissler, comparative Plains ethnologist

1871 Congress unilaterally decided to stop making treaties with tribes (sovereign nations) and substituted "agreements"

1871-1901 William Jones, Fox anthropologist educated at Harvard, murdered in the Philippines during fieldwork

1873 Charles Abbott found stone tools on his farm near Trenton and suggested they were ancient

1873-1958 John Swanton, prolific Northwest Coast and Southeast scholar

1874 Olympia (Greece) excavated with funds from German government (to 1880)

1874-1941 Elsie Clews Parsons, comparative Southwesternist, wealthy fieldwork patron, <u>Pueblo Religion</u> (1939)

1874-1961 Berard Haile, Franciscan priest, scholar of Navajo

1875 Copper Chief, Upper Tanana leader in the Yukon, controlled the copper trade and made his sons Tutchone chiefs

1876 First Canadian Indian Act; Defeat of US 7th Calvary of George Custer

1876-1938 Zikala-Sha (Red Bird), Gertrude Bonin, Sioux reformer and short story writer

1876-1960 Alfred Louis Kroeber, Berkeley professor, Handbook of the Indians of California (1925), Cultural and Natural Areas of Native North America (1939)

1879-1933 Knud Rasmussen, Danish-Eskimo Arctic explorer and trader, across Canada to Alaska (1921-24) by dog sled during the Fifth Thule Expedition

1879-1955 Albert Einstein (1921 Nobel Prize)

1880 Bingo devised from tumbula, an Italian lotto game

1800-1940 Alexander Goldenweiser, prolific Iroquianist

1880s Bison herds exterminated

1880-1948 Juan Delores, Tohono O'odam Papago linguist

1881-1955 Arthur C Parker, Seneca archaeologist, museologist, and reformer

1881-1949 John Cooper, Catholic priest, researched Northeast, Plains, and South America

1881-1950 Frank Speck, comparative Algonkianist

1882 American navy ship shelled Tlingit town of Angoon

1883 Wild West Show of William ("Buffalo Bill") Cody (1846-1917)

1883-1984 Ruth Underhill, comparative Americanist, Tohono O'odam, Navajo

1883-1957 Robert Lowie, comparative Americanist, Crow

1884-1951 Canadian Indian Act banned the potlatch and spirit dancing

1884-1936 Mourning Dove (Humishhuma), Christine Quintasket, Colville writer and politician

1884-1939 Edward Sapir, brilliant linguist

1884-1961 John Peabody Harrington, BAE linguist and eccentric

1885 John Killbuck, Delaware and Moravian missionary to Yup'ik Eskimo mission, now a province of the Moravian church; William Whipple Warren, Ojibwe metis, History of the Ojibway People

1885-89 Saint Catharine's Milling v The Queen (Victoria) upheld native rights in Canada

1885-1936 Thomas T Waterman, native languages, place names, and art

1886 Canadian Pacific Railway done; International Phonetic Association founded, approved IPA letters in 1888

1887 General Allotment (Dawes) Act passed, reducing native lands by 100,000 acres

1887-1948 Ruth Benedict, guardian spirit complex, Southwest, California, Plains, and best seller Patterns of Culture (1934)

1887-1959 Edward Gifford, Californianist

1887-1949 Leonard Bloomfield, comparative Algonkian linguist

1888 Akowitz, a Ute, led Richard Wetherill to Cliff Palace and other Mesa Verde ruins

1888-1971 Ella Deloria, Sioux scholar

1888-1977 Robert Spott, Yurok scholar

1888-1935 TE Lawrence (of Arabia)

1890 Wovoka Ghost Dance; Wounded Knee massacre of Big Foot's Miniconju Sioux band; first US census to include Indiens; Daughters of the American Revolution founded

1891-1917 Trans-Siberian Railroad

1893-98 Spanish-American War, US acquired Cuba, Puerto Rico, Guam, and Philippines

1893-1955 Gladys Reichard, prolific researcher of Navajo and Salish

1893-1961 Leslie Spier, Sun Dance, regional trait comparisons

1895-1970 Lazaro Cardenas, Tarascan President of Mexico (1934-40)

1896 Prize by Alfred Nobel (1833-1896), Swedish inventor of dynamite

1897 First producing oil well on Osage lands; 30 September, Robert Perry arrived in New York with six Polar Eskimos, four of whom soon died and had their bones added to the collections of the American Museum of Natural History until reburied in Greenland on 1 August 1993, the orphan Minik became a displaced misfit dying in 1918 influenza epidemic

1898 Alaska-Yukon Gold Rush destroyed Tlingit trade monopoly with inland Athapaskans, 3 Tagish (Kate, Skookum Jim, Tagish Charlie) became millionaires; Edward Tylor became first Professor of Anthropology, after teaching at Oxford since 1883

1898-1993 Ruth Bunzel, Zuni, urban New York

1700s

1700 Hopi massacred neighboring town of Awatobi, which welcomed back Catholic priests after the Spanish Reconquest of New Mexico

1701 French founded Detroit

1702 Cotton Mather, Ecclesiastical History of New England (<u>Magnalia Christi</u>)

1701-13 Queen Anne's War

1705 Account of Virginia by Robert Beverley (c1673-1722)

1707-1778 Carl von Linne (Linnaeus), Swedish, classic biological classification (1735)

1708 Carolina had sold over 10,000 Florida converts from Spanish Catholic missions into slavery in the West Indies

1709 First Russian prisoners sent to Siberia

1709-1747 George William Stellar, Kamchatka Peninsula (and the Northwest Coast) species for Bering expeditions

1710 British conquered Port Royal, Acadians fled to French Louisiana to become Cajuns; Treaty between Iroquois and Pennsylvania kept secret from New York

1711 Mobile becomes capital of Louisiana; war between North Carolina and Tuscarora, who fled to Iroquois (1722) near Buffalo, NY

1711-79 Eleazar Wheelock, Congregationalist minister, used money (11,000 pounds) raised in England by Mohegan Reverend Samson Occum to found Dartmouth College in 1769

1712 Fox (Mesquaki) massacred fleeing Detroit

1712-1778 Jean-Jacques Rousseau, French philosopher

1713-84 Junipero Serra, California Franciscan missions (1769-84)

1713-1784 Denis Diderot, French encyclopedist

1715 Yamasee War against South Carolina

1715-74 Sir William Johnson, British Indian Agent, 1772 account of Iroquois for American Philosophical Society

1716, 22, 29 Natchez Revolts as French massacred, enslaved, or scattered native survivors

1717 Thanadelthur (Slave Woman) died after opening fur trade between Chipewyan and York Factory (HBC); Smallpox inoculation in England

1718 New Orleans founded as capital of Louisiana; London Society of Antiquities

1718-47 David Brainerd, briefly missionary to Delaware

1723-36 Chinese encyclopedia

1727 History of Iroquois by Cadwallader Colden (1688-1776)

1728 Vitus Bering (1681-1741), Dane, explored for Russia to fatal shipwreck

1728? Ch'ing (Manchus) set up modern Tibetan form of government

1728-1779 James Cook, global circumnavigation of 1768-71, 1772-75, and 1776-80, killed in

Hawaii

1730 Fox massacred fleeing Chicago; John and Charles Wesley start Methodism at Oxford

1733 Georgia penal (convict) colony

1737 William Penn's sons arrange "Infamous Walking Purchase" to steal last Delaware lands in their homeland

1738 John Wesley and George Whitfield, "Great Awakening" in Georgia

1738-1822? Nancy Ward, last and youngest Cherokee Beloved Woman (giga')

1739 Moravians to Georgia, then moved Pennsylvania at Nazareth and Bethlehem

1739-1823 William Bartram, toured the South (1773-77, book 1791)

1741-1808 Samuel Kirkland, missionary to Oneida Iroquois

1743-1826 Thomas Jefferson, Minister to France (1785-89), responded to Count Buffon's (1707-88) Natural History (1778, 1786, 1791) about the inferiority of America with his own Notes on the State of Virginia, exposed Mound Builders, and instructions for the Lewis and Clark Expedition (1804-06)

1744 Russian fur traders to Aleutian Islands

1744-48 King George's War

1745-92 Samuel Hearne, explored western Subarctic guided by Matonabbee, a Chipewayan leader

1746 Culloden massacre of Highland Scots by William Augustus, Duke of Cumberland, namesake of flowering sweet william called stinking willie in Scotland

1749-1832 Johann Wolfgang Goethe, German writer

1751 British began New Year on 1 January

1752 Britain adopted Gregorian calendar (3-13 September dropped); Erhardt massacre delayed Moravian Labrador mission

1752-1836 Betsy Ross, US flag

1753 Royal Charter for the British Museum

1754 Albany Conference between English Colonies and Iroquois, a fertile ground for League of the Iroquois and Founding Fathers

1754-63 Seven Years or French and Indian War

1755 Braddock routed at Fort Duquesne (Pittsburgh); Samuel Johnson, English Dictionary (to 1773)

1756-1791 Wolfgang Amadeus Mozart

1758-98 George Vancouver, officer with James Cook, captain of 1790-95 voyage

1758-1801 Brotherton Reservation (NJ)

1759 British conquered Quebec, both generals (Louis Joseph Montcalm, James Wolfe) killed

1760 James MacPherson faked Ossian Tales, Scottish literary classic

1760-1884 Peter DuPonceau, linguist and director of the American Philosophical Society

1761-1849 Albert Gallatin, Secretary of Treasury (1801-13), founder of City University of New York, linguist, 1836 A Synopsis of the Indian Tribes within the United States East of the Rocky Mountains, and in the British and Russian Possessions in North America

1763 Royal Proclamation (7 October) affirmed territorial rights of American natives (still the basis of native rights in Canada); Pontiac Revolt of former native allies of French against British

1767 Jesuits suppressed in Spain

1769 San Diego Mission first to concentrate native peoples and protect the Manila Galleon; between 1769-1823, 21 missions extend to Sonoma; Dartmouth College founded (see 1711)

1769-1859 Alexander von Humboldt, German explorer and scientist

1770 Boston Massacre, Crispus Attikus, native and African, first American martyr; Jens Haven began Moravian mission to Labrador Inuit aided by Merkok and her son Tutauk, to 1926 when its trading posts sold to the Hudson Bay Company

1773 Boston Tea Party, Americans dressed as natives; Jesuit Order dissolved by Pope Clement XIV (to18)

1773-1847 Frances Slocum (Weletawash, Maconaquash), adopted Indiana Delaware and Miami

1774 Shawnee Revolt, Lord Dunmore's War, James Logan's, a Mingo (Ohio Iroquois), entire family massacred and his tragic speech reported by Thomas Jefferson

1775 History of the American Indians by John Adair (c1709-83) compared Southeast tribes with Biblical Hebrews, seeking "lost tribes"

1776 South Carolina and Virginia suppress Cherokee independence

1776-83 American Revolt (Revolution)

1777 Battle of Oriskany split Iroquois, Oneida against Seneca, Cayuga, Onondaga, Mohawk; Chicamauga towns, separatist Cherokee warriors under Dragging-Canoe, son of Little Carpenter

1777-1846 John Pickering, lawyer and linguist, On the Adoption of a Uniform Orthography for Languages of North America (1820) adopted by the American Board of Foreign Missions for its translations

1778 Delaware, in first treaty negotiated by the US founders, proposed a 14th state composed entirely of native tribes led by a Delaware; Captain James Cook visited the Northwest, while exploring the world; his crew brought sea otter pelts to China, sparking sea fur trade

1779 Armies of Generals John Sullivan and James Clinton destroyed Iroquois towns and fields

1780 American Philosophical Society incorporated at Philadelphia from the 1727 incentive of Benjamin Franklin

1782 Massacre of a hundred Christian Delawares by Americans at Gnadenhuetten (Ohio)

1782-1866 Lewis Cass, American politician and Great Lakes scholar

1783 Treaty of Paris ended US Revolution, without mention of native rights

1784 Grand River Reserve (Ontario) established for pro-British Iroquois; Deed of Declaration for Methodism

1784-1846 Isaac McCoy, Baptist missionary in Michigan and Kansas

1785-1863 Jakob Grimm, with brother Wilhelm (1876-1859), folklorists and comparative linguists of Indo-European languages, especially Germanic

1786 Jean Francois La Perouse, French global expedition

1786 Grigori Shelikhov to Alaska

1786-1836 Davy Crockett

1787 Northwest Ordinance provided model for converting the Old Northwest (Ohio and the midwest) into territories and included a clause specifying "The utmost good faith shall always be observed towards the Indians; their land and property shall never be taken from them without their consent; and in their property, rights and liberty, they shall never be invaded or disturbed, unless in justified and lawful wars authorized by Congress ..."

1788-1865 Christian Juergensen Thomsen arranged artifacts in Royal Copenhagen Museum into Stone, Bronze, and Iron Ages, defining European prehistoric archaeology

1789-1851 LJM Deguerre, developed photography

1789-1851 James Fenimore Cooper, American novelist noted for good / bad Indien images

1790 American Army of General Josiah Harmar defeated by natives in Ohio

1791 Army of General Arthur St Claire defeated by natives in Ohio

1792 Captain George Vancouver explored Northwest; Captain Gray of Boston in Columbia River for US claim

1793 Alexander McKenzie overland across Canada to namesake river; Orthodox clergy sent to Alaska; John Thomas Evans searched in vain for Welsh-speaking descendants of Prince Madoc among Missouri River tribes, arriving in 1797 among Mandan

1793-1864 Henry Rowe Schoolcraft, Superintendent of Sault Ste Marie Agency (1832-41), married to metis Jane Johnson, defined totem (from Ojibwe dodem = clan, town), Algic Researches (1839), Oneonta: The Indian in His Wigwam (1844), Historical and Statistical Information Respecting the History, Condition and Prospects of the Indian Tribes of the United States, Collected and Prepared under the Direction of the Bureau of Indian Affair (1851)

1794 Russian Orthodox mission at Kodiak Island; ("Mad") Anthony Wayne, with disciplined American army, defeated confederated tribes in Ohio at Battle of Fallen Timbers; Jay Treaty confirmed Iroquois rights on both sides of US and Canada border

1795 Treaty of Greenville ceded native lands in Ohio

1796-1982 George Catlin, American painter, toured the West (1830-36) and South America (1852-58)

1797-1868 Frederic Baraga, Slovenian priest and bishop, Otchipwe Dictionary (1853) and Grammar (1850)

1797 Comparative native vocabularies published by Benjamin Barton Smith

1799 Sitka founded by Alexander Baranov and 550 baidarka (Aleut watercraft) to intimidate local Tlingit; Russian American Company given fur trade monopoly in Alaska by imperial charter from the Czar, roustabouts called promishleniki oppressed native men into service as hunters; most of the Orthodox clergy of Alaska died in shipwreck; Seneca Handsome Lake had vision to reformulate Iroquois religion; Rosetta Stone found (deciphered in 1821 by Jean Champollion (1790-1832)); Anglican Church Missionary Society founded

1600s

1603 Samuel Champlain to St Lawrence River

1607 Jamestown, Virginia, founded in a bog

1608 Quebec founded; Jesuit state in Paraguay

1609 Henry Hudson, sailing for Holland, claimed the North (later Hudson) River; Samuel Champlain aided Algonkians by shooting Mohawk chiefs, Iroquois begin hostilities to French; Garcilasco de la Vega, History of the Conquest of Peru

1610 Santa Fe founded, when capital moved from San Gabriel; Jesuit Relations, annual reports 1610-1791 from New France; Henry Hudson explored for England, left by his crew to die in Hudson's Bay

1611 King James Bible

1612 John Smith, Map of Virginia

1615 Dutch built trading fort on Hudson River

1616 William Baffin (1584-1622) and Robert Bylot to eastern Arctic

1617 Fifth Dalai Lama began centralizing Tibet

1618 Defenestrations of Prague

1620 New Plymouth founded by Pilgrims

1621 Potatoes to Germany; Nova Scotia and Newfoundland colonized

1622 Powhatan revolt against Virginia, English dead have mouths stuffed with dirt; Papal year began January 1 instead of March 25

1624 Dutch West India Company to Delaware River, Manhattan, and Fort Orange (Albany)

1626 Company of New France incorporated by Cardinal Richelieu

1626-1689 Christina, Queen of Sweden until she became a Catholic (in 1654)

1628-50 Taj Mahal built

1630 Massachusetts Bay

1632 Conquest of Mexico by Bernal Diaz del Castillo

1634 English Catholics to Maryland

1637 Massachusetts and Connecticut massacred Pequots to take over their wampum bead trade, survivors, forbidden their own name, become ("first") Mohegans; Harvard founded

1638 New Sweden founded by Peter Minuet, presuming on goodwill of fellow Protestant colonies who also claimed this territory

1639 Academie Francaise French dictionary (to 1694)

1640 Willem Krieft ordered the Dutch massacre of Delawares at Pavonia (NJ), John Underhill, "butcher of the Pequots" came from Massachusetts to slaughter

1641 Dutch bounty on native scalps

1642 Montreal founded; Maryland defeated Susquehannocks

1643 Roger Williams (1604-1684), A Key into the Language of America (Narraganset); Susquehannocks defeated Maryland with weapons from Sweden

1644 Second Powhatan Revolt in Virginia

1644-1718 William Penn, Quaker pioneer

1645 Sillery, first Jesuit reduction in Canada

1648 John Eliot, "Apostle to the Indians," began his "Red Puritan" missions; George Fox founded Quakers

1648 Semen Dezhnev saw Bering Strait

1649 Iroquois scattered Huron nation

1656 Timucuan revolt in Florida

1656-80 Kateri Tekawitha, Lily of the Mohawks (venerable 1943 by Pius XII, beatified 1980 by Pope John Paul II, canonized by Pope Benedict XVI 2012)

1658 Esopus War with Dutch

1659 Medard Chouart Des Groseilliers and Pierre-Esprit Radisson, brothers-in-law, urge French then English toward monopoly in Hudson's Bay (see 1670); Prussian State Library in Berlin founded

1660 Natick, first Red Puritan town

1661 John Eliot translated Bible into Massachusetts language, first book printed in US

1664 Second Esopus Revolt; Duke of York (later James II) takes Dutch colony renamed New York

1668 Fathers Claude Dablon and Jacques Marquette to Saulte Ste Marie, gateway to the interior of North America; Rupert House, first HBC trading post

1670 Hudson's Bay Company (HBC) charted, expanded from Great Lakes (1670-63) to north central Canada (1764-1821), Yukon (1822-85), and High Arctic

1673 Marquette and Louis Jolliet followed native map to Mississippi River

1676 Nathaniel Bacon Rebellion in Virginia

1677 Covenant Chain founded among Northeast tribes and colonies

1680 Pueblo Revolt, Spanish driven from New Mexico for 12 years

1681 France chartered its own Hudson Bay Company; Pennsylvania given to William Penn (a

Quaker tolerant of other Christian religions) as compensation for his admiral father's loan of money to the king

1681-1746 Joseph Francois Lafitau, Jesuit missionary, compared Hurons with Greeks and Romans (1724)

1682 Rene-Robert Cavelier de La Salle, given French trade monopoly, explored length of Mississippi River

1683 William Penn, General Description of Pennsylvania; Germans to North America

1685 Chinese ports opened to foreign trade

1685-1750 Johann Sebastian Bach

1686-1758 Hans Egede, Greenland Lutheran missionary (1721-36)

1688 Glorious Revolution, William and Mary to English throne

1689 Peter the Great became Czar of Russia

1690 John Locke, Second Treatise on Government, proclaimed "in the beginning all the world was America"

1691 Jacques Le Tort and company left Burlington (NJ) and explored as far as the Missouri River, meeting over 40 tribes; William and Mary College founded

1692 Clan MacDonald massacred at Glencoe

1697 Spanish conquered Tayasal (modern Flores), Itza capital, last Maya kingdom, on an island in Lake Peten

1696 Pierre Le Moyne, Sieur de Iberville, to Fort Maurepas at Biloxi

1697 Barthelemy d'Herbelot compiled Bibliotheque Orientale

1699 Russian New Year changed to 1 January from 1 September

1500s

1500 Newfoundland cod fishery drew ships from all over Europe, land fur trade began

1500-2 Corte-Real voyages naming Labrador end when two of three sons (Miguel, Gaspar, Vasco) of the Portuguese governor of the Azores vanish in eastern Arctic

1515 Bartolome de las Casas became convinced of the evil of enslaving natives

1517 Martin Luther attacked Papal indulgences

1519 Hernando Cortez (1485-1547), invaded Mexico, defeated Aztecs with native allies

1520 Smallpox spread from Cuba to Mexico

1524 Giovanni Verrazano, an Italian working for the French, claimed the Northeast; Alvarado founded Guatemala City

1528 Francis Drake explored California while plundering Manila Galleons

1534 Jacques Cartier wintered with Saint Lawrence Iroquoians

1535 Gonzalo Fernandez de Oviedo y Valdes, first historian of the New World; Don Antonio de Mendoza, first Viceroy of New Spain, commissioned Codex Mendoza from Aztec scribes to explain their culture to Emperor Carlos V, but the manuscript was captured by the French, then owned by famous scholars Andre Thevet, Richard Hakluyt, Samuel Purchas, and John Selden before becoming a treasure of the Bodleian Library at Oxford after 1654

1537 Pope Paul III declared that Indiens had souls to be converted, but African slaves work on mines and fields

1539 Juan Rodriguez Carillo sailed along California coast; Hernando de Soto, army of +900, and diseases invaded La Florida, wandering 4 years through Southeast; Francisco Coronado and army similarly invaded the Southwest

1547-55 Johann von Staden of Hamburg to Tupinamba of Brazil, first captivity narrative

1550-1650s Portuguese galleon, Nao da Macao, traded to Goa, Malacca, Macao, and Nagaskai

1551 Emperor Charles V created National University of Mexico

1559 Spanish Inquisition Index of forbidden books

1564-1815 Manila Galleons traded every six months between Philippines and Acapulco, Mexico; Jacques Le Moyne painted Florida natives

1564-1642 Galileo Galilei

1565 Pedro Menendez de Aviles massacred French Huguenot colony at Fort Caroline, then founded San Augustine in Florida

1567-1615 Don Felipe Guaman Poma de Ayala, First New Chronicle and Good Government explained to the King of Spain about Inka history and colonial injustices in Peru, manuscript in Royal Library in Christianborg Castle, Copenhagen, for 300 years

1570 Jesuit mission massacred on Chesapeake Bay

1572 Saint Bartholemew massacre of 2,000 Protestants in Paris

1573 Laws of Colonization passed in Spain to "protect" natives and assure the monarchy's control of exploration and settlement

1576 Martin Frobisher (1535-94) to eastern Arctic

1579 General History of the Things of New Spain, with Nahuatl text and block prints finished by native scribes trained by Father Bernardino de Sahgun

1580 Buenes Aires refounded after 1535-37 attempt

1581-1656 James Ussher, Archbishop of Armagh, Ireland, calculated the date of the creation from biblical genealogies as BC 4004 (see 1828)

1582 Gregorian calendar introduced (in Papal states, Spain, Portugal, France, Netherlands, Scandinavia), adding 14 days to Julian calendar, England held out until 1752

1585 Sir Walter Raleigh founded colony of Roanoke, which "disappeared," John White painted images of Virginia natives; Exploring eastern Arctic, John Davis (29 July, off Gothab, Greenland) had his orchestra play and officers dance in response to Inuit singing to them from the shore

1588 England, Netherlands, and tempest defeated Spanish Armada; Father Jose de Acosta, Jesuit in Peru, argued that humans came to the New World from Siberia (Tartar), although animal and plant life came off Noah's Ark

1592 Juan de Fuca (Apostolos Valerianos) supposedly explored the Northwest

1593 Henry IV, after 1589 converversion to Catholicism became French king, saying "Paris is worth a Mass"

1593-1682 Thomas Mayhew, founded 1641 Martha's Vineyard mission sustained by 4 generations of his family

1595-1617 Pocahontas

1596 Tomatoes to England from Mexico

1598 Juan de Oñate colonized Rio Grande Pueblos

1400s

1400s Athapaskans (ancestors of Navaho and Apache) to Southwest

1403 Only 3 copies of 22,937 volume Chinese encyclopedia (Yung Lo Ta Tien)

1405-33 Chinese Treasure Fleet, seven voyages with 100 junks, visited the Indian Ocean under the command of Zheng He, a eunuch born Na Ho, a Muslim in Yunnan

1409 Ganden Monastery founded by Gelugpa sect of Dalai Lama

1415 John Hus burned for heresy

1430 Itzcoatl orders the destruction of the records of Tenochtitan

1431 English burned Joan of Arc (Jeanne d'Arc) as a witch; Ankor Wat in Cambodia abandoned

1439 Prince Henry the Navigator founded naval institute at Sagres on Portugese coast to amass information for ocean exploration

1451-1512 Amerigo Vespucci, American explorer and booster

1453 Constantinople fell to Moslems

1454 Johannes Guttenberg perfected moveable type for printing from a 1440 prototype

1472 Dante's <u>Divine Comedy</u> printed (see 1265); John and Sebastian Cabot (Caboto in Italian) explored for England

1473-1543 Nicolas Copernicus, Polish astronomer of helocentrism (sun-centered universe)

1474 William Caxton printed first book in English

1474-1566 Bartolome de Las Casas, American apostle (see 1515)

1475-1541 Francisco Pizarro, conqueror of Peru

1478-1535 Thomas More, <u>Utopia</u> (1516)

1483-1546 Martin Luther (95 Theses, 1517)

1486 Dedication of Huitzilopochtli temple in center of Tenochtitlan, Aztec capital

1490-1577? Alvar Nuñez Cabeza de Vaca, treasurer of doomed Navareaz expedition, wandered with 3 others through the US South (1527 - 1537)

1490s Spain colonized Canary Islands (native Guanche Berbers slaughtered), staging area for exploration across the Atlantic

1491-1556 Ignatius Loyola, founder of the Jesuits

1491-1557 Jacques Cartier, French explorer, first voyage in 1534

1492 Columbus entered Caribbean; Jews expelled from Spain after Moors defeated

1493 Pope Alexander VI "gave" Americas to Spanish Crown

1495 Syphilis epidemic spread from Naples throughout Europe

1496 Ramon Pane, monk on Second Columbus voyage, described the New World

1497 John Caboto to north Atlantic coast (see 1472)

1498 Bartholomew Columbus census of half of Hispaniola listed 1,100,00 natives (all extinct a few decades later)

1300s

1300-2300 Burial Mound II (Hopewell) in Eastern North America

1300? Reincarnation institutionalized in Tibet

1305 Edward I set the size of an English yard and acre

1305-78 Papal See at Avignon in France "Babylonian Captivity"

1317 France adopted Salic Law forbidding royal women from the throne

1325 Tenochtitlan, Aztec capital; 500 ancestral Arikara massacred at Crow Creek, a South Dakota tributary of the Missouri River

1332-1406 Ibn Khaldun, Arab historian

1334-85 Kan-ami, Japanese Noh performer

1338-1453 Hundred Years War between England and France

1340?-1400 Chaucer, <u>Canterbury Tales</u>

1343 Doge Palace in Venice began

1348 Edward III created Order of the Garter (motto in French: Evil to him who thinks evil)

1348-51 Black Death (Bubonic Plague) killed off over a fourth of Europe

1351 Eclipse probably coincided with the founding of the League of the Iroquois

1365 Vienna University founded

1368-1644 Ming Dynasty in China

1391 First Dalai Lama

1200s

1200 Chichen Itza abandoned

1200-1540 Temple Mound II in Eastern North America (to present for some tribes despite population devastation)

1202 Fourth Crusade (to 1204); Court jesters introduced

1206 Temujin took the name Genghis Khan

1209 Cambridge University founded

1210 St Francis founded Franciscans; Mongols began conquest of China

1212 Children's Crusade, most sold into slavery

1215 Magna Carta

1217-22 Fifth Crusade, against Egypt

1240 Alexander Nevsky defeated Swedish threat to Russia; Mongols burned Kiev; Sun Diata, Mande King, destroyed Kumbi capital in Ghana

1249 Sakya Pandit became Viceroy of Tibet under Mongols

1250 Mayapan founded (to 1451); Numic language expansion throughout the Basin; Hats fashionable in Europe

1252 Inquisition allowed the use instruments of torture

1253-1325 Amir Khusram, composer of ragas, inventor of sitar, in India

1265-1321 Dante Alighieri banished from Florence (1301-21), Divine Comedy (composed 1307-21, published 1472)

1266-1337 Giotto di Bondone, Italian fresco painter first to use perspective

1271-95 Marco Polo, with his father and uncle, visited China

1273 Thomas Aquinas (1225-1274), Summa Theologica

1280? First block printed books in Tibet

1283 England conquered Wales

1289 John of Montecorvino made Archbishop of Beijing (Peking)

1292 Scottish coronation stone moved from Scone to Westminster

1200s Stone statues on Easter Island

1100s

1132 Texcoco founded

1141 Empress Matilda driven from England, her cousin-foe Stephen returned to the throne

1147 Geoffrey of Monmouth, History of the English Kings

1150 Paris University

1151 End of Toltec Empire in Mexico

1167 Oxford University

1170 Thomas a Becket murdered at the altar of Canterbury Cathedral

1171 Henry II annexed Ireland

1182 Philip II banished Jews from France

1189 Third Crusade (to 1192)

1192 Minamoto Yoritomo, first Shogun of Japan, until 1868 Meiji Restoration of Emperor

1000s

1000-1600 Late Woodland in eastern North America

1000 Thule ancestors of Eskimo-Inuit developed along Bering Straits

1000 L'Anse au Meadow (Newfoundland) colonized by Vikings; Chinese perfected gunpowder; Tiahuanaco dominated Andes

1016-42 Danes ruled England

1021 Caliph al-Hakim declared himself divine and founded the Druse sect

1040 MacBeth defeated Duncan to become King of Scotland

1045-99 El Cid (Rodrigo Diaz), Spanish hero

1054 Eastern Orthodox Church independent from Roman Catholic Church

1057 Malcolm defeated MacBeth, then Lulach in 1058, to become King of Scotland

1059 Only cardinals can elect the Pope

1066 Battle of Hastings, Normans of William (the Conqueror) defeated British forces of Harold, weeks after he had defeated his brother Tostig and Norwegian invaders

1073 Sakya Monastery in Tibet

1086 Domesday Book, an inventory of England finished for the Norman crown

1096 First Crusade (of eight)

1098-1150 Over 300 Cistercian monasteries cleared forests and drained marshes

900s

900-1520 Postclassic in Mesoamerica

900 Alfonso II, King of Castile, expulsed Moors from Spain (until 1492); Medical school in Salerno; Toltecs at Tula (to 1110)

904 Pope Sergius III (to 911) elected, his mistress Marozia was mother of John XI, aunt of John XIII, and grandmother of Benedict VI

929 King Wenceslas of Bohemia martyred, as was his mother Ludmilla

932 Chinese began woodblock printed books

938 Beijing (Peking) founded

939 Ngo Quyen became first king of Dai Viet (Viet Nam)

962 Saint Bernard founded hospice in the Alps

965 Saint Dunstan imposed celibacy on English clergy

978 Chinese began (to 984) encyclopedia of 1000 volumes

981 Eric the Red to Greenland

993 Canonization of saints began

988 Prince Vladimir of Kiev converted to Orthodoxy

800s

800 (Christmas Day) Charlemagne (771-814) crowned Holy Roman Emperor of the West in Rome by Pope Leo III

813 School of Astronomy in Baghdad

814 Arabs adopted numbers (0-9) from India

826 King Harold of Denmark converted

830 Louis the Pious destroyed compilation of German epics by Charlemagne, his father

840 Danes founded Dublin and Limerick in Ireland

844 Scotland unified by Kenneth McAlpine

850 Zimbabwe built; German Jews developed Yiddish

860s Great Houses (pueblo apartments) in Chaco Canyon;

861 Vikings to Iceland

862 Vikings to Novgorod, begin Russian unification

863 Saints Cyril and Methodius began conversion of Russia, devised Cyrillic alphabet

871-99 Alfred, King of Wessex

879 Last date at Tikal

889 Last date at Washaktun, Seibal, other Maya cities

898 Last date at Chichen Itza

700s

700-1200 Temple Mound I in Eastern North America

700 Psalms first translated into Anglo-Saxon English; Easter eggs popularized

709 Lady Shok (died 749), wife of Shield Jaguar, offered blood from her tongue

712 <u>Kojiki</u> history of Japan

725 Copts (Egyptian Christians) revolted against Arabs, again in 739, 767-72; Saint Boniface (Wynfrith, an Anglo-Saxon, martyred 755) chopped down the Doner oak to force Germanic conversions he began in 716

716 Byzantine Emperor an iconoclast (opposed to images in churches), excommunicated in 730

731 Venerable Bede, <u>History of the English Church</u>

738 King 18 Rabbit of Copan sacrificed by Cauac-Sky of Quirigua

750s Teotihuacan abandoned; Hanlin Academy of Chinese arts and sciences founded

756 Papal States founded in Italy

757-96 Offa, King of Mercia and of England (in 779), built dike to keep out the Welsh

765 Japanese books with pictures

779 First major Tibetan monastery

780 Empress Irene, Byzantine ruler (to 802), restored the use of statues in churches

787 Danish Vikings invaded England; Council of Nicaea resumed use of images in churches

792 Legendary debate between Buddhisms of China or India in Tibet, won by Indic Mahayanas

794 Japanese capital moved from Nara to Kyoto (Heian)

600s

600? First Yarlung dynasty king in Tibet

603-83 Pakal (Sun Shield), King of Palenque (Maya)

606 Detailed examinations for Chinese civil servants

610 Vision of Mohammed

613 Brunhild, daughter of the Visigoth king and wife of Sigebert, Merovingian prince, dragged to death behind a wild horse by order of Pepin, founder of Carolingian kingdom of the Franks

620 Vikings invaded Ireland

622 Hegira, Mohammed fled Mecca to Yathrib (now Medina), first year of Moslem calendar

624 Buddhism established in Japan

631 Maya "star war" strategy

635 Catholic missionaries to China

638 Moslems conquered Jerusalem

639-42 Moslems conquered Egypt

641 Buddhism and writing to Tibet from China

645 Sutton Hoo ship burial; Nestorian Christians settled in China

664 Council of Whitby replaced Celtic Church with Roman Catholic forms

669 Theodore of Tarsus, a Greek monk, became Archbishop of Canterbury and reformed the English Church

675 Temple of the Inscriptions at Palenque

500s

529 Emperor closed School of Philosophy in Athens after 1000 years, professors and students dispersed throughout Persia and Syria

550 Saint David brought Christianity to Wales

552 Buddhism to Japan

563 Saint Columba founded monastery on Isle of Iona

570-632 Mohammed

400s

407 Romans abandoned England; First Mongol Empire

410 Goths, led by Alaric, sacked Rome

432 Saint Patrick to Ireland, where he had been a captive

450 Heroditus, "father of written history," visited Egypt

458-499 Hwui Shan, Afghan monk, left China and toured the Americas

476 Goths under Odovacar collapsed the Western Roman Empire

481-511   Clovis, King of the Franks, converted to Christianity (496), his four sons inherited power equally

300s

3-900 Classic period in Mesoamerica

313 Edict of Milan instituted tolerance of Christianity

326 Saint Helena (feast day 18 August), mother of Constantine, Roman Emperor, toured the Holy Land to locae places of Christ's life

330 Constantinople made capital of Roman Empire

354-430 Saint Augustine

372 Buddhism introduced into Korea

378 Tikal conquered Washaktun; Maya Tlaloc War system

200s

230 Sujin, first Emperor of Japan

100s

122 Hadrian's Wall built across northern England

166 Marcus Aurelius, Roman Emperor and philosopher, sent gifts to the Chinese Emperor, Huan Ti; Plague throughout the Roman Empire

0

0 Teotihuacan dominated Valley of Mexico; Ipiutak, Alaska, traded with Siberia

25 Later Han Dynasty (to 220)

29   Two Trung (Chong) sisters (Trac, Nhi) led revolt that removed Chinese overlords from present Viet Nam

30 Christ (born about 5 BC) crucified

43 Romans invaded Britain

51 Caractacus, captured British warrior, paraded in Rome dyed blue with woad

58 Mi Ti introduced Buddhism into China

70 Jews Revolt; Temple destroyed except for Wailing Wall, Diaspora of Jews throughout North Africa and Europe

77 Rome conquered Britain (to 407)

79 Vesuvius, near Naples, erupted and destroyed Pompeii, Stabiae, and Herculaneum

(Earlier Dates computed as 2000 + BC date)

2000

2000-now   Southwestern Co-traditions in US (Mogollon-Tanoans, Anasazi-Pueblos, Hohokan-Pimans, Hakatayan-Yumans)

2000-1000 Middle Woodland in eastern North America

2045   Julius Caesar (murdered 44 BC on the Ides of 15 March) became dictator of Rome, instituted Julian Calendar

2047 Alexandrian Library destroyed

2069-30 Cleopatra

2100 Lowland Maya temples and dated monuments

2120 First deciphered Maya date

2214 Great Wall of China begun

2221 Shih Huang Ti of Ch'in Dynasty styled First Chinese Emperor

2300-1700 Late Preclassic of Mesoamerica

2336-323 Alexander the Great, generals divided his empire: Ptolemy took Egypt, Seleucus took Syria, and Antigonus and Demetrius took Greece; His mother Olympias murdered for her tyranny

2347-183 Hannibal of Carthage (at the gates of Rome, 217)

2350 Sumerian Empire

2370 Huns to Europe

2400 Olmecs flourished

2427-347 Plato

2460 Age of Pericles in Athens

2469-399 Socrates, condemned to drink poison hemlock for heretical teaching corrupting youth

2477 Athens flourished

2500 Bantu expansion across Central Africa

2509 Traditional date of the founding of the Roman Republic

2551-2497 Confucius (K'ung Fu-tzu)

2563 Buddha (Prince Siddhartha Gautama) born at Lumbini (now Nepal)

2600 Tikal settled

2605-561 Nebuchadnezzar II, king of Babylon, sacked Jerusalem (2586), enslaved Jews in "Babylonian Captivity," built Hanging Gardens (2580); Edict (2538) of Cyrus the Great allowed some Jews to return to Judah

2621 Dracon imposed severe laws on Athens

2689 Assyrians destroyed Babylon

2753 Mythic founding of Rome by Romulus and Remus, after being suckled by a she-wolf

2776 First Olympic Games in Greece

2800 Traditional date for Homer's Iliad and Odyssey

2814 Carthage founded

2953 Dedication of Temple at Jerusalem

2994 Teutons moved west toward Rhine River

3000

3000 Olmec peak; David captured Jerusalem and made it capital of Israel; Dorset ancestors of Eskimo-Inuit occupied the Arctic

3000-2300 Burial Mound I (Adena) in Eastern North America

3000-2300 Middle Preclassic in Mesoamerica

3000-2000 Early Woodland in Eastern North America

3020 Saul, King of Israel

3100 First Chinese dictionary

3193 Troy destroyed by Greeks

3250 Exodus of Jews from Egypt

3300 Rock Temples at Abu Simbel, honoring Ramses II The Great

3379 Amenhotep IV became Akhenaton, worship of Aton = Sun as only god

3400 Poverty Point (Louisiana), a complex of octagonal earthworks and mounds began

3570 New Kingdom in Egypt

3728 Hammurabi the Great, law giver

3860 Stonehenge began

3830 First Dynasty of Babylonian kings

3950 Ur Empire ended

4000

4-3000 Early Preclassic in Mesoamerica; Late Archaic in Eastern America

4000 Europe Bronze Age; Arctic Small Tool tradition

4200 Jomon complex in Japan

4500 Knossos founded by Minoans on Crete (destroyed 3400); Indus Valley cities

4800 Old Kingdom of Egypt

5000

5000 Villages began in Tehuacan Valley; Phoenician traders; Northwest Coast exposed, maritime cultures began

5100 First Dynasty of Egypt

5113 13 August 3114 BC, the day called 4 Ahaw 8 Kumk'u, starting date for creation of Maya universe and the continuous Long Count of their calendar

5760 Jewish calendar began (3760 BC)

6000

6000 Canadian Shield exposed by glacial retreat

7000 Maize domestication began in Mexico; Sumerians; Jericho walled; England cut off as an island

7000-3000 Middle Archaic in Eastern North America (to 2000 in Plains)

9000-7000 American Early Archaic, mixed economy of hunting, fishing, and plant harvesting (tending but no farming)

9,000 Dog burials

10,000 Farming began in Middle East

10-8,000 Folsom complex

11,000 Woven sandals, Fort Rock Cave, Oregon

12-7000 Old Cordilleran Archaic in western North America

15-10,000 Beringia open, grassy plain between Siberia and Alaska

13-10,000 Clovis complex

15,000 Desert Tradition in arid western North America (to present among Nevada and Utah tribes in ritual contexts)

18,000 Genetic date for human arrival in the Americas

?50-10,000 Paleo-Indiens, Asiatic big game hunters, entered Americas

SIMILARITIES:
Native America

The Americas are a very special place because humans have developed here in ways unknown to the rest of the world, responding to local and regional climates, habitats, terrains, and fellow beings.

Yet, like all humans, natives shared basic concepts and relationships from which to build in varied ways. While these ancient human+land interactions are most susceptible to archaeological research, they continue to color and mold contemporary relations with the landscape. They survive, sometimes subtly, in language use, rituals, and behaviors. Indeed, Americanists have worked long and hard to amass just such information about Native America, particularly in terms of obvious details of technology and food economy. Yet, because few speak native languages or correctly record them, they have dealt mostly with such surface tangibles, avoiding the crucial but unseen concepts which underlie these outward manifestations.

Any of these obvious features have, of course, been given form, substance, and coherence by the over-all importance of engendering, the projection of Mind~Man~Woman onto the conditioning of enjoyment, content, and context for all events. Regardless of specific details, in order for any aspect of the concrete world to have meaningful significance, it must be engaged by gender, filtered through existing concepts, and given import within a culturally defined worldview. Wrongfully called looking toward the past, it is actually using the past to make sense of the future. Nylon nets and motor boats now do the work of handwoven nettle twine and canoes, but fishers still begin and end by thanking the fish for providing food.

Hence, then as now, Native America was profoundly anthropocentric. Most often these human genders have attributes such that Mind is inclosive, Man is inclusive, and Woman is exclusive, but Yuchi, Keres, and Kootenay provide telling counter examples. Similarly, in the universal tension between exclusive Human (own) Culture and inclusive (other) Nature, the overarching Mind is also their ultimate inclosive mediator.

Often women symbolize Nature because their own physiological cycle of menstruation and gestation is recognized to coincide with phases of the moon and rhythms of the tides, and thus closer to or more integrated into Nature than men.

While the enormously complex symbolism of menstrual blood and pubic hair in Native America has been slighted, suffice it to say that female puberty rites and monthly seclusion were widespread, enforcing a belief that menstrual blood was extremely dangerous, to men if not also to the rest of the world. It, along with corpse bones and ghost powder, is used in powerful sorcery and counter-magic in awesome rites dealing with cosmic order. Tohono O'odam Papago warn that contact with a menstruant will cause deer to avoid hunters, all-powerful crystals that are the insignia of a shaman to rot, and tobacco plants to shrivel up.[77]

Overall, depending on local conditions, recognized gender emanations conform to variable axial tensions used to articulate distinct cultures. While over a dozen tensions have been recorded for all human cultures, the human metaphor most informs other echos in the Americas, because, after all, it was and is humans who make these recognitions. Even the spirits, still the original owners of America, have human form in their own holy homes.

Thus, while all cultures, at some level, regard the same anthropocentric echo as universal,

77. Ruth Underhill 1939: 163.

each expresses it as ideas projected onto local images and objects, as concrete manifestations of an underlying concept, much as items in a medicine bundle serve to harness and represent abstract cosmic forces. Thus Crow Rock Bundles include a pair that over time produces pebbles. Similarly, neighboring cultures often reverse the inclusive/exclusive polarities of genders, as was done by Iroquois and Delaware of the Northeast, or Tewa and Keres Pueblos of New Mexico. All of these factors add to the incredible dazzle of details for which Americanists are both famous and infamous.

What must never be lost sight of, then, is that the Americas reflect only a portion of the human condition. To better understand humans, natives must be understood both in terms of themselves and by comparison with other peoples and cultures. Indeed, in other modalities, gender was and is equally important in the culture of India, where the Hindu meditation mantra "OM" is believe to represent unity because the "O" is considered in some sects to be open and feminine, while the "M" is closed and masculine. Moreover, only men should recite this mantra.

Similar engendered associations and restrictions were also vital to upholding life in the Americas, but lacking nation states, each culture, allowing for its political organization from band to chiefdom, was free to express itself as time, place, neighbors, and spirits allowed.

Just before 1900, the American government began to come to terms with a national "inferiority complex" concerning its lack of "history" when compared with Europe and Asia. As a young nation state, Americans lacked "both an ancient history and a cultural tradition rich in art, architecture, or literature."[78] Its response was a "scenic nationalism" that regarded majestic landscapes as compensation for these deficiencies. As "earth monuments" to American greatness and as future inspirations, the Yosemite Valley of California and Yellowstone in Wyoming were set aside as National Parks, rivaling in grandeur the ancient monuments of Europe (and Asia). In deciding to set these extremely rugged and remote places apart, the government also marked them as worthless for economic exploitation.

The irony in all this legislation, of course, was its immigrant white-only mindset. Certainly, in Cahokia, Chaco Canyon, Abbott Farm, the Mandan Okeepa, Pawnee animal lodges, Blue Lake, and Big Horn Medicine Wheel, as well as countless sacred shrines across the continent, Native America matched in time depth and effort the impressive cultural and religious feats of Europe (and of Asia). Yet, because they seemed so "naturally" a part of the landscape, as well as having been produced by "other" ancestors, settlers refused to see them as monuments to comprehensive human history, art, or civilization. If recognized at all, regard was distorted by misconceptions about non-native races of Mound Builders or other preposterous originators, who now linger on only in the Book of Mormon. By settler consensus, the goal of European colonization was "to get the land subdued and the wilde nature out of it," that is, remove every and any thing indigenous, including these ancient human beings and their works.[79]

Yet what makes America distinctive in the world community was and is its native inhabitants. They settled here first and they learned to know the land better than anyone who came, who destroyed much more than they ever learned. Indeed, what distinguishes United States law from that of other nation states is the existence of legally binding treaties with tribes

78. Richard White, "It's Your Misfortune and None of My Own", A New History of the American West 1991: 410.
79. Walter Crockett, a settler on Whidby Island in Puget Sound, wrote these incisive words 15 October 1853, See Richard White, Land Use, Environment, and Social Change, The Shaping of Island County, Washington 1980: 35.

on reservations. What sets apart the regional style of the Southwest is its native character, still strong after half a millennia of presures by Spanish and other Europeans.

More than their monuments, Indiens also deserve to be known for their brilliant ideas in the solution of very human concerns and problems, as expressed particularly in their rituals. A key feature of these public events was that there was literally something for everyone, as the Okeepa makes all too clear. The more practical and pragmatic members were satisfied by being involved in doing something, while those usually oblivious could be attracted by the dazzle of costumes, aromas, and feats of appearing or disappearing. Some spectators could be entertained by watching their relatives and friends take on new personas. Those more mystical could look beyond the obvious to be inspired by glimpses of divinity. Because these rituals involved so much of the exterior, and were often held outdoors, they could be widely seen and experienced, but, always, for some, their consequences included much that was interior.

Today, tribes, regardless of their origins, survive because they know and appreciate such virtues of tradition and community, something older and venerable for guiding present communal actions according to past understandings. Though land was taken away and religions oppressed, natives maintain their position of moral superiority because they knew how to defer to age-old practices, and to use them in new, creative, and exciting ways. That is what tradition is about, keeping together a close, caring, and continuing community linked from the past into the future.

If America is to survive, it too must learn similarly to delight in diversity, to honor landforms, and to defer to the elders, and, especially, to never again deny other realities. As a first step, the thousands of years of native civilizations in the Americas must receive their due. Hero Twins, Hare, Raven, and Coyote deserve to be as well known as St. Paul of Tarsus because all worked to make a better world.

After all, to paraphrase Shakespeare, "The measure of all things is human" in multiple emanations and incarnations, whether biological, spatial, metaphorical, or spiritual.

ABBREVIATIONS USED FOR SERIALS

AA American Antiquarian
AAA American Antiquity
AA-M Memoirs Of the Society for American Archaeology
AAA American Anthropologist
AAA-M Memoirs of the American Anthropological Association
ABC Anthropology in British Columbia
AE American Ethnologist
AES-M Memoirs of the American Ethnological Society
   -P Proceedings of the American Ethnological Society
AL Anthropological Linguistics
AMNH-AP Anthropological Papers of the American Museum of Natural History
An Anthropos
APS-P Proceedings of the American Philosophical Society
  -T Transactions of the American Philosophical Society
AR Anthropological Records
BAAS Reports of the British Academy for the Advancement of Science
BAE-AP Anthropological Papers of the Bureau of American Ethnology
   -AR Annual Report of the Bureau of American Ethnology
   -B Bulletins of the Bureau of American Ethnology
CA Current Anthropology
CUCA Columbia University Contributions to Anthropology
E Ethnology
EH Ethnohistory
En Ethnos
FMNH-AS Anthropological Series of the Field Museum Of Natural History
ICA Selected Papers of the Annual International Congress of Americanists
IJAL International Journal of American Linguistics
IURC Publications of the Indiana University Research Center In Anthropology, Folklore,
   and Linguistics
JAF Journal of American Folklore
JAR(SWJA) Journal of Anthropological Research, formerly SWJA
M Man
MAI-INM Museum of the American Indian, Heye Foundation, Indian Notes and
   Monographs
MS Mercury Series, National Museum of Canada
NARN Northwest Anthropological Research Notes (now JONA)
PA Plains Anthropologist
PP Papers of the Peabody Museum of Harvard University
SMC Smithsonian Miscellaneous Collections
SWJA Southwestern Journal of Anthropology, now JAR
UA-P Anthropological Papers of the University of Alaska
UA-AP Anthropological Papers of the University of Arizona
UC-PAE University of California Publications in American Archaeology and Ethnology

UNM-AP Anthropological Papers of the University of New Mexico
UM-AP Anthropological Papers of the Museum of Anthropology of the University of
 Michigan
UW-AP Anthropological Papers of the University of Washington
VFPA Viking Fund Publications in Anthropology
YUPA Yale University Publications in Anthropology

BIBLIOGRAPHY

Adair, James. 1930. History of the American Indians. New York: Promontory Press.
 508pp. [1775].

Allen, Grover. 1920. Dogs of the American Aborigines. Museum of Comparative
 Zoology of Harvard, Bulletin 63: 429-517.

Anonymous. 1930. Index to Volumes 1 to 40 of the Journal of American Folklore. JAF-
 M 14. 106pp.

Asher, Brad. 1995. A Shaman-killing Case on Puget Sound, 1873-1874. American Law
 and Salish Culture. Pacific Northwest Quarterly 86 (1): 17-24. Winter 1994/95.

Bailey, Garrick A, ed. 1995. The Osage and the Invisible World. From the works of
 Francis La Flesche. Norman: University of Oklahoma Press.

Balikci, Asen. 1970. The Netsilik Eskimo. New York: Natural History Press. 264pp.

Ballard, W. L. 1975. Aspects of Yuchi Morpho-phonology. pp. 163-187 in Crawford,
 ed.
 1978. The Yuchi Green Corn Ceremonial: Form and Meaning. University of
 California, Los Angeles, American Indian Studies Center.

Barnett, Homer. 1953. Innovation: The Basis of Cultural Change. New York: McGraw-
 Hill. 462pp.

Barry, Barry. 1972. The Beginning of the West: Annals of the Kansas Gateway to the
 American West, 1540-1854. Topeka: Kansas State Historical Society.

Basso, Keith. 1996. Wisdom Sits In Places. Landscape and Language among the
 Western Apache. Albuquerque: University of New Mexico Press.

Bauxar, J. Joseph. 1957. "Yuchi Ethno-Archaeology." EH 4 (3): 279-301, 4 (4):369-
 464.

Bean, Lowell John. 1974. Mukat's People: The Cahuilla Indians of Southern California.
 Berkeley: University of California Press. 201pp.

Bean, Lowell, and Florence Shipek. 1978. Luiseño. California. Robert Heizer, ed.
 Handbook of North American Indians 8: 550-563.

Benedict, Ruth Fulton. 1923. The Concept of the Guardian Spirit in North America.
 AAA-M 29. 97pp.
 1960. Patterns of Culture. New York: Mentor Books. 254pp. [1934].

Berger, Peter and Thomas Luckman. 1966. The Social Construction of Reality: A
 Treatise in the Sociology of Knowledge. Garden City: Doubleday. 219pp.

Berlin, Isiah. 1953. The Hedgehog and the Fox: An Essay on Tolstoy's View of History.
 London: Weidenfeld and Nicolson. 86pp.

Bharati, Agehananda. 1965. The Tantric Tradition. London: Rider and Co. 350pp.

Bicchieri, Marco. 1972. Hunters and Gatherers Today: A Socio-Economic Study of

168

Eleven Such Cultures in the Twentieth Century. New York: Holt, Rinehart, and Winston. 494pp.

Bidney, David. 1967. Theoretical Anthropology. New York: Schocken Books. 528pp. [1953].

Black, Lydia. 1988. The Story of Russian America. pp. 70-82 in Crossroads of Continents. Cultures of Siberia and Alaska. William Fitzhugh and Aron Crowell, eds. Smithsonian Institution Press.

Black Hawk. 1964. Black Hawk: An Autobiography. Urbana: University of Illinois Press.

Blodgett, Harold. 1935. Samson Occom. Dartmouth: Manuscript Series 3. 230pp.

Boas, Franz. 1916. Tsimshian Mythology. BAE-AR 31: 29-1037.

    1918. Kutenai Tales. BAE-B 59. 387pp.

Boas, Franz and others. 1915. Anthropology in North America. New York: G.E. Stechert and Co. 378pp.

    1916. "Phonetic Transcription of Indian Languages: Report of Committee of American Anthropological Association. SMC 66 (6): 1-15.

Bonneyea, Biren. 1933. General Index to Annual Reports 1-48 of the Bureau of American Ethnology. BAE-AR 48.

Bourke, John. 1891. Scatological Rites of All Nations. A Dissertation upon the Employment of Excrementitious Remedial Agents in Religion, Therapeutics, Divination, Witchcraft, Love-Philters, etc., in all Parts of the Globe. Washington: W.H. Lowdermilk and Co. 496pp.

Bowers, Alfred. 1950. Mandan Social and Ceremonial Organization. University of Chicago Press. 407pp.

    1965. Hidatsa Social and Ceremonial Organization. BAE-B 194. 528pp.

Brasser, Ted. 1974. Riding On The Frontier's Crest: Mahican Indian Culture and Culture Change. MS 13. 91pp.

Brinton, Daniel. 1896. "Left-Handedness In North American Aborginal Art. AAA 09 (5): 175-181.

    1901. The American Race. Philadelphia: David McKay. 392pp.

Brown, Joseph Epes and Black Elk. 1971. The Sacred Pipe: Black Elk's Account of the Seven Rites of the Oglala Sioux. London: Penguin Books. 144pp. [1953]

Brown, Paula and Georgeda Buchbinder, eds. 1976. Man and Woman in the New Guinea Highlands. AAA-SP 8. 108pp.

Buckley, Thomas, and Alma Gottlieb. 1988. Blood Magic. The Anthropology of Menstruation. University of California Press.

Buckstaff, Ralph. 1927. "Stars and Constellations of a Pawnee Sky Map." AAA 29 ():279-285.

Bunzel, Ruth. 1932. Introduction to Zuni Ceremonialism. BAE-AR 47: 469-544.

Burt, Jesse and Robert Ferguson. 1973. Indians of the Southeast: Then and Now. Nashville: Abingdon Press. 304pp.

Calloway, Colin G. 1987. Crown and Calumet. British-Indian Relations, 1783-1815. Norman: University of Oklahoma Press. 345pp.

Calloway, Colin G., ed. 1988. New Directions in American Indian History. Norman: University of Oklahoma Press. 262pp.

Carpenter, Edmund. 1973. Eskimo Realities. New York: Holt, Rinehart, and Winston. 224pp.

Catlin, George. 1976. <u>O-KEE-PA</u>. A Religious Ceremony and Other Customs of the Mandans. Lincoln: University of Nebraska Press. [1867].

Chafe, Wallace. 1962. "Estimates Regarding the Present Speakers of North American Indian Languages." IJAL 28 (3): 162-171.

    1965. Corrected Estimates. IJAL 31 (4): 345-346

Chamberlain, Alexander. 1892. "Report on the Kootenay Indians of South-Eastern British Columbia." pp. 549-615 in Report of the British Association For the Advancement of Science Meeting in Edinburgh.

Chamberlin, Ralph. 1908. "Animal Names and Anatomical Terms of the Gosiute Indians." Proceedings of the Academy of Natural Sciences of Philadelphia.

    1911. "The Ethno-botany of the Gosiute Indians of Utah." AAA-M 2 (5): 331-405.

    1913. "Place and Personal Names of the Gosiute Indians of Utah. APS-P 52 (208): 1-20.

Chamberlin, Von Del. 1982. <u>When Stars Came Down to Earth</u>. Ballena Press.

Cobb, John. 1917. Pacific Salmon Fisheries. Department of Commerce: Bureau of Fisheries, Document 839. 255pp.

Cohen, Felix. 1942. <u>Handbook of Federal Indian Law</u>. Albuquerque: University of New Mexico Press. 662pp.

Cole, Douglas. 1973. "The Origins of Canadian Anthropology, 1850-1910." Journal of Canadian Studies 8:33-45.

Collier, John. 1963. <u>Indians of the Americas</u>. New York: Mentor Books. 191pp. [1947].

Crocker, Christopher. 1973. "Ritual and the Development of Social Structure: Liminality and Inversion." pp. 47-86 in <u>The Roots of Ritual</u>. James Shaughnessy, ed. Grand Rapids, Michigan: Wm. B. Eerdmans Publishing Co. 251pp.

Crosby, Alfred. 1972. <u>The Columbian Exchange</u>: Biological and Cultural Consequences of 1492. Westport, Connecticut: Greenwood Publishing Co. Contributions in American Studies 2. 268pp.

Crawford, James. 1973. "Yuchi Phonology." IJAL 39: 173-79.

    1975. <u>Studies in Southeastern Indian Languages</u>. University of Georgia Press.

    ms. A Yuchi Conversation.

Crowe, Keith J. 1991. <u>A History of the Original People of Northern Canada</u>. Montreal: McGill-Queen's University Press.

Culin, Stewart. 1903. <u>Games of the North American Indians</u>. BAE-AR 24.

Curtis, Edward. 1924+. <u>The North American Indian</u>. Norwood: Plimpton Press. 20 volumes.

Damas, David, ed. 1984. <u>Arctic</u>. Handbook of North American Indians 5: 511-513.

Davis, Edward. 1920. The Papago Ceremony of the Vikita. MAI-INM 3 (4): 157-177.

d'Azevedo, Warren, ed. 1967. <u>The Current Status of Anthropological Research in the Great Basin</u>: 1966. Reno: Desert Research Institute. 379pp.

    1986. <u>Great Basin</u>. Handbook of North American Indians 11. 852pp.

De Peyster, Arent. 1908. Collections of the State Historical Society of Wisconsin 18: 387-388.

Deloria, Ella Cara. <u>Waterlily</u>. Lincoln: University of Nebraska Press. 244pp.

Densmore, Frances. 1953. The Belief of the Indian in a Connection Between Song and the Supernatural. BAE-B 151 (37): 217-223.

Dent, Frederick. 1979. Federal and State Reservations and Indian Trust Areas. US Department of Commerce. 604pp.

Dewdney, Selwyn. 1975. The Sacred Scrolls of the Southern Ojibway. Toronto: University of Toronto Press for Glenbow-Alberta Insititute. 199pp.

Douglas, Mary. 1970. Purity and Danger: An Analysis of Concepts of Pollution and Taboo. London: Pelican Books. 220pp.

Driver, Harold, John Cooper, Paul Kirchoff, Dorothy Rainier Libby, William Massey, and Leslie Spier. 1953. Indian Tribes of North America. IJAL 19 (3): 1-30.

Driver, Harold and James Coffin. 1975. Classification and Development of North American Indian Cultures: A Statistical Analysis of the Driver-Massey Sample. APS-T 65 (3): 1-120.

Drucker, Philip. 1965. Cultures of the North Pacific Coast. Scranton: Chandler Publishing Co. 243pp.

Dubois, Cora. 1939. The 1870 Ghost Dance. AR 3 (1): 1-151.

Duff, Wilson. 1964a. The Indian History of British Columbia. The Impact of the White Man. ABC-M 5. 117pp.

    1964b. "Contributions of Marius Barbeau to West Coast Ethnology." Anthropologica 6 (1): 63-96.

Dwyer, Daisy Hilse. 1978. Images and Self-Images, Male and Female In Morocco. New York: Columbia University Press. 194pp.

Dyen, Isidore and David Aberle. 1974. Lexical Reconstruction: The Case of the Proto-Athapaskan Kinship System. London: Cambridge University Press. 498pp.

Eddy, John. 1977. "Medicine Wheels and Plains Indian Astronomy." pp. 147-169 in Native American Astronomy. Anthony Aveni, ed. Austin: University of Texas Press.

Eggan, Fred. 1966. The American Indian: Perspectives for the Study of Social Change. Chicago: Aldine Publishing Co. 193pp.

Eggan, Fred, ed. 1967. Social Anthropology of North American Tribes. Chicago: University of Chicago Press. 574pp. [1937].

Elliott, Henry. 1976. Biographical Sketches of Authors on Russian America and Alaska. Anchorage Historical and Fine Arts Museum, Occasional Paper 2. 52pp.

Elmendorf, William. 1960. The Structure of Twana Culture, With Comparative Notes on the Structure of Yurok Culture by A.L. Kroeber. Pullman: Washington State University Research Studies 28 (3): 1-576.

Epstein, Lawrence. 1975. "Blood and Thunder: Theories of Causation in Tibet." The Tibetan Society Bulletin 9: 40-45.

Ewers, John. 1955. The Horse In Blackfoot Indian Culture, With Comparative Material from other Western Tribes. BAE-B 159. 374pp.

    1965. "The Emergence of the Plains Indian as the Symbol of the North American Indian." Report of the Smithsonian Institute (1964): 531-544.

Farrell, Brenda. 1995. Do You See What I Mean?. Plains Indian Sign Talk and the Embodiment of Action. Austin: University of Texas Press.

Fenton, William. 1950a. "Problems Arising from the Historic Northeastern Position of the Iroquois." Essays in the Historical Anthropology of North America (In Honor of John Swanton). SMC 100: 159-251.

    1950b. The Role Call of Iroquois Chiefs: A Study of a Mneumonic Cane from the

Six Nations Reserve. SMC 111 (15): 1-73.

    1987. <u>The False Faces of the Iroquois</u>. Norman: University of Oklahoma Press.

Fenton, William and John Gulick. 1961. Symposium on Cherokee and Iroquois Culture. BAE-B 180. 275pp.

Fernandez, James. 1974. "The Mission of Metaphor in Expressive Culture." CA 15 (2): 119-145.

Fienup-Riordan, Ann. 1990. <u>Eskimo Essays</u>. Yup'ik Lives and How We see Them. "The Real People and the Children of Thunder," pp. 71-93. Rutgers University Press.

    1991. <u>The Real People and the Children of Thunder</u>. The Yup'ik Eskimo Encounter with Moravian Missionaries John and Edith Kilbuck. University of Oklahoma Press.

    1994. <u>Boundaries and Passages</u>. Rule and Ritual in Yup'ik Eskimo Oral Tradition. Norman: University of Oklahoma Press.

Fitting, James, ed. 1973. <u>The Development of North American Archaeology</u>. Garden City: Anchor Books. 309pp.

Flint, Richard Foster. 1971. <u>Glacial and Quaternary Geology</u>. New York: John Wiley and Sons. 892pp.

Fogelson, Raymond and Richard Adams, eds. 1977. <u>The Anthropology of Power</u>: Ethnographic Studies from Asia, Oceania, and the New World. New York: Academic Press. 42pp.

Forde, Daryll. 1931. Ethnography of the Yuma Indians. UCPAE 28: 83-277.

Fortune, Reo. 1932. Omaha Secret Societies. CUCA 14. 193pp.

Foster, George. 1944. A Summary of Yuki Culture. AR 5 (3): 154-244.

Foster, Laurence. 1935. Negro-Indian Relationships in the Southeast." University of Pennsylvania: Theses (Ph.D.) in Anthropology. 86pp.

Fowler, Catherine. 1970. <u>Great Basin Anthropology</u> ... A Bibliography. Reno: Desert Research Insititute, Social Science and Humanities Publication 5. 418pp.

Franklin, Fay, ed. 1981. <u>History's Timeline</u>. New York: Crescent Books.

Freeman, John and Murphy Smith. 1966. A Guide to the Manuscripts Relating to the American Indian in the Library of the American Philisophical Society. APS-M 65.

Gardiner, Howard. 1974. <u>The Quest for Mind</u>. New York: Vintage Books. 283pp.

Gearing, Fred. 1962. Priests and Warriors: Social Structure of Cherokee Politics in the 18th Century. AAA-M 93, AAA 65 (5), II.

Gifford, Edward. 1937. "Coast Yuki Myths." JAF 50 (196): 115-172.

    1939. "The Coast Yuki." An 34: 292-375.

Gilberg, Rolf. 1975. "Changes in the Life of the Polar Eskimos Resulting from a Canadian Immigration into the Thule District, Northern Greenland, in the 1860s." <u>Folk</u> 16-17: 159-70.

Goddard, Ives. 1975. "Algonquian, Wiyot, and Yurok: Proving A Distant Genetic Relationship." pp. 249-262 in <u>Linguistics and Anthropology</u>: In Honor of C. F. Voegelin. M. Dale Kinkade, Kenneth Hale, and Oswald Werner, eds. Lisse: The Peter de Ridder Press. 720pp.

Goldschmidt, Walter. 1951. "Ethics and the Structure of Society: An Ethnological Contribution to the Sociology of Knowledge." AAA 53 (4, Part 1): 506-524.

Golla, Susan. 1975. Skidi Pawnee Religion: A Structural Analysis. George Washington

University: MA Thesis. 95pp.

Goldman, Irving. 1975. The Mouth of Heaven: An Introduction to Kwakiutl Religious Thought. New York: John Wiley and Sons. 265pp.

Graburn, Nelson and Stephen Strong. 1973. Circumpolar Peoples: An Anthropological Perspective. Pacific Palisades, Ca: Goodyear Publishing Co. 236pp.

Grange, Roger. 1979. An Archeological View of Pawnee Origins. Towards Plains Caddoan Origins: A Symposium. Nebraska History 60 (2): 134-160.

Grayson, Donald. 1977. "Pleistocene Avifaunas and the Overkill Hypothesis." Science 195: 691-693.

Greenberg, Joseph. 1966. Language Universals. The Hague: Mouton and Co. 89pp.
    1975. "Research on Language Universals." Annual Review of Anthropology 4: 75-94. (G 9553).

Griaule, Marcel. 1975. Conversations with Ogotemmeli: An Introduction to Dogon Religious Ideas. Oxford: University Press. 230pp.

Griffin, Naomi. 1930. The Roles of Men and Women in Eskimo Culture. Chicago: University Press. 113pp.

Griffin, James. 1952. Archaeology of the Eastern United States. Chicago: University Press. 392pp.

Grun, Bernard. 1979. The Timetables of History. A Horizontal Linkage of People and Events. New York: Simon and Schuster Touchstone Books.

Gullemin, Jeanne. 1975. Urban Renegades. The Cultural Strategy of American Indians. New York: Columbia University Press. 336pp.

Haas, Mary. 1969. The Prehistory of Languages. The Hague: Mouton. 120pp.

Hall, Robert. 1977. "An Anthropocentric Perspective for Eastern United States Prehistory." AA 42 (4): 499-518.

Hallowell, A. Irving. 1926. Bear Ceremonialism in the Northern Hemisphere. AAA 28 (1): 1-175.
    1942. The Role of Conjuring in Salteau Society. Publications of the Philadelphia Anthropological Society II. Brinton Memorial Series. 96pp.
    1957. "The Impact of the American Indian on American Culture." AAA 59 (2): 201-217.
    1960. "The Beginnings Of Anthropology in America." pp. 1-90 in Selected Papers from the American Anthropologist 1888-1920. Frederica de Laguna, ed. AAA Special Publication. 930pp.
    1963. "American Indians, White and Black: The Phenomenon of Transculturation." CA 4 (5):519-531.
    1967. Culture and Experience. New York: Schocken Books. 434pp.

Halpern, A.L. 1953. "A Dualism in Pomo Cosmology." Kroeber Anthropological Society Publications 8/9: 151-159.

Harper, Kenn. 1989. Give Me My Father's Body. The Life of Minik, The New York Eskimo. Iqaluit (Frobisher Bay): Blacklead Books.

Harper, J Russell. 1971. Paul Kane's Frontier. Fort Worth: University of Texas Press.

Harrington, M.R. 1913. "A Preliminary Sketch of Lenape Culture." AAA 15: 208-235.

Harris, Marvin. 1968. The Rise of Anthropological Theory: A History of the Theories of Culture. New York: Thomas Y. Crowell Co. 806pp.

Hassrick, Royal. 1964. The Sioux. Life and Customs of a Warrior Society. Norman:

University of Oklahoma Press.

Hatt, Gudmond. 1916. Mocassins and Their Relation to Arctic Footwear. AMNH-M 3: 149-250.

Hayes, E. Nelson and Tanya. 1970. Claude Levi-Strauss: The Anthropologist As Hero. Cambridge: MIT Press. 264pp.

Helm, June, ed. 1966. Pioneers in American Anthropology: The Uses of Biography. Seattle: University of Washington Press. 247pp.

 1981. Subarctic. Handbook of North American Indians. Volume 6. Smithsonian Institution.

Hendry, Jean. 1964. Iroquois Masks and Mask-Making At Onondaga. BAE-B 191: 349-409. BAE-AP 74.

Henriksen, Georg. 1973. Hunters in the Barrens: The Naskapi on the Edge of the White Man's World. Memorial University of Newfoundland, Institute of Social and Economic Research Studies 12. 130pp.

Herman, Mary. 1956. "Wampum as Money in Northeastern North America." EH 3 (1): 21-33.

Herzog, George and others. 1934. "Some Orthographic Recommendations." AAA 36 (4): 629-31.

Hewitt, J.N.B. 1920. "A Constitutional League of Peace in the Stone Age of America: The League of the Iroquois and its Constitution." SI-AR (1918): 527-545.

Hickerson, Harold. 1970. The Chippewa and Their Neighbors: A Study in Ethnohistory. New York: Holt, Rinehart and Winston, Studies in Anthropological Method. 133pp.

Hilbert, Violet. 1985. Haboo. Seattle: University of Washington Press.

Hill, W.W. 1939. "Stability in Culture and Pattern." AAA 41 (2): 258-260.

 1944. "The Navaho Indians and the Ghost Dance of 1890." AAA 46 (4): 523-27.

Hirchfelder, Arlene. 1970. American Indian Authors: A Representative Bibliography. New York: Association of American Indian Affairs. 45pp.

Hittman, Michael. 1973. Ghost Dances, Disillusionment and Opiate Addiction: An Ethnohistory of Smith and Mason Valley Paiutes. Ph.D. Dissertation: University of New Mexico.

 1973a. "The 1870 Ghost Dance at the Walker River Reservation: A Reconstruction. EH 20 (3): 247-278.

 1990. Wovoka and the Ghost Dance, A Source Book. Yerington, NV: Yerington Paiute Tribe.

Hockett, Charles. 1966. "What Algonquian is Really Like." IJAL 32 (1): 59-73.

Hodge, Frederick Webb. 1907-10. Handbook of American Indians North of Mexico. BAE-B 30. 2 Volumes.

Hoijer, Harry, ed. 1946. Linguistic Structures of Native America. VFPA 6. 423pp.

Holder, Preston. 1970. The Hoe and the Horse on the Plains: A Study of Cultural Development Among North American Indians. Lincoln: University of Nebraska Press. 176pp.

Honigmann, John. 1976. The Development of Anthropological Ideas. Homewood, Illinois: The Dorsey Press. 434pp.

Howard, James. 1957. "The Mescal Bean Cult of the Central and Southern Plains: An Ancestor of the Peyote Cult ?" AAA 59 (1): 75-87.

 1968. The Southeastern Ceremonial Complex and Its Interpretation. Missouri

174

Archaeological Society Memoir 6.

Hudson's Bay Company. 1968. A Brief History of the Hudson's Bay Company. Winnipeg: HBC Archives.

Hudson, Travis and Ernest Underhoy. 1978. Crystals in the Sky: An Intellectual Odyssey Involving Chumash Astronomy, Cosmology, and Rock Art. Ballena Press Anthropological Papers 10. 163pp.

Hunter, Helen. 1940. The Ethnography of Salt in Aboriginal North America. University of Pennsylvania: Thesis (Ph.D.). 63pp.

Irwin-Williams, Cynthia, Henry Irwin, George Agogino, and C. Vance Haynes. 1973. "Hell Gap: Paleo-Indian Occupation on the High Plains." PA 18 (59): 40-53.

Jacobs, Melville. 1959. Folklore. Anthropology of Franz Boas. AAA 61 (5), Part 2: 119-138.

Jefferson, Thomas. 1964. Notes on the State of Virginia. New York: Harper Torchbooks.

Jenness, Diamond. 1955. The Faith of a Coast Salish Indian. ABC 3. 92pp.

Jennings, Francis. 1975. The Invasion of America: Indians, Colonialism, and the Cant of Conquest. New York: W.W. Norton. 370pp.

    1993. Chronology, pp 412-421 in The Founders of America. How Indians Discovered the Land, Pioneered in it, and Created Great Classical Civilizations; How they were plunged into a Dark Age by Invasion and Conquest; and How they are Reviving. New York: WW Norton.

Jewett, John. 1987. The Adventures and Sufferings of John R. Jewett, Captive of Maquinna. Annotated and Illustrated by Hilary Stewart. Seattle: University of Washington Press.

Jones, J.A. 1955. "Key to the Annual Reports of the United States Commissioner of Indian Affairs. EH 2 (1): 59-64.

Judd, Neil. 1967. The Bureau of American Ethnology, A Partial History. Norman: University of Oklahoma Press. 140pp.

Kan, Sergei. 1988. The Russian Orthodox Church in Alaska. History of Indian - White Relations. Handbook of North American Indians 4: 506-521.

    1989. Symbolic Immortality. The Tlingit Potlatch of the Nineteenth Century. Smithsonian Institution Press.

Kardiner, Abram and Edward Preble. 1961. They Studied Man. New York: Mentor Books. 255pp.

Kehoe, Alice. 1970. "The Function of Ceremonial Sexual Intercourse among the Northern Plains Indians." Plains Anthropologist 15: 99-103.

Kinietz, Vernon. 1940. Indians of the Western Great Lakes 1615-1760. University of Michigan, Museum of Anthropology, Occasional Contributions 10. 427pp.

Kinkade, M. Dale. 1971. "Roster of Linguists Studying North American Indian Languages." IJAL 37 (2): 114-121, 38 (3): 201-202.

Kinkade, M. Dale and J.V. Powell. 1976. "Language and the Prehistory of North America." World Archaeology 8 (1): 83-100.

Knight, Vernon, Jr. 1989. "Symbolism of Mississippian Mounds." pp. 279-291 in Powhatan's Mantle. Indians in the Colonial Southeast. Peter Wood, Gregory Waselkov, and M Thomas Hatley, eds. Lincoln: University of Nebraska Press.

Kroeber, Alfred. 1925. Handbook of the Indians of California. BAE-B 78. 995pp.

1927. "Arrow Release Distributions." UC-PAE 23 (4): 283-296.

1932. "Yuki Myths." An 27: 905-940.

1939. Cultural and Natural Areas of Native North America. Berkeley: University of California Press. 240pp. [1963].

Kroeber, Theodora. 1961. Ishi in Two Worlds: A Biography of the Last Wild Indian in America. Berkeley: University of California Press.

Kurath, Gertrude. 1964. Iroquois Music and Dance. BAE-B 187. 268pp.

1970. Music and Dance of the Tewa Pueblos. Santa Fe: Museum of New Mexico Press, Research Records 8. 309pp.

La Barre, Weston. 1970. The Peyote Cult. New York: Schocken Books. 260pp.

La Flesche, Francis. 1963. The Middle Five: Indian Schoolboys of the Omaha Tribe. Madison: University of Wisconsin Press. 152pp. [1900].

de Laguna, Frederica. 1972. Under Mount Saint Elias: The History and Culture of the Yakutat Tlingit. Washington: Smithsonian Contributions to Anthropology. Volume 7 in 3 Parts. 1395pp.

Laird, Carobeth. 1975. Encounter with an Angry God. Banning, California: Malki Museum Press. 190pp.

1976. The Chemehuevis. Banning, California: Malki Museum Press.

1979. Limbo. San Francisco: Chandler and Sharp.

1984. Mirror and Pattern: George Laird's World of Chemehuevi Mythology. Banning, California: Malki Museum Press.

Landes, Ruth. 1968. Ojibwa Religion and the Midewiwin. Madison: University of Wisconsin Press. 250pp.

1970. The Prairie Potawatomi: Tradition and Ritual in the Twentieth Century. Madison: University of Wisconsin Press. 420pp.

Lane, Michael. 1970. Introduction to Structuralism. New York: Basic Books. 456pp.

Langdon, Margaret. 1974. Comparative Hokan-Coahuiltecan Studies: A Survey and Appraisal. The Hague: Mouton. 114pp.

Lantis, Margaret. 1947. Alaskan Eskimo Ceremonialism. AES-M 11. 127pp.

Larrabee, Edward. 1976. Recurrent Themes and Sequences in North American Indian-European Contacts. APS-T 66 (7): 1-52pp.

Latorre, Felipe and Dolores. 1976. The Mexican Kickapoo. Austin: University of Texas Press. 401pp.

Leach, Edmund. 1970. Claude Levi-Strauss. New York: Viking Press. 142pp.

1976. Culture and Communciation: The Logic by Which Symbols Are Connected. Cambridge: University Press. 105pp.

Leacock, Eleanor. 1954. The Montagnais "Hunting Territory" and the Fur Trade. AAA-M 78. 59pp.

Leacock, Eleanor Burke and Nancy Oestreich Lurie. 1971. North American Indians in Historical Perspective. New York: Random House. 498pp.

Lieber, Michael. 1994. More Than a Living. Fishing and the Social Order on a Polynesian Atoll. Conflict and Social Change Series. Boulder, CO: Westview Press.

Leonhardy, Frank and David Price. 1970. "A Proposed Culture Typology for the Lower Snake River Region, Southeastern Washington." NARN 4 (1): 1-29.

Leon-Portilla, Miguel. 1992. The Broken Spears. The Aztec Account of the Conquest of Mexico. Boston: Beacon Press.

176

Levi-Strauss, Claude. 1944. "Reciprocity and Hierarchy." AAA 46: 266-268.

    1969. The Raw and the Cooked. Mythologique 1: Introduction to the Science of Mythology. New York: Harper and Row. 390pp. [1964]

    1973. From Honey to Ashes. Mythologique 2. 512pp. [1966].

    1978. Myth and Meaning. New York: Schocken Books. 54pp.

    1979. The Origin of Table Manners. Mythologique 3. 551pp. [1968].

    1981. The Naked Man. Mythologique 4. 746pp. [1971].

Liberty, Margot, ed. 1976. American Indian Intellectuals. Proceedings of the AES. St. Paul: West Publishing Co. 248pp.

Liljeblad, Sven, and Catherine Fowler. 1986. Owens Valley Paiute. pp. 412-34 in Great Basin. Warren D'Azevedo, ed. Handbook of North American Indians 11.

Lindsay, Nicholas Vachel. 1923. Collected Poems. New York: MacMillan and Co. (Our Mother Pocahantas pp. 105-8).

Lindquist, G.E.E. 1923. The Red Man in the United States, An Intimate Study Of the Social, Economic, and Religious Life of the American Indian. New York: xxxx

Lips, Julius. 1939. "Naskapi Trade: A Study in Legal Acculturation." Journal of the Society of Americanists 31: 129-195.

    1947. "Notes on Montagnais-Naskapi Economy (Lake St John and Lake Mistassini Bands). En 12 (1-2): 1-77.

Lowie, Robert. 1963. Indians of the Plains. Garden City: Anchor Books. 258pp. [1954].

    1956. The Crow Indians. New York: Holt, Rinehart, and Winston. [1935].

McClellan, Catherine. 1975. My Old People Say: An Ethnographic Survey of Southern Yukon Territory. NMM-PE 6 (1) in 2 Parts.

MacCannell, Dean. 1976. The Tourist: A New Theory of the Leisure Class. New York: Schocken Books. 214pp.

McCoy, Isaac. 1840. History of the Baptist Indian Missions: Embracing Remarks on the Former and Present Conditions of the Aboriginal Tribes, Their Settlement within the Indian Territory and Their Future Prospects. Washington: William M. Morrison. 611pp.

McFeat, Tom. 1966. Indians of the Northwest Coast. Seattle: University of Washington Press. 270pp.

McGee, Emma. 1915. Life of W J McGee. Farley, Iowa. 240pp.

McNickle, D'Arcy. 1973. Native American Tribalism: Indian Survivals and Renewals. London: Oxford University Press. 190pp.

Makarius, Laura. 1973. "The Crime of Manabozo." AAA 75 (3): 663-675.

Malefijt, Annemarie de Waal. 1974. Images of Man. New York: Alfred Knopf. 410pp.

Malinowski, Bronislaw. 1954. Magic, Science and Religion. Garden City: Doubleday Anchor Books. 274pp. [1948].

Malouf, Carling. 1940. A Study of the Gosiute Indians of Utah. University of Utah: MA Thesis.

    1974. The Gosiute Indians. American Indian Ethnohistory: Shoshone, California, and Basin-Plateau Tribes. David Horr, ed. New York: Garland Publishing Co. 172pp.

Malouf, Carling and Elmer Smith. 1947. "Some Gosiute Mythological Characters and Concepts." Utah Humanities Review 1 (4): 369-377.

Margolin, Malcolm, ed. 1981. The Way We Lived. California Indian Reminiscences, Stories, and Songs. Berkeley: Heyday Books.

Martin, Calvin. 1978. Keepers of the Game: Indian-Animal Relations and the Fur Trade. Berkeley: University of California Press. 226pp.

    1987. The American Indian and the Problem of History. Oxford University Press. 232pp.

Mason, Otis Tufton. 1894. Woman's Share in Primitive Culture. New York: D. Appleton. 295pp.

Mattingly, H., trans. 1948. Tacitus on Britain and Germany. Penguin Classics.

Mead, Margaret and Ruth Bunzel. 1960. The Golden Age of American Anthropology. New York: George Braziller. 630pp.

Merriam, Lewis. 1928. The Problem of Indian Administration. Brookings Institution.

Michael, Henry. 1963a. Studies in Siberian Ethnogenesis. Arctic Institute of North America, Anthropology of the North: Translations From Russian Sources 2. 313pp.

    1963b. Studies in Siberian Shamanism. Artic Institute of North America, Anthropology of the North: Translations From Russian Sources 4. 229pp.

Miller, Jay. 1972. "Priority of the Left." M 7 (4): 646-647.

    1974a. "Why the World Is on the Back of a Turtle." M 9 (2): 306-8.

    1974b. "The Delaware As Women: A Symbolic Solution." AE 1 (3): 507-14.

    1975a. "Kwulakan: The Delaware Side of Their Movement West." PA 45 (4): 45-6.

    1975b. Delaware Alternative Classifications. Anthropological Linguistics 17 (9): 434-444.

    1977. "Delaware Anatomy: With Linguistic, Social, and Medical Aspects." AL 19 (4): 144-166.

    1979. A `Struckon' Model Of Delaware Culture And The Positioning Of Mediators. AE 6 (4): 791-802.

    1980a. A Structural Study Of The Delaware Big House Rite. Papers in Anthropology 21 (2): 107-133.

    1980b. "High-Minded High Gods in North America." An 75: 916-19.

    1980c. "The Matter of the (Thoughtful) Heart: Centrality, Focality, or Overlap. JAR 36 (3): 338-42.

    1982. "People, Berdache, and Left-Handed Bears: Human Variation in Native North America. JAR 38 (3): 274-87.

    1983. Numic Religion: An Overview of Power in the Great Basin of Native North America. Anthropos 78: 337-354.

    1984. The Tsimshian and Their Neighbors Of The North Pacific Coast. Jay Miller and Carol Eastman, eds. Seattle: The University of Washington Press. 344pp.

    1988. Shamanic Odyssey: The Lushootseed Salish Journey to the Land of the Dead. A Comparative Study of the Lushootseed (Puget Salish) Ritualized Journey to the Land of the Dead, in terms of Death, Potency, and Cooperating Shamans in North America. Ballena Press Anthropological Papers 32. 215pp.

    1989a. Delaware Traditions From Kansas: Nakoming to Isaac McCoy. Plains Anthropologist 34 (123): 1-6.

1989b. The Early Years Of Watomika (James Bouchard), Delaware and Jesuit. American Indian Quarterly 13 (2): 165-188.

1989. An Overview of Northwest Coast Mythology. NARN 23 (2): 125-141. 1989.

1990. Mourning Dove, A Salishan Autobiography. Indian Lives Series. Lincoln: University of Nebraska Press. 210pp. [Paperback, 1994]

1990. Introduction, Notes for Coyote Stories by Mourning Dove. Lincoln: Bison Books, University of Nebraska Press.

1991a. "A Kinship of Spirit." pp. 305-337 in AMERICA IN 1492. The World of the Indian Peoples Before the Arrival of Columbus. Alvin Josephy, ed. New York: Random House.

1991b. Delaware Masking. Man in the Northeast 41: 105-110.

1991c. Delaware Personhood. Man in the Northeast 42 (Fall): 17-27.

1991d. Art, Attitude, and Appropriation. American Woodturner 6 (4): 17, 1991.

1992. Earthmaker. Tribal Stories from Native North America. New York: Perigree Books. 176pp.

1994. The 1806 Purge Among the Indiana Delaware: Sorcery, Gender, Boundaries, and Legitimacy. EH 41 (2): 124-266.

1995. Mourning Dove: Editing in All Directions to "Get Real." SAIL (Studies in American Indian Literatures, Series 2) 7 (2): 65-72, Summer.

1996. Changing Moons: A History of Caddo Religion. PA 41 (157): 243-259.

1997a. Old Religion Among the Delawares. EH 44(1): 113-134.

1997b. Back to Basics: Chiefdoms in Puget Sound. EH 44(2): 375-387.

1997c. Tsimshian Culture. A Light Through the Ages. Lincoln: University of Nebraska Press.

ms. Keres Culture.

Miller, Virginia. 1979. Ukomno'm: The Yuki Indians of Northern California. Ballena Press Anthropological Papers 14. 117pp.

Mooney, James. 1928. The Aboriginal Population of America North of Mexico. SMC 80 (7):1-20. (Pub 2955).

Moore, John. 1974. "Cheyenne Political History, 1820-1894." EH 21 (4): 329-359.

Moriarity, James. 1969. Chinigchinx: An Indigenous California Indian Religion. Los Angeles: Southwest Museum, Frederick Webb Hodge Anniversary Publication Fund, Volume X. xpp.

Morgan, Lewis Henry. 1959. Indian Journals. Leslie White, ed. Ann Arbor: University of Michigan Press. 229pp.

1963. Ancient Society. Eleanor Leacock, ed. New York: The World Publishing Co. 570pp. [1877].

Muldoon, James. 1975. "The Indian as Irishman." Essex Insititute Historical Collections 111 (94): 267-289.

Murphy, Robert. 1971. The Dialectics of Social Life: Alarms and Excursions in Anthropological Theory. New York: Basic Books. 261pp.

Nabokov, Peter. 1967. Two Leggings: The Making of A Crow Warrior. New York: Thomas Y. Crowell.

1991. Native American Testimony. A Chronicle of Indian - White Relations from Prophesy to the Present, 1492-1992. New York: Penguin Books.

Needham, Rodney, ed. 1973. Right and Left: Essays on Dual Symbolic Classification. Chicago: University of Chicago Press. 449pp.

Neihardt, John. 1961. Black Elk Speaks: Being The Life History of a Holy Man of the Oglala Sioux. Lincoln: University of Nebraska Press. 221pp.

Nettl, Bruno. 1954. North American Indian Musical Styles. Philadelphia: American Folklore Society 45. 51pp.

Newcomb, William. 1961. The Indians of Texas: From Prehistoric to Modern Times. University of Texas Press. 404pp.

_____ 1974. North American Indians: An Anthropological Perspective. Pacific Palisades, Ca: Goodyear Publishing Co.

Nichols, Frances. 1954. Index to Schoolcraft's Indian Tribes of the United States. BAE-B 152. 257pp.

Olson, Ronald. 1933. Clan and Moiety in Native America. UC-PAE 33 (4): 351-422.

Oosten, Jarich Gerlof. 1976. The Theoretical Structure of the Religion of the Netsilik and Iglulik. Meppel: Krips Repro. 107pp.

Opler, Morris. 1977. The Creek Indian Towns of Oklahoma in 1937. University of Oklahoma, Papers in Anthropology 13.

Ortiz, Alfonso. 1969. The Tewa World: Person, Time, Being, and Becoming in a Pueblo Indian Society. Chicago: University Press. 197pp.

Ortner, Sherry. 1974. "Is Female to Male as Nature Is to Culture." pp. 67-87 in Woman, Culture, and Society. Michelle Rosaldo and Louise Lamphere, eds. Sanford: University Press.

Oswalt, Roger, James Deetz, and Anthony Fisher. 1967. The North American Indians: A Sourcebook. New York: MacMillan. 752pp.

Pandey, Triloki Nath. 1972. "Anthropologists at Zuni." APS-P 116 (4): 321-337.

Park, Willard. 1937. "Paviotso Polyandry." AAA 39 ( ):366-8.

_____ 1938. Shamanism in Western Native America. Evanston: Northwestern University Press. 163pp.

Parks, Douglas, and Waldo Wedel. 1985. "Pawnee Geography, Historical and Sacred." Great Plains Quarterly 5 (Summer): 143-76.

Paz, Octavio. 1974. Conjunctions and Disjunctions. New York: Viking. 148pp.

Pearson, Bruce. 1973. A Grammar of Delaware: Semantics, Morpho-Syntax, Lexicon, Phonology. University of California at Berkeley: Ph.D. Dissertation.

Perrone, Bobette, H. Henrietta Stockel, and Victoria Krueger. 1989. Medicine Women, Curanderas, and Women Doctors. Norman: University of Oklahoma Press. 252pp.

Phinney, Archie. 1934. Nez Perce Texts. CUCA XXV (25). 497pp.

Piaget, Jean. 1970. Structuralism. New York: Basic Books. 153pp.

Pierce, Richard. Russian and Soviet Eskimo and Indian Policies. History of Indian - White Relations. Handbook of North American Indians 4: 119-127.

Pope, Saxon. 1962. Bows and Arrows. Berkeley: University of California Press. 83pp.

Powell, Jay and Vickie Jensen. 1976. Quileute. An Introduction to the Indians of La Push. Seattle: University of Washington Press.

Powers, Marla. 1986. Oglala Women: Myth, Ritual, and Reality. University of Chicago Press. 241pp.

Powers, William. 1975. Oglala Religion. Lincoln: University of Nebraska Press. 233pp.

Price, Monroe. 1973. Law and the American Indian. Readings, Notes, and Cases.

Indianapolis: Bob Merrill. 807pp.

Prince, Dyneley. 1912. "An Ancient New Jersey Indian Jargon." AAA 14: 508-524.

Prucha, Francis Paul. 1975. Documents of United States Indian Policy. Lincoln: University of Nebraska Press. 278pp.

1984. The Great Father: The United States Government and the American Indians. Lincoln: University of Nebraska Press.

Quimby, George. 1979. "A Brief History of WPA Archaeology." pp. 110-123 in The Uses of Anthropology. (See xxxx).

Radin, Paul. 1944. The Story of the American Indian. New York: Liveright Publishing Co. 391pp. [1927].

Rasmusen, Knud. 1931. The Netsilik Eskimos. Reports of the Fifth Thule Expedition 8.

Ray, Arthur J. 1988. The Hudson's Bay Company and Native People. History of Indian - White Relations. Handbook of North American Indians 4: 335-350.

Ray, Verne. 1933. The Sanpoil and Nespelem: Salishan Peoples of Northeastern Washington. UWPA 5. 237pp.

1939. Cultural Relations in the Plateau of Northwestern America. Los Angeles: Southwest Museum. 154pp.

Rees, Alwyn and Brinley. 1961. Celtic Heritage: Ancient Tradition In Ireland and Wales. London: Thames and Hudson. 428pp.

Reichard, Gladys. 1934. "Understatement or Naivete." American Speech 9 (3): 19x-204.

1951. Navaho Grammar. New York; J.J. Augustin. AES-PXXI (21). 393pp.

Reichel-Dolmatoff, Geraldo. 1971. Amazonian Cosmos: The Sexual and Religious Symbolism of the Tukano Indians. University of Chicago Press. 290pp.

Rice, Stuart. 1931. Methods in Social Science, A Case Book. University of Chicago Press. 822pp.

Riddington, Robin. 1968. "The Medicine Fight: An Instrument of Political Process Among the Beaver Indians." AAA 70 (6): 1152-1160.

1969. "Kin Categories Versus Kin Groups: A Two-Section System Without Sections." E 8 (4): 460-67.

1976. Wechuge and Windigo: A Comparison of Cannibal Belief Among Boreal Forest Athpaskans and Algonkians. Anthropologica 18 (2): 107-129.

1978. Swan People: A Study of the Dunne-Za Prophet Dance. NMM-MS 38. 132pp.

1980. Trails of Meaning. pp. 265-68 in The World Is Sharp as a Knife. An Anthropolgy in Honor of Wilson Duff. Donald Abbott, ed. Victoria, BC: British Columbia Provincial Museum.

1988. Trail to Heaven. Knowledge and Narrative in a Northern Native Community. Ames: University of Iowa Press. 301pp.

1990. Little Bit Know Something. Stories in a Language of Anthropology. Ames: University of Iowa Press. 281pp.

Ritzenthaler, Robert and Pat. 1970. The Woodland Indians of the Western Great Lakes. Garden City: Anchor Books. 178pp.

Roe, Peter. 1982. The Cosmic Zygote. Cosmology in the Amazon Basin. New Brunswick: Rutgers University Press.

Rohner, Ronald. 1966. "Franz Boas, Ethnographer on the Northwest Coast." Pioneers in American Anthropology, The Uses of Biography. June Helm, ed. Seattle: University of Washington Press. AES-M 43: 150-247.

Romero, Javier. 1970. Dental Mutilation, Trephination, and Cranial Deformation (in Middle America). Handbook of South American Indians. T. D. Steward, ed. Volume 9: 50-67. Austin: University of Texas Press.

Romney, A. Kimball. 1957. "The Genetic Model and The Uto-Aztecan Time Perspective." Davidson Journal of Anthropology 3: 35-41.

Rooth, Anna Birgetta. 1957. The Creation Myths of the North American Indians. Anthropos 52: 497-508.

Rosman, Abraham and Paula Rubel. 1971. Feasting with Mine Enemy. New York: Columbia University Press.

Rossi, Ino, ed. 1974. The Unconscious in Culture: The Structuralism Of Claude Levi-Strauss in Perspective. New York: E.P. Dutton.

Rossman, Douglas. 1988. Where Legends Live. A Pictorial Guide to Cherokee Mythic Places. Cherokee, NC: Cherokee Publications. 48pp.

Rostlund, Erhard. 1952. Freshwater Fish and Fishing in Native North America. Berkeley: University of California Publications in Geography 9. 313pp.

Royce, Charles. 1899. Indian Land Cessions. BAE-AR 18 (2): xxxx.

Sabo III, George. 1992. Paths of Our Children: Historic Indians of Arkansas. Arkansas Archaeological Survey, Popular Series 3. 144pp.

Sapir, Edward. 1915. Abnormal Types of Speech in Nootka. Ottawa: Canada Department of Mines, Anthropology Series 62 (5): 1-21.

    1916. Time Perspective in Aboriginal American Culture: A Study in Method. Ottawa: Canada Department of Mines, Geological Survey Memoir 90, Anthropology Series 13. 87pp.

    1929. "Central and North American Languages." Encyclopedia Britannica 5: 138-141.

    1949. Language. New York: Harcourt, Brace and World. 242pp. [1921].

Schaeffer, Claude. 1949. "Wolf and Two-Pointed Buck: A Lower Kutenai Tale of the Supernatural World." PM 22 (1/2): 1-22.

    1965. "The Kutenai Female Berdache: Courier, Guide, Prophetess, and Warrior. EH 12 (3): 193-236.

    1966. Bear Ceremonialism of the Kutenai Indians. Browning: Museum of the Plains Indian, Studies in Plains Anthropology and History 4. 54pp.

    1969. Blackfoot Shaking Tent. Calgary: Glenbow-Alberta Institute Occasional Paper 5. 38pp.

Schele, Linda, and David Freidel. 1990. A Forest of Kings. The Untold Story of the Ancient Maya. New York: William Morrow pp. 26-33.

Scherman, Katharine. 1981. The Flowering of Ireland. Saints, Scholars, and Kings. Boston: Little, Brown and Co.

Schoenberg, Wilfred. 1962. A Chronical of Catholic History of the Pacific Northwest: 1743-160. Portland: Catholic Sentinel Printing. 570pp.

Schmidt, Fr. Wilhelm. 1933. High Gods in North America. Oxford University Press. 149pp.

Sebeok, Thomas, ed. 1976. Native Languages of the Americas. New York: Plenum Press. Volume I. 630pp.

182

Shapiro, Warren. 1970. "The Ethnography of Two-Section Systems." E 9 (4): 380-388.

Shafer, Robert. 1952. "Athapaskan and Sino-Tibetan." IJAL 18 (): 12-19.

Sharp, Henry. 1976. "Man:Wolf::Woman:Dog." Arctic Anthropology 13 (1): 25-34.

Sheehan, Bernard. 1973. Seeds of Extinction: Jeffersonian Philanthropy and the American Indian. Chapel Hill: University of North Carolina Press.

Shelford, Victor. 1963. The Ecology of North America. Urbana: University of Illinois Press. 610pp.

Siebert, Frank. 1967. "The Original Home of the Proto-Algonquian Languages." Contributions To Anthropology: Linguistics I (Algonquian). NMM-AS 78 (Bulletin 214): 13-47. 162pp.

Simmons, Leo. 1969. Sun Chief: The Autobiography of a Hopi Indian. New Haven: Yale University Press. 460pp. [1942].

Sinclair, A.T. 1909. "Tatooing of the North American Indians." AAA 11 ( ): 362-400.

Slotkin, J.S. 1965. Readings in Early Anthropology. Chicago: Aldine. 530pp.

Smith, Marian. 1940. The Puyallup-Nisqually. CUCA 32. 336pp.

Snellgrove, David, and Hugh Richardson. 1968. A Cultural History of Tibet. New York: Frederick A. Praeger. pp. 275-76.

Speck, Frank. 1909. Ethnology of the Yuchi Indians. University of Pennsylvania Museum 1 (1): 1-154.

    1915a The Family Hunting Band as the Basis of Algonkian Social Organization. American Anthropologist 17: 289-305.

    1915b. The Eastern Algonkian Wabanaki Confederacy. American Anthropologist 17: 492-508.

    1917. "Game Totems Among the Northeastern Algonkians." American Anthropologist 19: 9-18.

    1928. Native Tribes and Dialects of Connecticut. BAE-AR 43: 205-287.

    1933. "Notes on the Life of John Wilson, the Revealer of Peyote, as Recalled by His Nephew, George Anderson." The General Magazine and Historical Chronicle 35: 539-556.

    1935. Naskapi, The Savage Hunters of the Labrador Peninsula. Norman: University of Oklahoma Press.

    1945. The Iroquois: A Study in Cultural Evolution. Cranbrook Institute of Science. Bulletin 23. 94pp.

Spencer, Robert, Jesse Jennings, and others. 1977. The Native Americans: Ethnology and Backgrounds of the North American Indians. New York: Harper and Row. 584pp. [1965].

Spier, Leslie. 1921. The Sun Dance of the Plains Indians: Its Development and Diffusion. AMNH-AP 16 (7): 453-529.

Spier, Leslie, Irving Hallowell, and Stanley Newman, eds. 1960. Language, Culture, and Personality: Essays in Memory of Edward Sapir. Salt Lake City: University of Utah Press. [1941].

Spindler, George and Louise. 1957. "American Indian Personality Types and Their Sociocultural Roots." The Annals of the American Academy of Political and Social Science : 147-156.

Spiro, Melford, ed. 1965. Context and Meaning in Cultural Anthropology: in Honor of A. Irving Hallowell. New York: The Free Press. 442pp.

Spitzka, Edward Anthony. 1903. "A Study of the Brain of the Late Major J.W. Powell." AAA 5 (4): 583-643.

Spuhler, James. 1951. "Some Genetic Variations in American Indians." Reprint of pp. 172-202 in The Physical Anthropology of the American Indian.

Staden, Hans. 1557. The True History of His Captivity. Marburg, Germany. Republished 1929. The Argonaut Series. Malcolm Letts, trans. and ed. New York: Robert M. McBride and Company.

Standing Bear, Luther. 1978. Land of the Spotted Eagle. Lincoln: University of Nebraska Press. 259pp. [1933].

Stemple, Ruth. 1963. Author - Subject Index to Articles in Smithsonian Annual Reports 1849-1961. SI #4503. 200pp.

Steward, Julian. 1931. "The Ceremonial Buffoon of the American Indian." Papers of the Michigan Academy of Science, Arts, and Letters. 14: 187-207.

    1938. Basin - Plateau Aboriginal Sociopolitical Groups. BAE-B 120. 346pp.

Stewart, T.D. 1973. The People of America. New York: Charles Scribner's Sons. 262pp.

Stewart, T.D. and Marshall Newman. 1951. "A Historical Resume of the Concept of Differences in Indian Types." AAA 53 (1): 19-36.

Stocking, George. 1974. "The Boas Plan for the Study of American Indian Languages. pp. 454-484 in Tradition and Paradigms: Studies in the History of Linguistics. Dell Hymes, ed. Bloomington: University of Indiana Press.

Straus, Anne S. 1975. "Northern Cheyenne Ethnopsychology." Ethnos 5 (3): 326-57.

    1978. "The Meaning of Death in Northern Cheyenne Culture." Plains Anthropologist 23 (79): 1-6.

Strong, William Duncan. 1927. "An Analysis of Southwestern Society." AAA 29 (1): 1-61.

Sullivan, Lawrence E. 1989. Native American Religions: North America. New York: MacMillan Publishing Co. 220pp.

Susman, Amelia. 1976. The Round Valley Indians of California. An Unpublished Chapter in Acculturation in Seven (or Eight) American Indian Tribes. Contributions of the University of California, Archaeological Research Facility 31. 120pp.

Suttles, Wayne. 1977. "The 'Coast Salish' of the Georgia - Puget Basin — Another Look." Puget Soundings. April.

    1987. Coast Salish Essays. Seattle: University of Washington Press. 320pp.

Suttles, Wayne, ed. 1990. Northwest Coast. Handbook of North American Indians. Volume 7. Smithsonian Institution.

Svensson, Frances. 1973. The Ethnics in American Politics: American Indians. Minneapolis: Burgess Publishing Co. 53pp.

Swan, James. 1870. The Indians of Cape Flattery, At the Entrance to the Straight of Fuca, Washington Territory. Smithsonian Contributions to Knowledge 16 (#220). 108pp.

Swanson, Earl, ed. 1970. Languages and Cultures of Western North America: Essays in Honor of Sven Liljeblad. Pocatello: The Idaho State University Press. 288pp.

Swanton, John. 1928. Social Organization and Social Usages of the Indians of the Creek Confederacy. BAE-AR 42: 25-472.

    1928a ReligousS Beliefs and Medical Practices of the Creek Indians. BAE-AR 42:

184

473-672.

    1928b. Aboriginal Culture of the Southeast. BAE-AR 42: 673-726.

Tantaquidgeon, Gladys. 1972. <u>Folk Medicines of the Delaware and Related Algonkian Indians</u>. Harrisburg: The Pennsylvania Historical and Museum Commission, Anthropological Series 3. 145pp. [1942].

Tedlock, Dennis. 1985 <u>Popul Vuh</u>. The Mayan Book of the Dawn of Life. New York: Simon and Schuster Touchstone Books.

Thompson, Stith. 1966. <u>Tales of the North American Indians</u>. Bloomington: Indiana University Press. 386pp. [1929].

Toelken, Barre. 1979. <u>The Dynamics of Folklore</u>. Boston: Houghton Mifflin. 395pp.

Tooker, Elizabeth. 1970. <u>The Iroquois Ceremonial of Midwinter</u>. Syracuse: University Press. 189pp.

Trowbridge, Charles Christopher. 1939. Shawnee Traditions. Vernon Kinietz and Erminie W. Voegelin, eds. University of Michigan, Museum of Anthropology, Occasional Contributions 9. 71pp.

Turney-High, Harry Holbert. 1941. Ethnography of the Kutenai. AAA-M 56. 202pp.

Umiker-Sebeok, D. Jean and Thomas A. Sebeok. 1978. <u>Aboriginal Sign Language of the Americas and Australia</u>. Volume 2: The Americas and Australia. New York: Plenum Press. 445pp.

Underhill, Ruth. 1938. "A Papago Calendar Record." UNM-AS 2 (5): 1-66.

    1939. Social Organization of the Papago Indians. CUCA 30. 280pp.

    1946. <u>Papago Indian Religion</u>. CUCA 33. 359pp.

    1965. <u>Red Man's Religion</u>. Chicago: University Press.

Vanstone, James. 1965. The Changing Culture of the Snowdrift Chipewyan. NMC-B 208 (-AS 74). 131pp.

    1974. <u>Athapaskan Adaptations</u>: Hunters and Fishermen of the Subarctic Forests. Chicago: Aldine. 145pp.

Varenne, Herve. 1977. <u>Americans Together</u>: Structural Diversity in a Midwestern Town. New York: Teacher's College Press. 242pp.

Voegelin, Charles. 1952. The Boas Plan for the Presentation of American Indian Languages. APS-P 96 (4): 439-451.

Wagner, Gunter. 1931. Yuchi Tales. AES-P 8. 357pp.

Walker, Deward. 1970. <u>Systems of North American Witchcraft and Sorcery</u>. University of Idaho, Anthropological Monographs 1. 295pp.

    1972. <u>The Emergent Native Americans</u>: A Reader in Culture Contact. Boston: Little and Brown. 818pp.

Walker, Willard. 1969. "Notes on Native Writing Systems and the Design of Native Literacy Programs." AL 11 (5): 148-166.

    1975. "The Proto-Algonquians." pp. 633-647 in <u>Linguistics and Anthropology</u>: In Honor of C.F. Voegelin. M. Dale Kinkade, Kenneth Hale, and Oswald Werner, eds. Lisse: The Peter de Ridder Press. 720pp.

Wallace, Anthony F.C. 1952. The Modal Personality Structure of the Tuscarora Indians, As Revealed by the Rorschach Tests. BAE-B 150. 120pp.

    1969. <u>The Death and Rebirth of the Seneca</u>. New York: Vintage Books. 395pp.

Walsh, Jane MacLaren. 1976. <u>John Peabody Harrington</u>: The Man and His California Indian Fieldnotes. Ballena Press: Anthropology Series 6. 58pp.

Ward, Martha C. 1989. Nest in the Wind. Adventures in Anthropology on a Tropical Island. Prospect Heights, Il: Waveland Press

Warren, William. 1885. History of the Ojibways, Based Upon Traditions and Oral Statements. Collections of the Minnesota Historical Society 5. 527pp.

Washburn, Wilcomb, ed. 1964. The Indian and the White Man. Garden City: Anchor Books. 480pp.

1988. History of Indian - White Relations. Handbook of North American Indians 4. Smithsonian Institution.

Weinman, Paul. 1969. A Bibliography of the Iroquoian Literature. New York State Museum and Science Service Bulletin 411. 254pp.

Weltfish, Gene. 1971. The Lost Universe: The Way of Life of the Pawnee. New York: Ballantine Books. 617pp. [1965].

White, Leslie. 1966. The Social Organization of Ethnological Theory. Rice University Studies 52 (4): 1-66.

White, Raymond. 1963. Luiseño Social Organization. UC-PAE 48 (2): 91-194.

White, Richard. 1980. Land Use, Environment, and Social Change. The Shaping of Island County, Washington. Seattle: University of Washington Press.

1991. "It's Your Misfortune and None of My Own." A New History of the American West. Norman: University of Oklahoma Press.

Widmer, Randolph J. 1988. The Evolution of the Calusa. A Nonagricultural Chiefdom on the Southwest Florida Coast. Tuscaloosa: University of Alabama Press.

Wildschut, William. 1975. Crow Indian Medicine Bundles. John Ewers, ed. Contributions from the Museum of the American Indian, Heye Foundation, 17. 178pp. 68 plates.

Willey, Gordon. 1966. An Introduction to American Archaeology. Volume I: North and Middle America. Englewood Cliffs: Prentice-Hall. 526pp.

Winter, George. 1948. The Journals and Indian Paintings of George Winter, 1837-1839. Indianapolis: Indiana Historical Society.

Wissler, Clark. 1917. The American Indian. New York: MacMillan.

1926. The Relation of Nature to Man in Aboriginal America. New York: Oxford University Press. 248pp.

Witherspoon, Gary. 1975. Navaho Kinship and Marriage. Chicago: University Press.

1977. Language and Art in the Navajo Universe. Ann Arbor: University of Michigan Press. 214pp.

Witthoft, John. 1949. Green Corn Ceremonialism in the Eastern Woodlands. UM-AP 13. 91pp.

Wolff, Hans. 1951. "Yuchi Text With Analysis." IJAL 17; 48-53.

Woodman, David. Unravelling the Franklin Mystery: Inuit Testimony. Montreal: McGill-Queen's University Press.

Wright, Muriel. 1977. A Guide to the Indian Tribes of Oklahoma. Norman: University of Oklahoma Press. 300pp.

Yanovsky, Elias. 1936. Food Plants of the North American Indians. United States Department of Agriculture, Miscellaneous Publication 237. 83pp.

Zeisberger, David. 1910. History of the North American Indian. Archer Butler Hulbert and Rev. William Nathaniel Schwarze, eds. Columbus: Ohio Archaeological and Historical Quarterly 19 (1-2): 1-189.

Important general sources are the Handbook of American Indians North of Mexico (BAE-B 30) and the Handbook of North American Indians (20 volumes, already published 4 Indian-White, 5 Arctic, 6 Subractic, 7 Northwest Coast, 8 California, 9 Southwest, 10 Southwest, 11 Great Basin, 12 Plateau, 13 Plains, 15 Northeast, 17 Languages).

[p78 Powell 52.08 oz / McGee 49.73 oz]
NA-BIB

ACKNOWLEDGEMENTS

Throughout, my families of Millers, Toulouses, Dunns, Liebers, and Chesnins. More individually, Florence Hawley Ellis, Cynthia Irwin Williams, Philip Bock, Nibs Hill, Stanley Newman, Mary Elizabeth Smith, John Dunn, Luceen Latorre Dunn, Michael Hittman, Bruce Rigsby, Alfonso Ortiz, Robin Fox, Margaret Bacon, Yehudi Cohen, Warren Shapiro, Mark Leone, Esther Goldfrank, Karl Wittfogel, Raymond Fogelson, Sam Stanley, William Fenton, Fred and Joan Eggan, Alice Kehoe, Don and Catherine Fowler, Sven and Astrid Liljeblad, Terry Strauss, Colin Calloway, Raymond De Mallie, Douglas Parks, Harvey Markovitz, Ruth Hamilton, Violet Brown, Donald Fixico, and LaVonne Brown Ruoff.

Ernie and Lynne Hill, John and Helen Clifton, Oliver and Kristi Clifton, Marjorie Halpin, Viola Garfield, Erna Gunther, Wayne Suttles, Dale Kinkade, J V Powell, Dell and Virginia Hymes, Warren Snyder, Patrick Twohy SJ, Michael Fitzpatrick SJ, Ray Bucko SJ, Vi and Don Hilbert, Robert Rudine, Janet Yoder, Pam Amoss, Christopher Roth, Pam Cahn, Ed Davis, Lawrence Webster, Isadore and Jackie Tom.

Gladys Tantaquidgeon, Nora Thompson Dean, Lucy Blalock, Lillie Whitehorn, Isabel Arcasa, Adeline and Larry Fredin, Jim Rementer, Linda Poolaw, T B and Pearl Charlie, Christine Sam, Fred Bruner, Barney Leader, Agnes Wagosh, Frances Ashanany, Christine and Charles Quintasket, Juliann Timentwa, Herman Friedlander, Sue Matt, Jerome and Mary Miller, Shirley Palmer, Lucy Covington, Emily Peone, Richard and Nora Dauenhauer, Marilyn Richen, Ann Schuh, Joanne Kfouri, Donna Steinburn, Glenn Williams and Dottie Heck, Roland Wildman, Gerald Eck, Diana Riesky, Gerry DeLay, Larry and Michiko Epstein, Hiroko Roe, and Monday Nite.

Index

#f = scattered entries before and after this specified page number
#0 = scattered entries for the next ten pages after this specified decade: 10f, 20f ... 130f

T

Taikomol, 80f, 90f
Teotihuacan, 126
Tewa, 20, 35, 58, 164
Three Moons, 80
Tirawahat, 16, 54, 60
Tlingits, 134f, 140f
tobacco, 11, 22, 37f, 52, 75f, 83, 94f,
    100f, 128, 131f, 163
tree, 26, 57, 65f, 77, 81f, 91f, 124f, 143
trophies, 55, 89
Tsimshian, 9, 16, 26, 33, 42f, 51f, 60,
    146
Tsityostiinako, 92
Tsoyaha, 98
Tupinamba, 110f, 154
Turtle, 16, 25, 40, 61, 99, 102
Tuscaroras, 57, 147f
Tuscalusa, 122
Two Leggings, 29f
tysic, 4, 9, 16, 20f, 33f, 54, 64, 75, 87
Tyuonyi, 96

U

Ukiyo, 145
Ulysses, 109

V

Veniaminov, Ivan, 135, 145
Vi, 46, 140
virginity, 78

W

Weltfish, Gene, 28
wergild, 70
whale, 51, 62f, 69f, 83, 132
Whaling, 51, 68f
Williams, Roger, 108, 130, 153
Winnebagos, 54
Wishrams, 57
witches, 32, 44, 92f, 134f, 155
Wotan, 109

X

Ximinez, Fr Francisco, 123

Y

Yana, 50

Z

Zuni, 23, 41, 116

Sold @ Amazon.com

www.ingramcontent.com/pod-product-compliance
Lightning Source LLC
Chambersburg PA
CBHW080248290526
45790CB00005B/1735